Conscience and Purpose

CONSCIENCE AND PURPOSE
*Fiction and Social Consciousness
in Howells, Jewett, Chesnutt, and Cather*

PAUL R. PETRIE

THE UNIVERSITY OF ALABAMA PRESS
Tuscaloosa

Typeface: AGaramond

∞

The paper on which this book is printed meets the minimum requirements of American National Standard for Information Sciences—Permanence of Paper for Printed Library Materials, ANSI Z39.48–1984.

Library of Congress Cataloging-in-Publication Data

Petrie, Paul R., 1964–
Conscience and purpose : fiction and social consciousness in Howells, Jewett, Chesnutt, and Cather / Paul R. Petrie.
p. cm. — (Studies in American literary realism and naturalism)
Includes bibliographical references.
ISBN-13: 978-0-8173-1484-2 (cloth : alk. paper)
ISBN-10: 0-8173-1484-9
1. American fiction—History and criticism. 2. Ethics in literature. 3. Chesnutt, Charles Waddell, 1858–1932—Ethics. 4. Howells, William Dean, 1837–1920—Ethics. 5. Jewett, Sarah Orne, 1849–1909—Ethics. 6. Literature and society—United States. 7. Cather, Willa, 1873–1947—Ethics. 8. Social ethics in literature. 9. Conscience in literature.
I. Title. II. Series.
PS374.E86P48 2005
813.009′353—dc22
2005008009

Portions of chapter 3 first appeared in *Jewett and Her Contemporaries: Reshaping the Canon,* edited by Karen L. Kilcup and Thomas S. Edwards. (Gainesville: University Press of Florida, 1999, pp. 99–120. Reprinted by permission of the University Press of Florida.)

Portions of chapter 4 first appeared in *Studies in American Fiction* 27 (1999), edited by Mary Loeffelholz. (Copyright © 1999 by Northeastern University Press. Used by permission.)

Portions of chapter 4 first appeared in *American Literary Realism* 33 (2001), edited by Gary Scharnhorst. (Copyright © 2001 by the University of Illinois Press. Used by permission.)

Contents

Acknowledgments

I am grateful to the many readers and advisers who contributed valuable insights and suggestions at various stages of this book's production, including Clare Eby, William Curtin, and especially Brenda Murphy, who oversaw this project in its dissertation stages and later encouraged me to pursue it as a book. Thanks are also due to the Connecticut State University system for its award of a CSU Research Grant and to the Southern Connecticut State University English Department for its grant of reassigned time from teaching, both of which were indispensable to the completion of this project—as was the interest and support shown by many of my colleagues at SCSU. For permission to reuse portions of this text first published elsewhere, I thank the University Press of Florida for portions of chapter 3 first published in *Jewett and Her Contemporaries: Reshaping the Canon,* Northeastern University for portions of chapter 4 first published in *Studies in American Fiction,* and the University of Illinois Press for portions of chapter 5 first published in *American Literary Realism.* Many thanks as well to the editorial staff at the University of Alabama Press who were infinitely patient with this rookie author.

Finally, I want to express my deepest gratitude and love to Allison Tate Hild, who patiently endured a decade's worth of drafts and revisions, hopes and anxieties, and elations and dejections as this work took its slow course to completion, and to my two children, Maxwell and Claudia, whose curiosity about their Dad's work and whose firm prioritization of play were equally indispensable to the maintenance of my sanity and to the book's completion.

Introduction

As I completed the manuscript of this book, the National Endowment for the Arts, in a study based on analysis of twenty years of U.S. census and polling information, reported that "for the first time in modern history, less than half of the adult population now reads literature," a casualty of "our society's massive shift toward electronic media for entertainment and information" (vii). In this respect, the report only confirms what most of us have long assumed on the basis of anecdotal evidence and firsthand classroom experience. Perhaps more unexpectedly, though, "Reading at Risk" explicitly links the comprehensive decline in numbers of readers and time spent reading to its broader and more troubling implications for the entire culture. "More than reading is at stake," NEA chairman Dana Gioia notes in his preface to the report. "As this report unambiguously demonstrates, readers play a more active and involved role in their communities. The decline in reading, therefore, parallels a larger retreat from participation in civic and cultural life. The long-term implications of this study not only affect literature but all the arts—as well as social activities such as volunteerism, philanthropy, and even political engagement" (vii). In short, "Reading at Risk" asserts through its statistical analysis of a huge sampling of American readers and their reading habits what many of us in the profession of teaching literature accepted, either as an unarticulated intuition or as an article of faith, when we chose this profession: that literature matters, not merely as personal entertainment but as a vital part of the life of the society in which it participates.

This book addresses one phase of the history of literature's vital engagement with its society—a history that now may be drawing toward its close. The book examines one particularly comprehensive and influential conception of why and how the literary arts should engage their readers in the shared civic life of American democracy, in order to understand how that conception informed the creation of a number of late-nineteenth- and early-twentieth-century American fictions. William Dean Howells, the powerful novelist, editor, essayist, and mentor whose importance eventually would be acknowledged in his christening by his contemporaries as "the Dean of American letters," constructed in his *Editor's Study* columns in *Harper's Monthly* magazine (1886–92) a literary aesthetic based on an impassioned commitment to literature as a uniquely potent and crucial instrument for constructive public discourse about contemporary American social realities. This book reconstructs the terms of his socially and ethically purposive aesthetic and then traces its impacts on and implications for the work of a number of turn-of-the-century American fiction writers—Howells himself included—who wrote in the wake of Howells's pervasive influence.

Chapter 1 revisits Howells's most sustained body of critical writing and finds that most branches of his literary aesthetic thinking arise from and/or contribute to a single, loosely constructed but pivotal conception: that the chief end of literature is to perform a public role of cultural mediation, enlarging the sphere of social understanding and sympathy by employing fiction as a tool for communication across the cultural boundaries dividing classes, regions, and ethnicities in the late-nineteenth-century United States. The chapter traces the theoretical consequences of Howells's attempt to fuse aesthetics and social ethics in a scheme of artistic valuation that sought to measure aesthetic success according to the real-world effects of fiction upon the minds, hearts, and conduct of its audience. The theoretical conundrums in which this attempt landed him—along with their pragmatic resolutions—foreshadow the difficulties that he, along with the other writers of fiction this book explores, experienced in putting a social-ethical literary aesthetic into practice in fiction. Chapter 2 investigates the consequences of his aesthetic for Howells as a novelist, as he attempted to practice in his fiction what he advocated in the *Editor's Study*. *The Minister's Charge* (1886), *Annie Kilburn* (1888), and *The Vacation of the Kelwyns* (published posthumously in 1920 but begun during the 1870s) all were written during the gestational years of Howells's literary aesthetic, and like the *Editor's Study* itself, they grapple with the practical implications of a fiction undertaken on the assumption of identity between aesthetic and social-ethical values. More specifically, these novels grapple with the problem of a readership/citizenry's probable responses to the sympathetic knowledge of the cultural Other that Howells's aesthetic described as the primary end of serious literature. Each novel enacts the Howellsian social-ethical aesthetic, taking more or less for granted literature's power to communicate culturally alien realities in emotionally moving ways across deep social divisions in contemporary society. But each in its own way wrestles anxiously with the prospects for concrete, ethically informed social, economic, and political action undertaken on the basis of the sympathetic knowledge thus produced. These fictions ask: once an urban middle-class readership has gained the kinds of knowledge that the new literature according to Howells's aesthetic affords, what then should they—or indeed *can* they—do with that knowledge?

Chapters 3 through 5 explore selected fictions by a number of late-nineteenth- and early-twentieth-century writers as they, too, struggle with the implications of Howellsian social-ethical aesthetics for their own literary practice. Sarah Orne Jewett, Charles W. Chesnutt, and Willa Cather represent distinct literary generations as well as different genders, ethnic and regional origins, literary training and influences, and diverse literary practices and career trajectories. But all three writers, by virtue of their particular historic moments, wrote in a cultural world definitively shaped by the powerful Howellsian conception of literature's social-ethical purposes, and all three wrote in part in response to the assertions, assumptions, and expectations about the purposes and modes of literary fiction left them by the decisive cultural presence of Howells's aesthetic. Whatever their differences from each other and from Howells—and there were many—these three writers' fictions were shaped by their interactions with Howellsian ideas about fiction's social-ethical duties and the artistic mode(s) best suited to fulfilling them. Interpretation of key texts by each of them in the context of Howellsian aesthetics reveals a series of fictions that developed a variety of strategies to adopt, adapt, and/or resist Howells's aesthetic imperative, struggling creatively to adjust it to variant aesthetic goals, authorial doubts about its viability or limitations, or alternative conceptions or prioritizations of literary purpose and procedure.

Chapter 3 focuses on the two works by Howells's near contemporary and lifelong acquaintance, Sarah Orne Jewett, that are most closely allied to the sort of social and ethical purposes that he envisioned for the new literature, pursuing a literary aesthetic marked by close observation and documentation of commonplace social realities and aimed at enlarging the bounds of sympathy across regional and class-based cultural borders. But both works seek to expand the range and purposes of Howellsian literary representation and to subsume them within an alternative model of reader interaction with textually represented social realities, one that makes room for a spiritualized and mysticized sense of both the bases of local reality and of literary communication with its readers. *Deephaven* (1877) exhibits a marked tension and vacillation between these two aspects of Jewett's emerging aesthetic, while *The Country of the Pointed Firs* (1896) employs a new, reader-participatory narrative mode, grounded in a supra-social sense of human community, to fuse social-ethical with mystical literary purposes.

Chapter 4 focuses on the first and last published works of Charles W. Chesnutt to argue that their author's adoption of the Howellsian aesthetic to further his racial reform goals coexists uneasily with his use of his fiction to question the prospects for success of his own literary project in a time of ongoing political and legal reinstitution of black slavery in all but name. Having adopted a writing career with the explicit purpose of using imaginative literature to improve white readers' understanding of African Americans, Chesnutt includes in *The Conjure Woman* (1887–99) a number of tales that not only pursue the ethical transformation of their probable readership but subtly question the capacity of that audience to receive and act upon the cross-cultural communication of African-American realities via plantation-dialect fiction. Shifting the focus of critique from audience to reformer, *The Colonel's Dream* (1905) self-consciously explores the limitations placed on reform—whether literary or extraliterary—by the reform temperament itself. Confronting the apparently immovable fact of white American racism, the novel's more polemic approach paradoxically both depicts the failure of its Southern reformer-hero and calls for renewed effort in the reform cause. The novel thus constitutes both a continuation of the Howellsian project with which Chesnutt began his career and a detailed critique of the psychological and emotional qualities that both motivate the reformer and endanger the success of his efforts on behalf of reform.

Chapter 5 addresses the sole author in this book who rejected Howellsian aesthetics outright: Willa Cather. The three early works discussed here, all of which were written during the author's transition from work as a journalist and editor for the muckraking *McClure's* magazine to a full-time literary career, document the painstaking process by which their author sought to free herself from the pervasive presence of Howells in the early-twentieth-century cultural landscape. The chapter traces Cather's struggle to subordinate regional literary materials and a mimetic prose imbued with the traces of Howellsian assumptions about literature's social-ethical purposes to aesthetic ends that rejected overt ethical aims and made social description the symbolic expression of a mythic typology of human character and reality. "Behind the Singer Tower" (1912), Cather's only attempt at an overtly socially purposive fiction, reveals in its very indecision about its final aims the difficulty its author faced in seeking to make socially descriptive writing suggest a mythic rather than a social and ethical basis for human reality. Similarly, Cather's first novel, *Alexander's Bridge* (1912), attempts to make material realities and social relationships express the mythic, essential selfhood of the novel's hero but despite the clarity of its intentions repeatedly founders on the competing exigencies of a lingering social understanding and construction of character and human reality. Finally, *O Pioneers!* (1913) succeeds in putting mimetic linguistic reference of regional social realities to consistently mythic and heroic aesthetic uses, constructing its characters and their society alike as the ephemeral, material expressions of a fully idealized conception of human reality—an approach opposite to that of Howells in most ways.

A few words on recurring terms and assumptions are in order here. This book both is and is not an influence study in the traditional sense of the term. W. D. Howells figures prominently throughout the book both in his own right and as a significant presence in the careers if not always directly in the lives of each of the three other writers; given his shifting but always prominent cultural significance throughout the period and his documented functions as editor, reviewer, mentor, social acquaintance, and/or cultural icon for each of the three, it would have been virtually impossible for any of them to have escaped his influence entirely. Nevertheless, the importance of Howells for this book is only partially bound up with his status as an influence on the other authors who comprise three-fifths of the study. My attempt herein is to trace not just Howells's direct and personal literary influence but (to reverse the terms of the subtitle of Michael D. Bell's book *The Problem of American Realism: The Cultural History of a Literary Idea*) to reconstruct part of the literary history of a cultural idea, an aesthetic that defined artistic excellence by the ethical work fiction could do in the ongoing public discourse about the momentous social changes taking place in turn-of-the-century America. Hence the ubiquity in these pages of the adjective "Howellsian," which I mean to suggest a loosely bound package of values and assumptions about literature's role in contemporary society that stems from the root aesthetic conception outlined above. The aesthetic program detailed in the pages of the *Editor's Study* is unique in its particular synthesis of aesthetic, social, and ethical ideas and in its alliance of literary mimetic strategies we may term Realist with a particular conception of literature's social responsibilities. But the *Editor's Study* is important primarily for its forceful, consistent, and influential articulation of ideas that, taken piecemeal, are neither unique to Howells nor limited in their currency to the years of the highest ascendancy of Howells's influence. After all, in her Deephaven sketches of the late sixties and early seventies Jewett was writing fiction pursuant to "Howellsian" literary goals more than a decade before Howells himself fully articulated those goals in the *Editor's Study;* likewise, Howells himself was already practicing, fitfully and experimentally, his emerging sense of a literary social ethics in his editorial decisions at the *Atlantic Monthly* and in travel essays such as *Suburban Sketches* (1872) before the *Editor's Study* and before he had turned to fiction as the literary genre best suited to his nascent conception of literary purpose. Further, the genesis of the Howellsian aesthetic may be traced to literary debates and examples—prominent among them Stowe's *Uncle Tom's Cabin,* a critically important book not only for Howells but for Chesnutt as well—that significantly predate the ascendancy of literary Realism and that would continue in other guises long after Howells's statues had been cut down around him and lay moldering in the literary historical moonlight. In one sense, this book addresses only a single brief chapter in a much longer history of literary theory and practice concerned with the morality (or immorality) of fiction. The term "Howellsian," of course, does not refer to the entire span of that history but to a specific but nevertheless somewhat open-ended and capacious conception in the late-nineteenth century of literature's rightful place in the ethical life of contemporary society; my use of the term is an attempt to reference in a single gesture the particular history of that idea as it was developed and deployed by Howells himself and the consonances of his ideas with other, closely allied notions of literary purposes and concomitant aesthetic means. As the other authors in this study—and indeed as Howells himself—encounter the Howellsian aesthetic, they inevitably re-understand (not to say misunderstand) his ideas in the ways that are most amenable to their own particular personal and literary characteristics, needs, purposes, and desires. Such creative misreading is an unavoidable feature of any process of intellectual interchange, but it is uniquely authorized, even encouraged, by the pragmatic, "anti-theoretical" nature of Howells's aesthetic writing: since the *Editor's Study* promulgates not a rigid artistic dogma but an evolving set of recurring ideas organized loosely around the central principle of literature's social-ethical use-value, the term "Howellsian" is useful, too, as a way of suggesting the radically antidogmatic nature of Howells's aesthetic thinking. Made for use in the "real" literary and social world, the Howellsian social-ethical aesthetic was designed to accommodate flexibly the particular uses and revisions that subsequent authors chose to undertake.

Accordingly, Howellsian aesthetic influences extend beyond the boundaries of texts that we would consistently term Realist. Even though three of its four subject authors wrote works whose relation to Realism has become something of a vexed critical issue and one of them—Cather—is by most accounts not a Realist at all, this book is a study of American literary Realism albeit in a somewhat particular sense. Howells bound his literary-ethical idea so closely to his articulations of Realism that in his wake they seemed to be one and the same, inseparable aspects of a single model of literary enterprise. Indeed, Howells fused his social-ethical conception of literary purposes with a particular formulation of Realism as a distinct set of subject matters and formal, stylistic, and procedural practices for attempting their mimetic representation in literature. That said, my interest in Realism through the course of this book is primarily upon the former rather than the latter aspect of Howells's literary thought and practice. In other words, the book's interest in Realism emphasizes not its formal or narratological properties per se but its attempted enactments of the particular set of social purposes and ethical raison d'être upon whose basis Howells constructed the most efficient literary method he could for pursuing them. Despite the fact that Howells developed his social-ethical literary imperative as an integral part of a theory of Realism, this book subordinates its consideration of Realism to the more fundamental conception of literature as a socially and ethically purposeful act of cross-cultural communication. Such an emphasis is warranted by Howells's own critical practice in the *Editor's Study* and elsewhere; he often praises works that we would not readily classify as "Realist" for those qualities in them that correspond to his sense of literary purposes.

Lastly, a word on my choice of the terms "ethics" and "ethical" throughout this work. While it is standard practice to employ the words "morality" and "ethics" (and their linguistic variants) interchangeably, I have chosen the latter here to suggest the collective dimension of moral interrelationship that stands at the center of Howells's aesthetic reasoning and fictive practice. If a merely personal morality had been all that was at stake for Howells in his construction of a modern literary aesthetic, his grounds for objection to the literature of morally spotless, idealized heroes and heroines would have been narrowed almost to the vanishing point. A significant portion of his criticism of contemporary literature based itself on his sense that it simply was not morally sufficient for literature to devote itself to the individual dimension of human life but that the literary work should instead be other-centered in its outlook and subject matter, and should encourage its readers—albeit through the unavoidably individual act of reading—to adopt an analogous outlook in their dealings with others in their society. Accordingly, I have chosen to use the word "ethical" throughout the book to indicate the social and public emphasis that Howells's aesthetic places upon its particular entrance into the larger debate about literature and morality. For closely related reasons, the term "ethical" is repeatedly deployed in the book as part of the (admittedly clumsy) formulation "social-ethical." I employ this term as the adjectival form of the

common formulation "social ethics" to suggest that for Howells consideration of the social could not be divided from issues of ethics. "Morality
penetrates all things, it is the soul of all things" (*Study* 50), he wrote, and
morality was accordingly and irreducibly a matter of social interrelationship as well as an individual concern. Elsewhere, Howells developed the
idea of "complicity" to express the inescapable condition of ethical interdependence, which in his view binds all people to each other through webs
of influence of which they remain largely ignorant. Oddly, the term "complicity" appears nowhere in the pages of the *Editor's Study* even though the
concept gained explicit expression elsewhere (in the 1886 novel, *The Minister's Charge*) early in the columns' run and even though it significantly
informs Howells's thinking therein. My use of the term "social-ethical" is
meant to suggest the core Howells idea that no department of human
endeavor—least of all a literature concerned with social representation—
could truthfully claim nonparticipation in an ethical field of interdependence. For Howells, the "social" and the "ethical" were but two faces of a
single reality that literature could face or not but with which it was necessarily involved in any case.

Conscience and Purpose

1
W. D. Howells's Literary Antitheory
Toward a Social-Ethical Aesthetic in the *Editor's Study*

Virtually all considerations of William Dean Howells's aesthetic principles acknowledge the pivotal role his impassioned ethical concerns played in their development. Howells's increasing preoccupation during the 1880s and '90s with the divisive cultural impacts of contemporary social and economic change, as documented by a long list of scholars, resulted in a corresponding movement of his literary thinking toward core values that could accommodate his increasing unease with the ever more divisive effects of emergent American capitalism, industrialization, urbanization, and immigration. Howells's ardent public advocacy of literary Realism and his concomitant production of the novels of the mid-1880s and early 1890s that still constitute the core of the Howells canon both resulted from his increasingly radicalized social and economic attitudes, which seemed to Howells to demand an aesthetic response commensurate to the deeply disruptive historical transformations of the late-nineteenth-century United States. While most critical attention to these matters has been trained upon Howells's fiction, this chapter will revisit his aesthetic theory, which gained its most extensive and influential formulations in the *Editor's Study* columns of *Harper's Monthly* magazine between 1886 and 1892. While virtually all scholars agree that Howells's social, political, and ethical anxieties deeply influenced his aesthetic thinking during this period of his career, the relationship between Howells's politics and his aesthetics is at once more integral and more useful in understanding his fiction and his influence upon subsequent writers than is usually recognized. In the *Editor's Study*, Howells attempted to construct a theory of literary art in which aesthetic principles would emerge integrally from considerations of social ethics, so that the "right thing" in life would merge seamlessly with the "good thing" in art, and vice versa. The wide-ranging occasional pieces that constitute the *Editor's Study* are founded consistently upon the notion that all legitimate aesthetic value proceeds from a preexisting social-ethical imperative: namely, that modern literature above all else should function as a vehicle for public communication aimed at mediating the deepening alienations between classes, regions, and ethnicities in an increasingly divided post-Civil War society. By fostering cross-cultural sympathies, Howells argues, literature not only would fulfill its social-ethical duties but also guarantee its own aesthetic excellence.

Rereading the *Editor's Study* through the lens of this central conception of literature's social and ethical aims reveals an underlying logical unity in Howells's aesthetic thinking that formalist approaches (such as, most recently, that of Michael Davitt Bell) have tended to suppress. But this unity is not without its internal inconsistencies, the most persistent of which is the paradox of a theory of art which, as Bell notes, habitually disparages art itself. Howells's elevation of the ethical use-value of the literary work to the status of shibboleth for its aesthetic value has the effect of subsuming literature itself within an antecedent, extra-aesthetic standard of value, thereby all but erasing art as an autonomous category. Literature would live up to its rightful purposes, Howells argues, only when the artifice of fiction so effaces itself as to disappear entirely into real life, allowing literary works to become routinely usable and practically useful parts of readers' everyday lives. Readers would then gain a literature so closely united to commonplace life that they would be left, as Howells in *Literature and Life* later confessed himself to be, with "a confusion as to which is which" (iv)—a confusion, it should be added, born not of life's imitation of art but of art's faithful imitation of life.[1] Paradoxically, however, Howells's positing of an art so successful at "hiding the joint" ("Novel-Writing" 15) between literature and extraliterary reality that it gives the appearance of having erased the distinction between the two entirely ends by reinforcing the notion of aesthetic autonomy that it seeks to counter, inadvertently reinscribing a conception of art as absolute illusion. Thus Howells's foundation of his literary thinking upon a principle of social-ethical purpose produced an apparently irresolvable theoretical contradiction.

But Howells's vision of literary usefulness not only creates this conundrum, it also provides a key to its resolution, and the terms of that resolution reconfirm the value of rereading the *Editor's Study* through Howells's conception of literature as a socially and ethically purposive activity. Howells's central aesthetic principle is instrumental rather than ontological, deriving not from what literature is, in and of itself, but rather from what literature does, for actual readers in the historical world. The conceptual corner into which Howells seems to have painted himself in the *Editor's Study* is only a conundrum when read as an abstract assertion of a universally valid aesthetic principle within an internally consistent and self-supporting theoretical system; understood, instead, as one in a series of pragmatic tactical maneuvers in a public campaign for a new, socially and ethically responsible literature, the apparent logical contradictions of Howells's theory of art resolve themselves into effective rhetorical argumentation. Howells's conception of literary art, then, is best understood not as an internally coherent, closed system of aesthetic theory but as a process of occasional and pragmatic actions—like the fiction for which the theory calls—aimed at furthering the specific social-ethical goals which for Howells comprised literature's raison d'être. Whatever internal consistency the *Editor's Study* can justly claim for itself depends on the recognition that Howells's aesthetic principles emerge from a particular, prior functional value which would create and evaluate literature according to the ethical work it attempts in the social, historical world. The ethical rootedness of Howells's fiction in the commonplaces of everyday life has led John Updike to characterize Howells the fiction writer as an "anti-novelist"—a writer dedicated to frustrating novel readers' expectations by creating marginally (un)likeable heroes, deliberate anticlimaxes, and story lines that resist the shapeliness and closure of conventional plotting. Likewise, Howells the aesthetician is best understood (to borrow from Updike) as an "anti-theorist," whose dedication to making literature an ethically useful element of the shared life of the society led him to abandon theoretical consistency in favor of the practical pursuit of literary art's rightful social-ethical purposes.

Society, Audience, Authorship

The sources of Howells's social, ethical, and aesthetic radicalization during the period of the *Editor's Study* have been thoroughly documented elsewhere, but a brief summary of the major strands of influence in the development of Howells's social and ethical stance in the mid-1880s will help to situate the aesthetic formulations which arose from them.[2] W. D. Howells inherited just enough of the staunch Swedenborgianism of his father, William Cooper Howells, to become what Edwin Cady terms an "agnostic Swedenborgian" (*Road* 150), convinced of the ethical, humanistic dimensions of the faith but skeptical of its mystical dimensions and unable to believe in its certitudes.[3] From his immersion in the abolitionist, radical Republican politics of antebellum Ohio, primarily gained, as was his education in political reporting and publishing, through his father's print shop, Howells learned not only the intricacies of politics but also the informed willingness to risk livelihood and reputation for the sake of egalitarian and communitarian principles.[4] Such principles saw continued professional exercise when Howells took on journalistic and editorial duties first at the *Nation* and then at the *Atlantic,* both of which journals were dedicated to far-ranging public discussion of politics, science, literature, and society; these experiences constituted for Howells, as Robert Hough has asserted about his *Atlantic* editorship, "a liberal education about contemporary America" (23), as well as a standing invitation to understand writing and publishing as an active authorial engagement with the political and cultural life of the society.[5] Howells's encounters during the decades of the *Editor's Study* with the works of Tolstoy and of a range of socialist writers including Laurence Gronlund, Edward Bellamy, and William Morris pushed him, from within the framework of his youthful democratic principles, to consider the necessity of far-reaching reform of current political, economic, and social arrangements. His distress at the drastically escalating disparities of the Gilded Age between owners and workers, "Americans" and immigrants, came to a head with his lonely and unsuccessful defense of the Haymarket Anarchists in 1887, during the second year of the *Editor's Study.*[6] "I should hardly like to trust pen and ink with all the audacity of my social ideas," he wrote Henry James in 1888, "but after fifty years of optimistic content with 'civilization' and its ability to come out all right in the end, I now abhor it, and feel that it is coming out all wrong in the end, unless it bases itself anew on a real equality" (*Life* 1:417).

In the *Editor's Study*, Howells bent his full critical energies toward making literature a public vehicle for securing this "real equality." Literature, he consistently asserted, should dedicate itself to introducing to each other citizens from the various divided sectors of society, in the hope that such acquaintance would improve their behavior toward each other, from the level of personal morality to that of reordering the economic and social structures that enforced intra- and intercultural divisions. Howells, holding as an article of faith that "Men are more like than unlike one another," called upon literary artists to

> make them know one another better, that they may be all humbled and strengthened with a sense of their fraternity. Neither arts, nor letters, nor sciences, except as they somehow, clearly or obscurely, tend to make the race better and kinder, are to be regarded as serious interests; they are all lower than the rudest crafts that feed and house and clothe, for except they do this office they are idle. (96)

This passage—perhaps the central statement of the social-ethical aesthetic principle that underwrites all of the *Editor's Study*—frames the entire literary enterprise as valuable primarily for its extraliterary effects in the individual and social lives of real readers. In order for the literary branch of the arts to perform such an office, writers must reconceive the role and function of literature, not as mere entertainment, nor as exercises in harmless escapism or personal moral idealism, nor as self-validating aesthetic activity, but as socially and ethically purposeful communication between members of a vast audience who also comprise the contemporary American polis. Further, the aesthetic success of literature is absolutely dependent on its fulfillment of these extraliterary purposes. As Clara Kirk puts it, for Howells, if the arts as "a form of communication . . . fail to reach the ordinary man, they fail as art" (Kirk, *Art* 147).[7]

Howells's recurring concern with issues of audience in the *Editor's Study* is directly traceable to this conception of literary art as public communication. In the midst of an exploding market for magazine fiction and a corresponding boom in book publishing, Howells worried that despite its

unprecedented popularity, fiction in the United States had little importance for most of the population except as cheap entertainment or salable
commodity. "Nothing perhaps is so illusory as the supposition of interest
in literature and literary men on the part of other men," he wrote late in
1888. For most readers, fiction "is an amusement, a distraction, a decora-
tion, taken up for a moment, an hour, a day, and then wholly dropped out
of sight, out of mind, out of life" (164)—a state of affairs that Howells
found acutely distressing. Even the most avid readers, Howells complained,
harbor toward favored authors only "such maudlin affection as the *habitue*
of an opium-joint perhaps knows for the attendant who fills his pipe with
the drug"; less zealous readers become "merely contemptuous" of literature,
regarding the novel "as an amusement, like horse-racing and card-playing"
(74). Either way, in Howells's view, literature generally failed to make itself genuinely useful to its readers, and consequently the majority of the
American audience regarded literature as fundamentally irrelevant to the
commonplace demands of daily life—precisely those areas to which Howells felt literature should directly address itself. Resisting the temptation
to which a later generation of literary Modernists would capitulate with
gusto, Howells refused to turn such observations into raillery against the
cloddishness of the reading public, choosing instead to take the opportunity to reassert the need for a new sense of literature as ethically purposive
communication. Public indifference to things literary stems not from the
failure of readers but from the failure of literature to communicate anything of real worth to its audience. If the mass of readers finds fiction
frivolous or contemptible, far removed from "the serious business of life"
(74), "they are very little to blame for it . . . for it is only in the rarest instances that literature has come home to their business and bosoms" (164).

Such a conception of audience had far-reaching implications for both
authorship and its product. It meant, first and foremost, a revolution in the
subject matter to which fiction should devote itself, coupled closely with a
new conception of the literary modus operandi offering the best approach
to this material; only by attempting an objective representation of the
commonplace world comprised of the quotidian social experiences of its
own audience could literature gain a solid basis for ethically purposeful
communication between authors and readers. Implicit in Howells's plea for

establishing a common ground between literature and life is a particular set of assumptions about the nature and the artistic representability of that life, the recurring assertion of which is such a commonplace of both Howells's own criticism and later Howells scholarship as to require little further comment here. Postmodern complications notwithstanding, Howells's root contention is simple: fiction must be created from direct, accurate observation rather than from prior—or a priori—literary types.[8] In an often-quoted passage of the *Editor's Study,* Howells made the point by employing an analogy between authorship and scientific fieldwork. Literature should turn its attentions from "the ideal grasshopper, the heroic grasshopper, the impassioned grasshopper, the self-devoted, adventureful, good old romantic card-board grasshopper" of established literary conventions and should devote its energies instead to describing, science-like, "the simple, honest, and natural grasshopper," which alone is "real" (111–12). In social terms, modern literature's usefulness to its readers depended, according to Howells, on a firm grounding in the everyday experiences of representatively average, commonplace lives. Edwin Cady has referred to this Howellsian literary orientation to reality as "a theory of Common Vision," and he emphasizes the "useful ambiguity" of the word "common," which may simultaneously suggest both "average, ordinary, normal, democratic" and "shared, general, normative, perhaps even universal" (*Common* 5). Rather than chasing after implausible idealizations of human character and conduct, literature must maintain the utmost "respect for probability, the fidelity to conditions, human and social, which can alone justify the reading or writing of novels" (*Study* 36). An empirical method of literary observation and representation thus guaranteed that fictive subject matter would coincide with the quotidian lives about which and for which literature must communicate in order to fulfill its social-ethical mission.

Recognition of these authorial obligations called for comprehensive rethinking of the nexus of intersections among art, artists, readers, and life. "It is the conception of literature as something apart from life, superfinely aloof, which makes it really unimportant to the great mass of mankind, without a message or a meaning for them" (74), Howells wrote. Conversion of literature into a medium for truthful social communication required authors and readers alike to abandon the conception of art as a privileged and autonomous realm. For the audience, the remaking of literature as a communicative rhetorical transaction based in commonplace social reality would remove the gulf between lived and literary experience, making literature directly accountable to the social and ethical uses to which real readers, inhabiting shared social territory with fictive characters, could put it. Authors, too, were reconceived as co-occupants of this shared space, and the vocation of authorship accordingly altered. The Romantic notion of literature as a series of aesthetic monuments to the creative genius of individual artists working in relative isolation from the mundane concerns of everyday life had to give way to a conception of literature as an ongoing, collective participation in a shared social enterprise:

> The whole field of human experience was never so nearly covered by imaginative literature in any age as in this; and American life especially is getting represented with unexampled fulness. It is true that no one writer, no one book, represents it, for that is not possible; our social and political decentralization forbids this, and may forever forbid it. But a great number of very good writers are instinctively striving to make each part of the country and each phase of our civilization known to all the other parts; and their work is not narrow in any feeble or vicious sense. (98)

Literature would fulfill its communicative function not through any single, culturally comprehensive and permanently valid American masterwork, but through the patient, piecemeal efforts of dozens of new American fictionists, each writing from his or her own fund of local cultural experience and observation. Consequently, "We shall probably never have a great American novel as fancied by the fondness of critics," nor is this consequence to be lamented (3). The representation of American life in fiction must occur "not in some typical embodiment long dreamed of as the business of a great American novel, but in details of motive and character slowly and honestly assembled by many hands from its vast spaces and varieties" (3). Howells thus envisioned the social work performed by modern fiction as a continual, collaborative literary dialogue aimed at mediation of cultural differences within a radically decentered society.[9]

Language, Style, Form

Just as these macroconceptions of literature, as a practice and as a body of individual works, refer ultimately (via fiction's central communicative capacity) to the keystone principle of literature's social and ethical responsibilities, so too do Howells's microconceptions of acceptable language, style, and form. Insofar as these elements of the literary work facilitate clear communication and therefore contribute to the greater purpose of making the members of a society know each other better, they are aesthetically good. But when the "apparatus" of art calls attention to itself and away from the subject of its communication, it becomes an obstacle to literature's performance of its rightful social function and hence results in bad art. Accordingly, Howells follows up his oft-quoted clarion call, "Let fiction cease to lie about life," with specific advice concerning the kind of language that will achieve that goal: "let it not put on fine literary airs; let it speak the dialect, the language, that most Americans know—the language of unaffected people everywhere" (81). The language of fiction, in other words, in order to fulfill its primary communicative function effectively, should be transparent and middling, drawn from the colloquial field that the new literature shared with its characters, authors, and readers. The choice of such language—founded, as Daniel Borus notes, upon the assumption of direct correspondence between words and the things that they name, which would be readily communicable by using a neutral, near-universal, a-rhetorical idiom (22–23)—rather than calling attention to itself, would allow readers direct access to the "facts" the literary work strives to represent, putatively unmediated by the distracting artificialities of self-conscious literary aesthetics.[10]

Howells cites as a prime example U.S. Grant's *Personal Memoirs,* whose successful literary communication of its content is achieved through the author's praiseworthy indifference to questions of mere style. "The author's one end and aim," Howells writes in terms easily generalizable beyond Grant himself,

is to get the facts out in words. He does not cast about for phrases, but takes the word, whatever it is, that will best give his meaning, as if it were a man or a force of men for the accomplishment of a feat of arms. There is not a moment wasted in preening and prettifying, after the fashion of literary men; there is no thought of style, and so the style is good . . . with a peculiar, almost plebeian, plainness at times. (34)

Directing his words as a general would his soldiers, Grant chooses and deploys them solely according to the practical merits of the rhetorical situation. His language, drawn from a shared, commonplace vocabulary, is valuable not in and of itself but only for its capacity to get the particular job done: to communicate clearly to an audience inhabiting the same linguistic and social world that the author and his subjects inhabit. Books like Grant's are "possessed of their subject rather than possessed of their manner" (35), Howells claims. Aesthetic "preening and prettifying" can have no place in a literature so forthrightly devoted to plain facts. In such work, as Daniel Borus remarks, a common, widely shared vernacular replaces a specialized literary language determined by a cultural elite; "the goal of this new discourse was to provoke in readers a sense of their commonality both as readers and as citizens and to stimulate an active participation in social life" (133). Grant and his literary kin, according to Howells, achieve pure literary communication by adopting an essentially antiliterary language and style, measured against existing late-nineteenth-century standards.[11]

Elsewhere in the *Editor's Study,* Howells coins the term "literosity" (49) to denote any literary technique, manner, or style that fails to meet the communicative standard exemplified by Grant by interfering with an audience's direct and unhampered interaction with the realities represented in fiction. Favorably reviewing *The Mayor of Casterbridge,* for example, Howells praises its achievement, as he had Grant's, as something "exist[ing] apart from any beauty of style or felicity of phrase" (49). Hardy's excellence consists in his "very frank and simple way of dealing with every kind of life, and of approaching men and women as directly as if they had never been written about before" (49). The novelist's

first sense of people is apparently not a literary sense, but something very much more natural. He studies their exterior graphically, and deals with their souls as we do with those of our neighbors, only perhaps a little more mercifully. This absence of literosity, if we may coin a word as offensive as the thing, accounts for an occasional bluntness of phrase, which we have sometimes felt in Mr. Hardy's work, and for here and there an uncouthness of diction—or call it awkwardness; but we gain infinitely more than we lose by it. (49)

Hardy's aesthetic success arises from his humane dedication to faithful communication of his subjects' lives rather than from a devotion to artistic style for its own sake. His penetrating and sympathetic interaction with his characters models the kind of interaction Howells wishes all literature to promote among its readers. In Hardy's studious avoidance of literosity, a term that Howells would use with increasing frequency in the pages of the *Editor's Study*, resides a primary resource in literature's quest to perform its social and ethical functions.

From the same source arises Howells's virulent opposition to the twin aesthetic mistakes of aestheticism and what he calls "effectism," both of which distract readerly attention from literature's rightful purpose as social mediation and divert it either toward the literary work itself or to the reader's own emotional responses to it. Aestheticist theories of literature, according to Howells, are misguided precisely because they prize literosity to the exclusion of literature's social-ethical objectives. Hence the inaugural essay of the *Editor's Study*, in praising the latest novels of Mary Noailles Murfree, G. W. Cable, and S. Weir Mitchell, unfavorably contrasts the aestheticist insistence on the deliberate uselessness of art with the Realist "disposition to look at [life] keenly and closely in the right American manner, and to question the results with the last fineness for their meaning and their value" (3) for actual readers and the society they comprise. "There is conscience and purpose in it all," Howells continues, "and it is all far from the make-believe 'Greek' theory of art for art's sake—as if the Greekest of the Greek art were not for religion's sake, as the Greeks understood it" (3). The invocation of classical literature's seamless contiguity with the communal values of cult and polis serves to commend the best contemporary writing for its devotion to analogous social purposes in contemporary U.S. society. The fundamental error of aestheticism, he argues, is that it mistakes a single effect of literature for its primary end, subordinating truthful social representation to the personal emotional gratification readers derive from the aesthetic play of the text. Accordingly, Howells takes issue with Spanish novelist Juan Valera's self-declaration as "an advocate of art for art's sake," maintaining that the Spanish novelist's practice is more true than his theory. "If it is true," Howells writes, quoting from Valera,

> that "the object of a novel should be to charm through a faithful representation of human actions and human passions, and to create by this fidelity to nature a beautiful work," and if "the creation of the beautiful" is solely "the object of art," it never was and never can be solely its effect as long as men are men and women are women. If ever the race is resolved into abstract qualities, perhaps this may happen; but till then the finest effect of the "beautiful" will be ethical, and not aesthetic merely. (50)

In other words, the emotional effect of the novel's beauty upon the reader is for Howells only a pleasant side effect of its success as a faithful representation of shared social reality for specific ethical purposes; it is only a means to a larger end. Since real readers, after the act of reading is ostensibly complete, necessarily take their personal responses to the literary text with them, back into the world of ethically invested social interactions, aesthetics cannot reasonably pretend that the act of reading takes place in an ahistorical realm of pure ideality, insulated from the demands and vagaries of "real life." The aesthetic success of any literary work is to be measured, finally, in terms that go beyond the limited space defined by the solitary reader of the individual text, to the effects of that textual transaction upon the behavior of reader-citizens toward each other in the social world to which readers, authors, and characters alike belong.

Aestheticism, Howells asserts, abrogates literature's fundamental responsibilities by ignoring the implications for art of the essentially social and historical nature of human existence, along with its concomitant ethical implications, overemphasizing the status of the textual artifact per se. "Effectism"—a term that Howells borrows from Spanish novelist and critic Palacio Valdés—stands similarly condemned. Valdés defines effectism as "the itch of awaking at all cost in the reader vivid and violent emotions, which shall do credit to the invention and originality of the writer" (224), and Howells predictably objects to the distracting overemphasis on both author and reader that such a literary practice produces. Measured against the literary-ethical imperative at the core of Howells's aesthetic, effectism—as a form of literosity—interferes with the rightful communicative function of literature by distracting readerly attention from the text's content and diverting it to the short-lived thrills afforded by sensationalism and sheer artistic novelty—hardly properties of the text that contribute to the social-ethical usefulness of readers' aesthetic experiences beyond the immediate act of reading. Like aestheticism, effectism cuts off literary art from its full embeddedness in the world of social and ethical interactions inhabited by its readers. "All arts," Howells later wrote, "decay when they begin to exist for themselves alone, or merely for the pleasure they can give, since truth beyond and beside them must be their incentive" (186).

Howells maintains that literary form, like language and style, also must avoid the readerly distractions created by literosity in order to fulfill its communicative functions and hence its social-ethical purposes. Since the truth of literature is a function of its faithful connectedness to the real life of its audience, the form of good literature will follow that function, rather than strive for a formal unity at the expense of truth to life. A novel, whatever its size, "is necessarily a group of episodes more or less loosely connected by a thread of narrative, and there seems no reason why this thread must always be supplied. Each episode may be quite distinct, or it may be one of a connected group; the final effect will be from the truth of each episode, not from the size of the group" (97). Form, according to this logic, is wholly a function of the communicative connection between the lives of the audience and those of the characters about whom they read, and it therefore must be driven by its faithfulness to the contours and qualities of the particular subjects of its representation rather than by self-referential attention to the internal consistencies of the text that performs that representation. Truthful social communication, in other words, may well require literary forms as open-ended and "baggy" (to borrow Henry James's pejorative)—as apparently inartistic—as life itself. The neater the resolutions and closures of the literary work of art, the more suspect it becomes for Howells as responsible ethical communication. The Howellsian novel in theory, as Everett Carter writes of it in practice, "simply runs off the edge of the canvas" in its determination to become "something very close to the texture of life itself" (131): an organicism not, as Carter would have it, of the work of art with itself and the mind of its creator but with the social life it represents and with the readers for whom it represents that life. Plot, dramatic form, architectonics—all the artistic trappings of the novel as it had been practiced and as it would continue to be developed, notably in the markedly different and decidedly formalist aesthetic of Howells's friend Henry James—can be aesthetically good only insofar as they further literature's social-ethical aim of making itself seamlessly contiguous with, and thereby ethically usable in, the lives of its readers.

Literary Use-Value

From roots to branches—that is to say, from the informing principle of social-ethical purpose to the conforming details of literary technique, language, style, and form—the *Editor's Study* arises from Howells's insistence that the use-value of the literary work for real readers in the world outside the boundaries of the text must be considered as a wholly integral part of that work's aesthetic worth. Howells's consequent de-emphasis of the idiogenetic qualities of the literary work—its relative aesthetic autonomy and self-referentiality, and its relatedness to other works of art—consistently calls for the critic's attention to be trained not only upon the text's internal properties but also on the literary work's effects and uses in a socially and ethically interactive historical world.[12] For Howells, literature's primary responsibility was an ethically purposeful engagement with social realities shared by author, audience, and fictive characters, undertaken "as a form of political intervention designed to repair the fissures that had run through nearly every aspect of American life" (Borus 139), and all aesthetic judgment therefore must remain cognizant of the literary work's relative success in meeting that responsibility. Howells's reconceptualization of fiction as a socially and ethically communicative act thus entailed a particular understanding of the use-value of literature, which became the source and measure of the idiogenetic aesthetic merit of any given literary text. In the *Editor's Study*, the social-ethical use-value of literature in the world beyond the text is in every respect contiguous with the literary work's status as art object.

Both Daniel Borus and Rodney Olsen have explored in some depth the importance of Howells's ideation of "use-value" to his thinking about literature and the literary vocation, but with significant differences whose explanation should help to clarify the emphasis of this argument. Borus, who founds his investigation of the literary "practices"[13] of Howells, James, and Norris upon the thesis that "the central historical determinant of the realist writing process was the consolidation of the literary marketplace as the locus of literary production, exchange, and circulation" (24), accordingly understands the use-value assigned to literature by Realist writers, including Howells, as an attempt "to rescue literature from the whims of the marketplace" (58). Recognizing the opportunity presented by the burgeoning literary marketplace to involve multitudes of new readers in "a democratic and socially meaningful art" (57), Borus argues, Realist writers were nevertheless dismayed by the tendency of market forces to reduce all fiction to "mere commodity" (58). Since the "serious" literary artist depended on a mass readership to further his literary goals, "Realists were therefore faced with the problem of preventing the exchange value of fiction from swamping its use value" (58). Howells's attempted solutions to this problem, Borus maintains, revert to individual readers' preferences as the ultimate source of aesthetic value, thus "enshrining the sovereignty of the individual subject" (62). And since this notion of autonomous individual choice "was the fundamental principle of the marketplace from which [Realists] had hoped to disengage literature" (62), Howells's attempts to establish literary use-value as something other than economic profitability were "compromised" (62). "Howells made narration conditional on the agreement of the audience to accept it," Borus continues, and thus

> focused attention on the author-audience relation. Realizing that no objective standard of art could be maintained in an era in which the literary marketplace held sovereignty, realists admitted that the ability to convince the readership was crucial. In effect, realist doctrine made value recoverable only at the moment of consumption. When the author was understood, the "work" of writing had been realized. (99)

Borus's close attention to the undeniable impact of the burgeoning capitalist system upon Howells's practice of literary Realism valuably situates Realist aesthetics within its late-nineteenth-century context and thus rescues it from an ahistorical formalist critique. But his assertion of the literary marketplace as a single-cause explanation of turn-of-the-century changes in authorial practice significantly limits our understanding of Howells's aesthetic project in the *Editor's Study*. Indeed, Borus's assertions about the aesthetic impacts of market capitalism on Howells's work rely heavily not on Howells's most extensive exposition of principles in the *Editor's Study* but on the later, shorter single essay entitled "The Man of Letters as a Man of Business," in which Howells engages most directly the economic issues at the core of Borus's thesis. The effect is to unduly skew interpretation of Howellsian aesthetics toward the economic and away from other, equally powerful motives for Howells's redefinition of literary use-value and his altered practice of authorship. While it would be ludicrous to maintain that pervasive changes in the business of literary publishing played no significant role in the formation of Howells's literary theory, Borus's persistently economic definition of literary use-value runs counter to Howells's core critical assumptions in the *Editor's Study* and leads to some highly questionable assertions about the nature of the author-audience relationship in his aesthetic; in Borus's argument, irresistible market values always trump literary authors' consciously held social and ethical purposes. Borus rightly notes the new, communicative basis upon which Howells attempted to place literary aesthetics; but surely Howells's recognition that this aesthetic communication was dependent on the literary marketplace—a recognition that gave him multiple theoretical and practical headaches, as Borus observes—does not lead logically to the equation (in the passage quoted above) of the act of understanding by a novel's reader with the act of consumption by its purchaser, as though buying a book were equivalent to reading and understanding it. Sovereign individual subjectivity may indeed underpin both consumer capitalism and the act of reading, but this fact by itself does not subject all aspects of the reader-text transaction to the forces of the marketplace nor make them understandable in purely economic terms. In fact, Howells's social-ethical conception of literary purpose led to a definition of literature's use-value that actively resisted understanding audience as a function merely of market forces, insisting instead on a conception of readers as individually and communally autonomous agents whose actions in the world would inevitably be influenced, for better or worse, by fiction's mimetic representations of the world. While Howells the businessman could not but be aware of the problematic ramifications of the fact that fulfillment of his aesthetic purposes was dependent in part upon selling books to prospective readers, the aesthetic that he develops in the *Editor's Study* cannot be understood, finally, as a function solely of the economic principles governing the literary marketplace.[14]

A more nuanced, multicausal explanation of Howells's conception of literary use-value emerges from Rodney Olsen's study of Howells's early life and works. Concentrating on "Howells' emotional, intellectual, and moral development" as both a product and a reflector of "the making of middle-class culture in the nineteenth century" (xv), Olsen sees the development of Howells's idea of literary authorship as the product of his personal negotiation of the midcentury cultural pressures surrounding issues of vocation, politics, gender, and religion. One of the most keenly felt of these tensions for Howells, Olsen argues, was between an imperative, middle-class ambition for personal economic success and a religious/ethical mandate toward conscientious, other-centered selflessness in one's public dealings. The result was that Howells was driven to conceptualize the literary vocation, and hence literature itself, not only as a respectable and potentially lucrative choice of profession but also as a publicly useful, communal enterprise. (See especially 16–19, 89, 256–58.)[15] Responding in his career to the influences of William Cooper Howells's Swedenborgianism as well as to antebellum cultural ideals of family, community, and political life, Howells accordingly worked to "make the literary vocation a force for class reconciliation and communal betterment" (258). Although Olsen confines his attention to the early Howells and so does not treat the *Editor's Study*, the multiple impetuses in Howells's life toward other-centered usefulness that Olsen identifies obviously bear a very close relationship to the formulation of literary use-value in the literary theory of the *Editor's Study*.

For Howells, the use-value of literature—its worth as public communication of shared social realities aimed at personal and collective ethical reform—constitutes not only the hallmark of "serious" literary endeavor but also the primary benchmark for aesthetic success. The root theoretical strategy in the *Editor's Study* is to subsume literature's aesthetic value within its use-value, which thereby encompasses not only the literary artifact's idiogenetic artistic qualities but also the effects of those qualities on the actions of real readers in the world beyond the immediate act of reading. In a long passage hailing the advent in modern literature of a new "art for humanity's sake," "working with an ethical purpose" of truthful representation of human life and character, Howells explicitly equates fulfillment of that purpose, figured here in terms of an explicitly Christian social ethics, with aesthetic excellence: "Christ and the life of Christ is [sic] at this moment inspiring the literature of the world as never before, and raising it up a witness against waste and want and war. . . . [I]n the degree that it ignores His spirit, modern literature is artistically inferior. In other words, all good literature is now Christmas literature" (169). The literary "masters of our time," Howells continues, "are conscious of a duty to man in their work, and they do it with a sense that it does not begin and end in themselves; that even art does not compass it all, and that to amuse or thrill their readers is no longer enough" (169). The ethical vocation of the literary artist precedes and includes his or her artistic vocation, not only requiring (as already demonstrated) a reconstitution of literature as primarily an act of communication, but redefining aesthetic excellence itself as a function of the literary work's success in pursuing its social-ethical goals. There can be no question of artistic excellence independent of a literary work's purposeful interaction with its society; there can be no aesthetic beauty not intimately bound up with the ethical effect of the work upon its audience. Contrary to recurring anti-Realist charges that the modern literary abandonment of ideal subject matter and elevated style render fiction morally pernicious and aesthetically ugly, Howells writes (of H. H. Boyesen) that "Perfect realism need not be ever less poetical because it is ever more conscientious" (206). On the contrary, "The finest work of our day teaches that to be morally false is to be aesthetically false" (195). Beauty in literature arises from truth, not vice versa; and truth is to be found not in the realm of a priori ideals but in the human, social world of ethical interrelationship. Only through conscientious performance of its public duty of truthful representation, of its readers for its readers, can literature hope to achieve aesthetic excellence.

The Disappearance of Art

As Howells argues ever more persistently for the keystone principle of social-ethical responsibility in literature, the *Editor's Study* strategically devalues all terms of art that might imply the existence of an autonomous realm of idiogenetic aesthetic reference in order to emphasize the literary use-value that alone can guarantee aesthetic worth. In fact, this strategy is so persistent as to cause Michael D. Bell to pronounce "Howells' insistence on the radical opposition of interest in 'style' and concern for 'truth'" to be "in effect, the central theoretical underpinning of his version of realism" (20, 21). "Is it possible, then," a rhetorically incredulous Bell goes on to ask, "that the apparent *problem* of Howellsian realism—its persistent denigration of the 'literary'—is in fact one of its principal *tenets?*" (21).[16] Bell here identifies what is in fact a central feature of Howells's aesthetic thought (although the interpretive conclusions Bell draws from this fact seem, as will become apparent, highly questionable). In order to understand Howells's theory of literature in the *Editor's Study*, one must understand the meaning of Howells's apparent devaluation of art itself.

As demonstrated previously, Howells subordinates form, style, and language to the use-value of literature as ethically purposeful communication. In order to make literature a usable part of the lives of actual readers, as many perceptual barriers as possible between literature and life must be removed. The tying of aesthetic standards to prior ethical standards—in Howells's words, the equation of literature's "lasting beauty" with its "final usefulness" (211)—entails the devaluation of any aspect of literary practice that reemphasizes the artificiality of art, thereby increasing the perceived distance between art and life. Since the aim of all good literature, in Howells's thinking, is to make the boundary between fiction and life so permeable as to yield an absolute contiguity of art and life, literosity is the enemy of good literature because it reinforces that boundary, calling readerly attention away from the shared life under literary representation and toward the idiogenetic qualities of the literary work or the reader's own, subjective responses to them. Thus Howells's repeated denunciations of literature and the literary—admittedly rather startling from the pen of a serious, practicing novelist—are inseparably linked to the social-ethical literary principle at the heart of the *Editor's Study*. Further, far from representing an opposition between artistic "style" and "truth" (as Bell would have it), Howells's aesthetic reasoning seeks to erase the distinction between the two. In short, the *Editor's Study* repeatedly appears to make the rather surprising assertion that in order for literary art to do its social-ethical work, art itself must disappear. Accordingly, Howells praises Charles Dudley Warner as one of "the few literary men, destined to be more, for whom literature does not suffice as an end, but who regard it consciously or unconsciously as a means, and who give their work enrichingly back to the life from which its materials came" (239). Similarly, the novels of W. H. White, by studiously avoiding any "merely decorative use of words," produce the sense "that you have witnessed the career of a man as you might have witnessed it in the world, and not in a book" (9). And most radically of all, Howells claims for *Anna Karenina* the power to erase wholly the boundary between life and art: "As you read on you say, not, 'This is like life,' but, 'This is life.' It has not only the complexion, the very hue, of life, but its movement, its advances, its strange pauses, its seeming reversions to former conditions, and its perpetual change; its apparent isolations, its essential solidarity" (17). Tolstoy, for Howells the chief exemplar of the new "Christmas literature" (169), succeeds artistically precisely because he seems not to be performing art at all, but seamlessly merging the lives and concerns of literary characters with the world as lived by actual readers.

Howells distributes comments like these liberally throughout the columns of the *Editor's Study*. But his rhetorical strategy of denigrating literary art in order to champion an expanded, social-ethically rooted literary aesthetic leads to what seems to be a glaring theoretical self-contradiction. For if the literary work can only fulfill its social-ethical purposes by so effacing its own artifice as to seem to disappear into life itself, then does that not make it the most illusionary artifice of all? Howells concludes his praise of *Anna Karenina* by asserting that the novel "is a world, and you live in it while you read, and long afterward" (17). In effect, the novel's successful erasure of the great divide between life and art perversely forces Howells to acknowledge what may be an unavoidable paradox of any mimetic theory of art: the more complete the artwork's resemblance to real life, the more it proves that its status is something different from real life. To the degree that the novel convinces its readers of its own reality, it has succeeded in creating an aesthetic illusion and thus has proven that art does indeed constitute an autonomous realm that is not life itself but operates according to its own rules and principles. Theoretically speaking, then, literature's quest for absolute ethical usefulness in the lives of its readers leads to a literary art that strives for absolute illusion, and in the process appears to reify art and extra-artistic reality as wholly separate and distinct entities. Upon this theoretical conundrum, in its apparent admission by Howells that the fusion of art and life is an impossibility after all, Michael D. Bell constructs his hostile interpretation of *Criticism and Fiction;* the terms of his misreading shed useful light on the nature of Howells's critical reasoning.

Bell professes to be interested in "realism and naturalism" not as designations for a "coherent formal tradition," which in his view "may be little more than figments of our literary-historical imaginations," but as functional cultural terms "used by generations of American fiction writers . . . to describe what they thought they were doing" (4). (Hence the subtitle of his book: *Studies in the Cultural History of a Literary Idea.*) Accordingly, Bell claims to be pursuing an understanding of Howells's critical thinking within its functional context: "William Dean Howells was no Auerbach, no Lukács, and if we wish to understand Howells we must try to understand him on his own terms and in his own context" (5). But Bell's explication of *Criticism and Fiction* proceeds to ignore these professions of contextual criticism by reading Howells through a prism of formalist assumptions that run counter to Howellsian thinking and virtually guarantee an antagonistic interpretation of his ideas. Bell's selection of *Criticism and Fiction* as his working text, rather than the *Editor's Study* or any other works of Howells's voluminous output of practical criticism, signals both his formalist assumptions and his lack of concern for cultural-historical contexts. Ignoring without comment the majority scholarly opinion that *Criticism and Fiction,* in Cady's words, does "deadly damage . . . to Howells' thought and prose by his own rupture of contexts" (*Critic* 75), Bell chooses a text whose primary weakness is that it gives to a six-year-long series of "opportunistic" (*Critic* 76) essays on current books and literary trends the false appearance of trying to be a systematic theory.[17] Consequently, the relatively independent critical comments contained therein, intended by Howells as pragmatic assertions of one type of literary practice against other historically specific conceptions of literature's rightful ends and means, are made to yield the false impression of constituting absolute and unconditional aesthetic principles. Bell's exclusive focus on *Criticism and Fiction,* in other words, enables him more easily to evade the intensely practical and expansively cultural intent of Howells's critical statements, reducing them to a collection of logical absurdities by suppressing their functional value as part of an ongoing cultural argument and treating them instead as a series of logically incoherent assertions in a systematic aesthetic philosophy—a status that not even *Criticism and Fiction* claims for itself.

Having rightly noted Howells's recurring opposition of terms such as "art," "style," "form," and the "literary" to "truth," "life," the "real," and the "human," Bell reads these oppositions as expressions of absolute ontological categories originating in a static realm of eternal aesthetic truth. He assumes, without explanation or argument, that art actually *is* primarily a matter of form and style. Thus Bell is surprised, and expects his readers to share his surprise, that for Howells "what apparently distinguishes a picture from a map"—the former, according to Howells, being modern fiction's appropriate goal—"astonishingly enough, is not consciousness of form, of pictorial composition, but attention to 'fact' and 'meaning'!" (19). Accordingly, Bell casts Henry James, whose objections on specifically formal grounds to Howells's theory and practice increased exponentially throughout their synchronous careers, in the role of "intelligently critical" (22) corrective to Howells's "naive" (22) theoretical blunders. James's protests against Howells's strategic devaluation of the literary then become not the words of "an aesthete rebuking a realist but [those of] a serious writer reminding his friend"—by implication *not* a serious writer—"that even realistic literature neither can nor should seek to evade the 'literary'—that realism involves not a rejection of style (if such a thing were even possible) but a particular *use* of style" (21).

Ironically, Howells's pronouncements on literary style—along with form, technique, language, and all the other tools the literary artist uses to represent reality in fiction—present precisely the kind of argument for a particular use of style that Bell here accuses Howells of lacking. Howells, as a practicing novelist, sensitive editor, and penetrating if perhaps overly sympathetic critic, can hardly be said to have been unaware that the creation of literary art requires the writer's adoption of form and style. But Howells consistently deploys the terms "form" and "style," as well as the other terms of art that the *Editor's Study* strategically disparages, not as the ontological absolutes upon which Bell's anti-Realist argument rests but as provisional categories, valid only insofar as they prove useful in his campaign for a literary aesthetic that would include consideration of the social-ethical effects of fiction on its readers and their society. For the formalist, whether Michael D. Bell or Henry James, the material of art matters only insofar as it gives occasion for the aesthetic selection and shaping the artist confers upon it; but for Howells, the idiogenetic aspects of art matter only insofar as they prove ethically useful to a real audience struggling to live in a real social world.[18]

Howells never intends his denigration of the terms of art as denials of the reality of art and aesthetic experience. On the contrary, his persistent denunciations of the "literary" constitute the primary tactic in an impassioned argument *in favor* of art, albeit an art based on antiformalist assumptions. The derogation of "art" in the *Editor's Study* is the result (as even Bell must grant) neither of Howells's "personal naiveté" nor of "the lack of theoretical sophistication in his literary contemporaries" (Bell 21), but neither is it the result, as Bell would have it, merely of Howells's personal need to prove himself a "real man" despite his feminized literary vocation. Instead, the key to correctly understanding Howells's aesthetic pronouncements in the *Editor's Study* consists in close attention to the kind of document Howells set out to write: not an internally consistent treatise on literary aesthetics but an array of pragmatic entries in a continuing cultural dialogue. Howells wields the antiliterary tenor of much of the *Editor's Study* as a means to an end; his denigration of the terms of art comprises a series of provisional attacks upon contemporary definitions of literature that run counter to the particular conception of literary use-value that is the keystone of his critical thinking.

Despite the fact that the *Editor's Study*, as Donald Pizer writes, "seldom dealt theoretically with the values and assumptions underlying [Howells's] discussion of current literature," there emerges from it nevertheless a "coherent critical position that ran like an undercurrent" (xvi) in the stream of Howells's purposely occasional speculations. The unity of Howells's major statement of literary theory arises not from its status as a theory, but from the same principle of literary use upon which Howells sought to establish literature itself. Criticism—his own included—could be for Howells nothing but a means to an end; only insofar as the *Editor's Study* proved useful in the campaign to make literature more responsive to the social and ethical needs of real readers could it be considered a worthwhile project. By reading the *Editor's Study* itself as another embodiment of the principle of social-ethical use that Howells sought to make the keystone of serious literary practice, one discovers the basis for understanding the numerous backtrackings, inconsistencies, and outright self-contradictions that sometimes seem to be the primary feature of the entire series of columns. Hence, in a work ostensibly devoted to "banging the babes of romance about" (qtd. in Cady, *Realist* 12), Howells does not hesitate to praise the romance of the past, when it "sought, as realism seeks now, to widen the bounds of sympathy" (22). Likewise, in a work that proselytizes for modern fictive practice, Howells thinks nothing of speculating that the pursuit of "real usefulness" in literature may someday cause fiction itself to "be superseded by a still more faithful form of contemporaneous history" (116). Similarly, he does not balk at criticizing an author of overtly ethical fiction (George Washington Cable) for allowing "the citizen, the Christian . . . to threaten the artist" (159)—not because art has suddenly become more important than ethics but because lack of due attention to idiogenetic considerations interferes with the achievement of social-ethical purposes. The provisional, use-driven nature of the *Editor's Study* even allows Howells, without blinking, to adopt the decidedly unrealist mode of allegory to express once again the key principle of his literary thinking by temporarily entering the world of idealist abstractions in order to make his thoroughly time-bound and conditional point: "The True and The Beautiful are one and the same; only The True is the one, and The Beautiful is the same" (290–91). Even allegory, Howells demonstrates, can be made to serve legitimate literary purposes under an aesthetic defined by its pragmatic social effects rather than exclusively by the artistic means by which those effects are achieved.

Ultimately, Howells practices literary theory according to the same "agnostic" principle of social and ethical use for which the theory argues in literature. Howells assumes the futility of searching for an immutable aesthetic ideal just as he assumes the final mystery of the existence of God: whatever may be known of either can be apprehended only through the

evidence available empirically through the experience of commonplace realities. Criticism, like literature, should concern itself not with speculative
abstractions but with immediate ethical usefulness in the temporal and
social world that readers and writers inhabit together. The *Editor's Study*,
finally, is Howells's antitheory of literature. The repercussions of its radical
reordering of the relations between literature and society would be felt by
contemporary and succeeding literary generations as unavoidable premises
or obstacles to the practice of writing fiction. The following chapters of this
book explore a representative range of significant literary responses to
Howells's social-ethical aesthetic, the first of which is Howells's own.

2
What Is To Be Done?
Howells's Social-Ethical Fiction

One of the most striking features of Howells's criticism in the *Editor's Study* is its catholicity. Not only did Howells review works from an exceptionally diverse range of genres, nations, regions, and kinds of authors, but more often than not he found something valuable in what he read. The number of texts and authors receiving outright pans in the columns of *Harper's Monthly* was relatively small. Instead, negative criticism tended to be aimed at classes of authors and books without, as it were, naming names, while Howells found some element or another to praise and encourage in large numbers of works that one probably would not consider to be particularly good examples of the type of literary art for which he consistently argued. Despite the perceptions of his Romanticist opponents and despite his own avowals, the strategy in the *Editor's Study* was less an affair of "banging the babes of romance about" (qtd. in Cady, *Realist* 12), as Howells wrote to Edmund Gosse early in 1886, than it was a mission to find and encourage, in whatever contexts they were found, qualities of writing amenable to the development of his expanded social-ethical aesthetic. This approach is quite in keeping with Howells's decentered and diffuse conception of the American literary enterprise: no one "Great American Novel" could reasonably be expected to perform all the cultural work necessary under the new aesthetic to make the various far-flung corners of the always-changing republic sympathetically known to each other.

Instead, artistic success was a matter of the ongoing, patient accrual of multiple literary points of view trained upon all aspects of contemporary life; the Great American Novel was to be metaphorically reconceived as a collective, multiauthored, and perpetual work-in-progress rather than as a single text by a single author of genius.

Howells's own fictions enact this principle of literary decentralization. Only *A Hazard of New Fortunes* even remotely embodies a socially comprehensive approach to Howells's social-ethical aesthetic ideal, and in fact even that novel has sometimes been faulted for not descending far enough into the working class to constitute a true social panorama, contenting itself instead with viewing life among "the other half" from safely this side of what Howells calls, always defining it from a middle-class perspective, the "sad knowledge of the line at which respectability distinguishes itself from shabbiness" (*Hazard* 49). In *Hazard,* Howells creates middle- and upper-class characters (Margaret Vance, Conrad Dryfoos) who move, work, or even live among the poor, but the working class, always seen through the eyes of its social "betters," has no character representative of its own. Even Gustav Lindau, whose sympathies and political commitments move him to align himself with the working class, makes his living with the tools afforded him by a middle-class education and lives among the working poor by choice rather than by compulsion.

Under the terms of Howells's social-ethical aesthetic, however, the artistic success of a work of fiction did not depend on the comprehensiveness of its representation of contemporary society. Howells the antitheorist, as the previous chapter argued, developed in the *Editor's Study* a pragmatic aesthetic that would measure artistic merit not merely by the idiogenetic aspects of the literary work but by its use-value in the historical world as effective communication of socially "other" realities. Such a definition of aesthetic success meant that virtually any literary representation of commonplace social actualities, regardless of the particular corner of American social experience upon which the individual writer chose to train his or her attention, would contribute to literature's legitimate aesthetic goals—as long as it enabled its readers to gain some measure of sympathetic knowledge about the people comprising the object of its mimesis. Nearly any of Howells's own fictions, then, can be read profitably as Howells himself was wont to read large numbers of his contemporary novelists:

as examples of the new aesthetic put into experimental practice. But the social-ethical aesthetic also assumed, with little discussion, that readers' acquisition of the kind of sympathetic understanding afforded by the new fiction would lead necessarily—somehow, some way—beyond the act of reading, to their undertaking socially and ethically constructive action in the normal course of daily social contacts, domestic and business life, social and political affiliations, and so on. Of special interest, then, are those of Howells's fictions in which he takes up the next logical question implied by his own aesthetic of social responsibility: What precisely *should be* that "somehow, some way" for the educated, middle- to upper-middle class people to whom, for whom, and about whom he primarily wrote? Once the reader has gained a measure of that sympathetic knowledge toward which all literature of aesthetic worth contributes, the question posed by these fictions—to borrow the title of the book by Leo Tolstoy which, along with his other works, were pivotal influences upon Howells during these years—is "What is to be done?"[1] A number of Howells's fictions written during and after the *Harper's Editor's Study* years explore the moral and practical travails of middle-class folk of average moral sensibilities as they struggle first to know the Other and then to act constructively upon that knowledge. In effect, Howells employs these fictions to grapple with that last and perhaps most problematic implication of his aesthetic model: if aesthetic success is linked inextricably to the actions of real readers operating in a world defined by their social and ethical interactions, what in fact are the prospects for gaining and acting upon that sympathetic knowledge of the Other at which the Howells aesthetic aims?

Howells's critical approach to the question of what readers should do with the sympathetic knowledge they gain from Realist fiction contains more than an echo of Harriet Beecher Stowe's confident admonition in the "Concluding Remarks" of *Uncle Tom's Cabin* to "feel right" (624), advice that she pins explicitly to the notion of moral sympathy between her white readers and the African-American subjects of her novel. Understood in its theological context, Stowe's counsel calls not (as is sometimes charged) for a quietist self-satisfaction with the status quo but for the morally committed action that alone, within an evangelical Christian theological system, can produce right feeling.[2] But Howells's fictive characters most decidedly do not "feel right" even in their most committed moments of social action, and Howells's prognosis for meaningful social transformation on the basis of sympathetic, cross-cultural knowledge, despite the repeated clarion calls of the *Editor's Study,* is anything but confident in his fiction. A significant and illuminating share of his fiction in and beyond the mid-1880s might best be described as a fiction of perplexed sympathy, in which Howells considers again and again the anguishing difficulties faced by those who would seriously pose to themselves Tolstoy's question and seek to act upon its answers. Each of the three novels whose discussion comprises the remainder of this chapter—*The Minister's Charge* (1886), *Annie Kilburn* (1888), and *The Vacation of the Kelwyns* (1920)—is situated during the closing decades of the nineteenth century and focuses on varieties and dynamics of cultural schism during a time when immediate contact among individuals of different social classes was still a regular, if increasingly infrequent and insubstantial, occurrence, particularly outside the depersonalizing spheres of the burgeoning urban centers. All three focus on the social divisions of which Howells had the most direct knowledge, via both experience and observation: those between urban and rural culture, the educated professions and manual labor, and the middle-to-upper economic classes and the working class. *The Minister's Charge* (1886) brings an uneducated rural laborer to the Boston metropolis, where his accidental sponsor confronts the difficulties of overcoming the social disparities that divide them from each other; *Annie Kilburn* (1888) focuses on its title character's largely unsuccessful efforts to know and to help the working poor in a formerly agricultural village amid its painful transition to an urban-industrial town; and *The Vacation of the Kelwyns* (1920) sends an upwardly mobile, educated, urban professional family to confront the alien social *moeurs* of the rural working class in the New Hampshire countryside. Each of the three begins its inquiry by placing members of different classes and cultural backgrounds into close proximity and then observes characters' ethical struggles with, and faltering attempts at, cross-cultural communication, sympathetic knowledge, and resultant action.

The Minister's Impossible Charge

The title of *The Minister's Charge* points at once to the novel's double plot-line and dual centers of interest. The farm boy Lemuel Barker becomes the charge of the Reverend David Sewell when he is lured from home to the city by the minister's well-meant but insincere praise of Barker's poetry. The novel traces Barker's gradual economic and social advancement from penniless bumptiousness to relative wealth and urban respectability, à la Horatio Alger.[3] But the novel interweaves with the episodes of Barker's "apprenticeship" (as the novel's subtitle puts it) the story of Sewell's attempts to act upon his growing sense of responsibility for his charge. This awareness issues ultimately in Sewell's sermon on "complicity": his charge to his parishioners and fellow citizens to recognize the moral obligations incumbent upon them because of their inevitable mutual involvement in the lives of their compatriots via the intricate and often invisible webs of social interrelationship. As Sewell puts it to himself with some exasperation just before he writes his sermon, "everybody seems to be tangled up with everybody else" (308); the idea of complicity is the ethical recognition of this social fact.

Edwin Cady finds in Sewell's complicity sermon not only the moral idea "on which the novel essentially closes" (*Realist* 6) but also the expression of "the best of Howells' own ethical thought to date" (*Realist* 6). Be that as it may, the essential problem of the novel is not the recognition of the individual's inevitable complicity, nor even the ethical responsibilities arising from that recognition, but the extreme difficulty of acting upon those responsibilities once they have been recognized and accepted. The culminating sermon on complicity really comes as something of an anticlimax; both the concept and the term itself have already been presented eighteen chapters before Sewell's sermon is delivered, when the minister's journalist friend, Evans, presents it to him in casual but earnest and extensive conversation. And in fact, Sewell has already accepted his share of the common responsibility for his charge by the end of the first chapter, when he sheepishly accepts his wife's upbraidings for having misled Barker with his disingenuous praise of his poems. *The Minister's Charge,* then, is less concerned with establishing the fact of complicity than it is with working out what a morally well-intentioned member of the upper-middle class should do with knowledge of that fact once he has achieved it. The strand of the novel that concerns Sewell's efforts in that direction (as distinct from the story of the rise of Lemuel Barker) develops almost exclusively as an exercise in frustration and futility.

The structure of the novel suggests the intractability of the problem that Sewell and the novel itself address. The two plotlines, one devoted to Barker's rise and the other to Sewell's moral and practical travails as he seeks to understand and to help his charge, stay for the most part separate from each other. Long chains of chapters recount Barker's progress with no reference whatsoever to Sewell, who for much of the novel is absent not only from Barker's life but also from his consciousness. Sewell, who is more centrally preoccupied with Barker than Barker is with him, nevertheless either forgets the younger man altogether for long stretches of time or fails to make contact with him despite his best efforts to do so. While the two plotlines are structurally counterpointed, the moments of contact between the two plots are almost always deployed to emphasize the fleeting and largely fruitless nature of Sewell's attempts to intervene constructively in Barker's life. Having been inadvertently successful in complicating Barker's life for the worse, Sewell's attempts to make meaningful contact with his involuntary charge are nearly always unsuccessful, if not disastrous, in their outcomes. The novel offers trope after trope, incident after incident of thwarted contact, miscommunication, and misunderstanding despite the would-be philanthropist's best intentions and real efforts—so much so that the sense of individuals' existential isolation threatens to outweigh the novel's more overt message of social and moral complicity.[4] The counterpointed plotlines serve primarily to emphasize Sewell's inability to act upon his recognition of complicity, a powerlessness that stems more from the conditions of contemporary urban life and social organization than from any personal failing of Sewell himself.

The opening sequence of chapters establishes the pattern of thwarted knowledge and failed communication that prevails throughout the rest of the novel. Chapter one introduces the novel's initiating action in split screen, as it were, establishing from the first the fundamental lack of understanding between the rural laborer and the urban professional. While Mrs. Sewell upbraids her husband for having falsely praised young Lemuel Barker's atrocious poetry, and Sewell argues the inconsequentiality of his action, Barker basks in the glow of the minister's praise and dreams of future greatness as he gazes at the moon rising over the stone fence of the family farmstead. One chapter later, much to the minister's dismay, his unthinking flattery has brought Barker to Sewell's doorstep in Boston. The utter lack of understanding between the professional-class urban vacationer who offers as a social palliative what the uneducated farm boy can only understand as sincere praise is further underscored by Sewell's treatment of Barker as a temporary guest in his home. Having belatedly confessed his fault, Sewell attempts to entertain Barker according to the best traditions of his middle-class social training. His efforts are met by an inscrutability so impenetrable that he begins to feel "as if he had been preaching to a dead wall" (15). He attempts conventional small talk about Barker's family and life in the country, shows Barker his collection of pictures (Aggasiz, Nilsson, Lincoln—"great Originals" [16] who rose from the peasantry to positions of fame and leadership), invites him to dine with his family, but is driven toward distraction by Barker's unrelenting impassiveness. Barker "did what Sewell bade him do in admiring this thing or that; but if he had been an Indian he could not have regarded them with a greater reticence. Sewell made him sit down from time to time, but in a sitting posture Barker's silence became so deathlike that Sewell hastened to get him on his legs again, and to walk him about from one point to another, as if to keep life in him" (17).

Sewell's disposition to treat Barker kindly proceeds not only from his professional and Christian vocations but also from the recognition, to be developed later in the novel as the doctrine of complicity, that his actions have already impacted Barker's life in ways that carry with them a measure of ethical responsibility for their outcomes. The comedic bumbling of his futile efforts to put Barker at his ease represents his first attempts to rectify the harm he considers he has done Barker by unintentionally luring him to the city. But just as Sewell's class assumptions permitted his false admiration of Barker's poetry by preventing a truer knowledge of Barker's personality, class assumptions again obstruct his efforts to know Barker in the city and to act accordingly. Sewell relies on the code of middle-class manners and *moeurs* on the assumption that they comprise a universal language of social interchange rather than a class-specific, exclusionary medium of communication. Comfortably situated within the structure of his class assumptions, he persists in his failure to imagine Barker's perspective sufficiently to understand the full awkwardness of the young man's position or to imagine his likely emotional responses to his situation. As Sewell's well-meant but clumsy efforts to make middle-class social pleasantries do the work of honest interpersonal communication fail, Sewell begins to blame

Barker for the failure and "to doubt whether Barker understood anything. He seemed so much more stupid than he had at home; his faculties were apparently sealed up, and he had lost all the personal picturesqueness which he had when he came in out of the barn, at his mother's call, to receive Sewell" (14–15). At dinner, Sewell temporarily escapes his unease in sophisticated banter with a chance visitor of his own class, with whom the conventions of parlor chatter can indeed serve as a mode of genuine communication. But as the genteel Miss Hope Vane regales Sewell with an account of her niece's newfound dedication to "the flower charity" ("Hundreds of bouquets are distributed every day. They prevent crime") (21), Sewell again fails to recognize the exclusionary effect of this idiom of parlor chatter on the class outsider, Barker. Only when Barker rises from the table does Sewell realize that he has forgotten his charge and "neglected this helpless guest" (23) despite his best intentions. Sewell's failure as a host results in part from his personal psychological necessity to escape an inherently uncomfortable situation. But the source of that discomfort is the intractability, despite Sewell's good intentions, of the class-specific cultural codes that define and limit each individual's behavior and modes of understanding.

After Barker leaves, the minister assesses recent events in terms that indicate that he both understands the nature of his failure and begins to see it in terms not merely personal but also sociological:

> If I could only have got near the poor boy. . . . If I could only have reached him where he lives, as our slang says! But do what I would, I couldn't find any common ground where we could stand together. We were as unlike as if we were of two different species. I saw that everything I said bewildered him more and more; he couldn't understand me! Our education is unchristian, our civilization is pagan. They both ought to bring us in closer relations with our fellow-creatures, and they both only put us more widely apart! Every one of us dwells in an impenetrable solitude! We understand each other a little if our circumstances are similar, but if they are different all our words leave us dumb and unintelligible. (26–27)

Sewell's diagnosis of his failed interaction with Barker is integral to the doctrine of complicity that he adopts explicitly later in the novel: already he understands the failure of cross-class communication as a function of education and social conditioning, and he recognizes that action taken for the benefit of others depends, in the first instance, upon the accurate understanding of those others, which can only come from clear communication. But intermixed with his fulminations against the social structure as the agent of thwarted communication is a partially self-contradictory assumption that the failure stems from Barker's inadequacies rather than from his own or those of the environing social system.

Little does Sewell realize just how much about Barker he has failed to understand. So seductive has been the narrative monopoly imposed by the minister's perspective to this point that it comes as a shock at the beginning of the next chapter when Howells suddenly immerses us for the first time in Barker's consciousness. Contrary to Sewell's anxious surmises, Barker has indeed "understood" a number of the elements of their recent discourse quite clearly, and that understanding has done nothing to aid the two men's free communication with each other. Barker grumbles to himself not only about Sewell's initial deception but also about his apparent inability to conceive Barker's real material and personal circumstances:

> There he made Barker think everything of his poetry and now he pretended to tell him that it was not worth anything; and he kept hinting round that Barker had better go back home and stay there. Did he think he would have left home if there had been anything for him to do there? Had not he as much as told him that he was obliged to find something to make a living by, and help the rest? What was he afraid of? Was he afraid that Barker wanted to come and live off *him?* He could show him that there was no great danger. If he had known how, he would have refused even to stay to dinner.
>
> What made him keep the pictures of these people who had got along, if he thought no one else ought to try? (28)

This revelation of Barker's interior life, which initiates the first series of chapters devoted to his rise, reveals the depths of the social divisions that the doctrine of complicity seeks to bridge. Sewell's well-bred and, in their way, sincere efforts to reach out to Barker fail because they are based on Sewell's class-bound conceptions of how a liberal Christian ought to help a social inferior. He does the best he can within the boundaries of his professional-class social training but, as he himself recognizes without being able to act upon the knowledge, both his own and Barker's class training prevents them from communicating with each other (to borrow a term from Ralph Ellison) on the lower frequencies. While class-specific *moeurs* and manners enable intra-class interactions, they thwart genuine interpersonal interactions across the borders of social class. Howells's rigid control of point of view during the opening chapters reinforces his middle-class readers' tendency to assume the truth and justice of Sewell's perspective on and actions toward Barker, who is presented as a sort of specimen exposition of the rural working class, in order to provide, when Barker's interiority is suddenly revealed in chapter four, the shock of realizing just how shallow and incomplete has been Sewell's and our supposed knowledge of the real life of the minister's charge. Sewell does learn more about Barker's character and circumstances by the end of the novel, but the problem of class-thwarted sympathetic knowledge that the beginning chapters lay out as a structural principle for the entire novel never entirely disappears. No matter how often the twin, class-identified plot trajectories of the book may come into contact, that contact remains fleeting and relatively insubstantial, hampered by the mutual misunderstanding born (as Sewell puts it) of an "unchristian" education and a "pagan" religion.

Perhaps the most glaring example of this class-thwarted understanding occurs in the unhappy end of Sewell's first and most traditionally charitable effort to assist Barker by securing for him a position as Miss Vane's man-of-all-work. Having temporarily lost track of Barker, who in the meantime has been cheated, robbed, and arrested on false charges of purse-snatching, Sewell at last rediscovers his charge, via the morning paper's police blotter, in the kitchen of the Wayfarer's Lodge for homeless men. Finding himself "baffled again" (85) by the question of what to do for—or perhaps with—Barker, who refuses to return home, Sewell impulsively stops at Miss Vane's house, "bent on repairing his wrong at any cost to others" (85), and in short order arranges for Barker to become the Vanes' odd-jobs man. The process of arranging Miss Vane's and Sewell's charitable effort carries within it the seeds of its own destruction; as in Sewell's previous encounter with Barker, the class divisions exert pernicious effects upon genuine interhuman interaction. While Sewell explains to Miss Vane all that has happened to Barker during the last two days, he and she both begin to see the story as a joke, so that Sewell "began really to be afraid she would do herself an injury with her laughing" (86). ("What—what—do you suppose-pose—they did with the po-po-*po*em they stole from him?" Miss Vane asks through her laughter. Sewell replies: "Well, one thing I'm sure they *didn't* do. . . . They didn't *read* it" [86].) Although neither Sewell nor Miss Vane mean any malice toward Barker as they transform his recent experiences into the stuff of comedy, their laughter nevertheless strikes readers who have accompanied Barker though his ordeal as unseemly at best. Their distance from Barker prevents them from having any truly sympathetic knowledge of his recent history; readers, on the other hand, having participated vicariously in the young man's bewilderment, anger, and humiliation, are well positioned to see the levity of his would-be benefactors as evidence of the pernicious effects of class on genuine interpersonal sympathy. As their conversation turns toward more serious consideration of the situation, the chapter continues to frame their projected actions on the problem posed by Barker in terms of charity to be doled out to a member of the deserving poor from the safe vantage point of their superior social station. Miss Vane immediately frames the project in terms of her niece's flower charity; Sybil Vane, her aunt reports, has been discouraged that the objects of her beneficence in the city hospitals "were mostly disgusting old men that hadn't been shaved. I think that now she wants to try her flowers on criminals" (87). "Why not let her reform Barker?" Sewell humorously replies, but the terms of his humor do not mask the fact that he has indeed begun to see Barker as his own personal reform movement. Miss Vane and Sewell continue to run through their charitable options, discarding each of them as impracticable or ineffective, until Miss Vane remembers that her furnace man has struck for higher wages and decides to offer the position to Barker. Barker accepts the offer in part because "his ignorance of city prejudices and sophistications probably suggested nothing against the honest work to his pride" (89). But if Barker remains for the time being in ignorance, his benefactors do not: before Barker's acceptance, Sewell fears that "Barker may fling your proffered furnace in my teeth" (88) as an affront to his personal dignity, and Miss Vane succeeds in hiring him only because "she treated him at once, not like a servant, but like a young person, and yet she used a sort of respect for his independence which was soothing to his rustic pride" (89). The narration makes it clear that her approach is strategic, a deliberate deployment of "tact" (89) to achieve the desired end of doing a kindness for a social inferior rather than an acknowledgment of any sort of democratic equality between Barker and herself.

The failure of this façade and Barker's consequent awareness of how his employer really views him and his work is what eventually will drive Barker back into the streets. Hope Vane's niece, Sybil, earnestly takes hold of the opportunity for charitable action Barker's advent presents to her, filling his room with arrangements of flowers from the household garden and adopting as her "great object" the task of "keep[ing] him from feeling that he has been an outcast, and needs to be reclaimed" (93). While Barker assumes himself to have been hired as a free laborer on a business basis to do honest work at an agreed-upon wage, Sybil (who is only a less skilled and more tactless representative of Miss Vane and her entire class) regards him simultaneously as a charitable object and as a servant subject to her whims and orders. She assumes, in short, that Barker really is an outcast who needs to be reclaimed, and her well-meant actions proceed from a condescension that ends in disaster. The scene opens with Barker's return to the Vane house after he has been romantically acquainting himself with the young woman who mistakenly accused him of stealing her purse. Hearing him enter, Sibyl Vane prevents him from retiring to his bedroom, in rapid succession encouraging him to eat a little supper, asking him to locate the cook in the house, ordering him to light the gas jets, reprimanding him for not obeying her orders quickly enough, and pleading with him to investigate a noise she thinks she has heard from the third floor. Sibyl's attitudes toward Barker are just as divided between the sympathetic impulse and the presumption of her own class prerogatives as her aunt's, but she has not yet learned the social tact that would hide her snobbery from the object of the Vanes' charity. She dances recklessly along the class boundary that she knows as part of her birthright but is still learning to manipulate, her vocalizations carrying the overtones, successively, of employer, mother, lover, sister, equal. Barker remains only dimly aware of the game she is playing, responding consistently with the deference he considers due an employer by an employee but also with the reticence and dignity he assumes as a social equal with the niece of the woman who pays his wages. The long-suffering Barker finally draws the line at Sibyl Vane's patronizing toying with him, rising "in clumsy indignation" (118) at her insistence that he confess having seen his former accuser that day. Her response to his adamant resistance is to fall back upon the privileged class position that she believes gives her the freedom to toy with him with impunity. Barker tells her, bluntly, that he wishes her to leave him alone.

> At these words, so little appreciative of her condescension, her romantic beneficence, her unselfish interest, Sibyl suddenly rebounded to her former level, which she was sensible was far above that of this unworthy object of her kindness. She rose from her chair, and pursued:
>
> "If you need a friend—a sister—I'm sure that you can safely confide in—the cook." She looked at him a moment, and broke into a malicious laugh very unlike that of a social reformer, which rang shriller at the bovine fury which mounted to Lemuel's eyes. . . . "I never expected to be treated in my own aunt's house with such perfect ingratitude and impudence—yes, impudence!—by one of her servants!" (119)

Sibyl's Aunt Hope, who has witnessed the very end of this outburst, only recapitulates her niece's mistakes by attempting to force Barker to defend himself against Sibyl's charges by recounting their conversation. She trades upon the presumed rights of both age and class when she sternly admonishes Barker for his "resentful" and "wicked" behavior in resisting her queries: "I tell you that you are not behaving rightly. Why don't you do what I wish?" (121). Barker of course has no desire to humiliate himself all over again by parading the content of his discussion with Sibyl before her aunt, and he protects his personal dignity against Miss Vane's class-authorized depredations by calmly refusing to answer and equally calmly accepting her dismissal. Still acting from his own presumption of social equality, and to Miss Vane's "unmeasured astonishment, he offered her his hand; her amaze was even greater . . . when she found herself shaking it" (121). The end of the chapter reveals a dejected Miss Vane berating her niece for having been the cause of Barker's firing. Although she has acted in unquestioning solidarity with her niece upon thoroughly ingrained class assumptions regarding the maintenance of social hierarchies and power, her un-easy response to her own actions hints at a dim recognition that something is seriously awry in the ways that class interferes with her intentions to know and help Barker. Her foul mood at chapter's end is the product of the contradiction between the handshake accepted as between equals and the accomplished fact, undertaken out of blind class loyalties, of her dis-missal of the minister's charge. For Sewell, the episode seems to confirm his earlier intuition that "the world seems so put together that I believe we ought to think twice before doing a good action" (25).

A major part of Barker's education during the succeeding chapters of the novel continues the process begun by his fateful argument with Sybil Vane and consists of his gradual awakening to social class realities be-yond the simple economic distinctions he has hitherto assumed to be the sum total of class difference. But for purposes of this argument, Barker's apprenticeship to the urban middle class concerns us only indirectly, as a means for Howells to investigate his middle-class readership's ability to at-tain and act constructively upon knowledge of the Other. In the wake of the failure of Sewell's charitable act toward Barker, undertaken by proxy and undermined by its basis in presumptive class differences rather than democratic egalitarianism, the novel reasserts the frustratingly bifurcated nature of life in an increasingly class-divided nation. With the best will in the world, and with a growing sense of understanding and respect for Barker's position, Sewell becomes ever less able even to communicate with his charge, let alone constructively intervene in his life. Having resigned himself to the impossibility of bringing about a rapprochement between Miss Vane and her former employee (pointed out to him, tellingly, by his wife in light of her experiences rehiring fired servants) Sewell ruefully con-fesses that she has successfully "proved that nothing can be done for Barker with the Vanes. And now the question is, what *can* be done for him?" (136) The question is a keynote not only for Sewell's task but for the task that the novel poses to its readers and its author; the answer remains as unclear to the reader as it does to Sewell even after another twenty chapters of his attempting to find an answer that will enable him to act. In the absence of an answer, Sewell decides that his provisional first step must be to find Barker, a task which he regards as a "useless quest" but which he undertakes anyway "because he did not know in the least what else to do" (136). The minister's recognition of the responsibility he bears for Barker, slight as are its real grounds, compels him to seek the knowledge of Barker that alone might show him how to act. But this impulse is repeatedly frustrated, and it is all Sewell can do merely to keep track of the whereabouts of his charge. Repeatedly spotting him from afar as one of the worshippers in his own congregation, he fails in his repeated attempts to find him before he escapes the church each Sunday. Barker becomes for Sewell "a lurking discomfort . . . in his soul" (136), the source of an irrepressible feeling of responsibility that can find no outlet in action.

When Barker's whereabouts finally become known to Sewell through his friend Evans, a permanent resident of the hotel where Barker is employed, the news comes hand in hand with the idea of complicity that undergirds both Sewell's and the novel's sense of the moral relationship of self to others in a nominally democratic and Christian society. Evans first defines complicity as an insight that occurred to him as he watched the performance of a Restoration comedy and became convinced of the audience's shared responsibility for the play's content and moral effects. As he continues to talk, he outlines a concept that progressively expands from a relatively narrow principle of shared responsibility for shared sin to an assertion of the inevitability of the effects of any individual's actions upon others and a concomitant acceptance of the ethical responsibilities thus entailed. After Evans has introduced Barker into the conversation, he confesses that the real impetus for the idea was Evans's offering of a tip and Barker's self-respecting refusal of it. The incident, alien as it is to our contemporary conception of the social meanings of tipping, is emblematic of the problem faced by those of Evans's, Sewell's, and Howells's class who wish to gain and act upon a sympathetic understanding of the class-divided Other in the late-nineteenth-century United States. Evans means the tip as a kindness, a small but meaningful material addition to Barker's economic standing. But Barker, who has consistently refused offers of money he has not earned, regards the proffered fee (as does Sewell) as a degradation to both giver and recipient. The tip represents a concrete effort to materially aid another human being and results from the implicit recognition of an ethical obligation of the wealthy toward the poor. But the material transaction, despite the good motive that underwrites it, has the effect of damaging the relationship between giver and recipient by reducing it to an

economic transaction that, moreover, reasserts the social differential between the two parties. In short, the well-intentioned action thwarts the
benign intent of the benefactor by psychologically and socially reinforcing
the divisions that are the root cause of class estrangement in the first place.

When Evans makes the leap from Sewell's account of his involvements
with Barker to his own interpretation of the Wayfarer's Lodge as evidence
of complicity, he translates a principle of interpersonal morality onto the
plane of social ethics and political action. The existence of the Wayfarer's
Lodge, Evans argues, shows that "the city of Boston has instinctively sanctioned" the idea of complicity by acting upon a recognition of the ethical
responsibilities of all for each. He continues: "It is—blindly perhaps—
fulfilling the destiny of the future State, which will at once employ and
support all its citizens; . . . it is prophetically recognizing my new principle
of Complicity" (165). Here, in Evans's only half-serious prophecy of an
American socialist state that is already in the making, is the logical political end point of the principle of complicity: a nation collectively reorga-
nized both politically and socially to enable unimpeded communication,
knowledge, and compassionate action among all its members by removing
the class boundaries that prevent these transactions under the current social
arrangements. The discussion ends by returning to the present and with it
the question of how the recognition of complicity might be translated into
immediate, constructive action before and preparatory to the advent of a
socialist state. Evans brings the conversation back to the "beautifully perfect case of Complicity" (165) that is Lemuel Barker, and he asks Sewell,
"What do you propose to do, now you've rediscovered him?" Sewell replies, frankly, that he does not know.

The final chapters of the novel offer very little in the way of mitigation
of the dead wall of blocked communication that thwarts Sewell's efforts to
live up to his own moral advice to his parishioners. While Sewell watches
from a distance, keeping tabs on what is visible of Barker's development to
their mutual acquaintance, Evans, he develops a fuller but still radically
incomplete knowledge of his charge without ever finding an effective way
to translate his new mindfulness into meaningful action. When Barker and
Sewell's paths do cross, their interactions are more cordial but no more
constructive than before. On one occasion, for instance, Sewell offers
Barker general advice on young men's relationships with women, but with-

out the requisite knowledge of Barker's complicated associations with two particular young women, his counsel is less than useful. Again, in the wake of Barker's loss of employment at Evans's hotel, he and Sewell discuss his prospects and the moral dimensions of his recent activities, but again to no avail in terms of concrete action. Sewell does succeed in securing for Barker a position reading for the invalid patrician Bromfield Corey but unknowingly fails to help avert a new crisis when he cannot recognize Barker's plea for counsel about his deteriorating relationship with his fiancée. Several chapters later, Sewell watches in helpless dismay as Barker proceeds toward a marriage that is sure to be permanently unhappy; all Sewell can find to do is to accede to Barker's request for a loan. In the end, Sewell preaches his sermon on complicity with the full conviction of its truth, but neither the sermon nor the novel satisfactorily maps a viable course of action for those who accept the essential ethical interdependence of all individuals in a society. On the whole, Barker is markedly more successful in his apprenticeship to the middle class than Sewell is in his to the principle of complicity.

In the meantime, as Sewell continues to grope for the answers to his questions, Barker encounters his particular train of successes and reverses essentially alone. Even though the problem of knowing how to act upon the insight of complicity is rooted in class difference, the novel gradually comes to develop its response to complicity in terms not primarily of class difference and collective action but of personal isolation and the failure of interpersonal communication. "Isn't it strange," Barker's friend Jessie Carver comments, "how little we really know about people in the world?" (280). The words have primary reference to her and Barker's now corrected misinterpretations of each other's dispositions, but they serve also as a gloss on the problem that the novel addresses but cannot resolve: having accepted shared responsibility for our fellows, how can we know them sufficiently to be able to take beneficial action on their behalf? While the novel, by allowing Barker a (limited) success on the Alger plan and by framing its responses to the plight of the nation's Barkers primarily in terms of individual, charitable action rather than collective reform or revolution, might seem to revert to an individualist ideology and ethic, its anxious portrayal of the inadequacies of Sewell's response works instead to undermine the success myth that ostensibly underpins Barker's half of the plot. When the patrician Bromfield Corey, for instance, speculates that the lesson of Barker is that American "life isn't stratified; . . . for the present, we're all in vertical sections" (262), his pronouncements are meant to be heard not as a statement of fact but, with all due suspicion about their source, as an optimistic assessment of what might still come to be despite contemporary socioeconomic trends. The speculations that Lemuel Barker provokes among members of the classes above him always have to do not with him alone but with the broader social and political problems that he represents. If *The Minister's Charge* reverts uneasily to the language of individual enterprise and individual morality in its grappling with the question of right social-ethical action in response to those problems, it also demonstrates Howells's deepening distress with the rapidly solidifying stratification of American society. This novel's more urgent concern is with the immediate, provisional possibilities for individuals who, recognizing their complicity with that stratification and its victims, wish to take action. But the collective terms of the novel's central ethical insight, the principle of complicity, ultimately imply the necessity of a collective response. In the next of Howells's "economic" novels, *Annie Kilburn,* the frustrated impulse toward meaningful ethical action becomes more unequivocally the product of class division, and the call to action becomes more explicitly—if no less anxiously—a call to collective as well as individual work.

"The Iron Wall of Uselessness": *Annie Kilburn* and the Failure of Charity

Near the end of *Annie Kilburn* (1888), the novel Howells began writing the same month he reviewed Tolstoy's *Que Faire* (*What Is to Be Done?*) in the *Editor's Study,* Dr. Morrell asks Annie Kilburn the question posed by Tolstoy's title: "[T]hey say poverty is on the increase. What is to be done?" (818). Despite its late appearance as an explicit query, Dr. Morrell's question has been the central problem of the novel from the first chapter, when Annie Kilburn resolves to return to her native Massachusetts, after the death of her father and long exile in Washington, D.C. and Europe, in order to "try to be of some use in the world—try to do some good" (645). "In Hatboro'" she says, "I think I shall know how" (645). Her decision, the narrator informs us, is impulsive and emotional; while she feels herself discontented with the "life of cheerful acquiescence in worldly conditions" (647) that her family wealth has heretofore enabled, she has no very secure knowledge of either the socioeconomic conditions of her home village or of the steps she might take to ameliorate them. The novel traces the process by which the returned village aristocrat seeks to gain a sympathetic knowledge of the cultural Other in her own town and to turn that knowledge to some account in the way of concrete philanthropic action. The novel's conclusions regarding the options and possibilities for such an ambition are considerably less than sanguine, but neither are they wholly pessimistic.

While historical ties of property, family, and personal history suggest Hatboro to Annie Kilburn as the right place for her to seek constructive connection with community, she discovers upon her return that the translation of philanthropic ideals into genuinely useful social action is anything but a simple matter. She quickly discovers that she does not in fact "know how" to do good in her home village—a lesson that is painfully impressed upon her as she travels through the village green on the way from the station to her ancestral home. On the green stands the new Civil War monument that she has commissioned, in large measure financed, and caused to be erected on the village green before her return from Europe. She is deeply mortified to find that the monument is wholly inappropriate to its social and architectural context; it is not part of the village but an imposition from without of her own philanthropic intentions upon the community. Having taken it upon herself, in the interests of patriotism and aesthetic good taste, to substitute for the villagers' "simple notion of an American volunteer at rest, with his hands folded on the muzzle of his gun" (651) a newly designed Winged Victory, she has inadvertently created a memorial whose "involuntary frivolity insulted the solemn memory of the slain" (652). Her charitable intention has been thwarted by her distance, literal and figurative, from the recipients of her generosity. The incident prefigures the outcome of her further attempts to understand, communicate with, and "be of some use" to Hatboro's nascent working class.

The first obstacle in Annie Kilburn's quest for social usefulness is the complexity of the social and cultural divisions that partition Hatboro, which complicates her attempts even to know who it is she should be trying to know. The third chapter describes in some detail the welter of changes that the newly industrialized rural community has undergone in its "expansion from a New England village to an American town" (744). "As formerly," the narrator writes, "some people were acceptable, and some were not; . . . there was an aristocracy and a commonalty, but there was a confusion and a more ready convertibility in the materials of each" (744). The older and relatively soft division between the professional class and the farmers still exists, but the new preeminence of the factory owners and merchants has rendered the cultural and political leadership of lawyers, doctors, and ministers somewhat moot (as evidenced, for instance, by the leading role taken by the merchant-class petty tyrant, William Gerrish, who nearly succeeds in rallying sufficient community opposition to the socially liberal Reverend Peck to oust him from his pastorate). The transformation of former farmers' daughters into hat-factory operatives has increased the distance between the middle class and the laboring class, now mere factory operatives instead of self-employed freeholders. But Reverend Peck is a former "hand," as is Annie's childhood friend, Lyra Wilmington, who has married into wealth and social prominence via Hatboro's leading manufacturer, and at least one of the factory workers is also a landlord for some of his fellow workers. The railroad, as in many other mill towns, divides the respectable middle-class district from "Over the Track," (706) where the mill workers are housed in tenements, yet the Wilmingtons' fashionable home is situated on this same wrong side of the tracks. To complicate matters further, the wealthier people are themselves divided into an older group of long-term, year-round Hatboro natives and a burgeoning colony of leisure-class summer residents who have built their "cottages" just over the hill in South Hatboro.

As a result of this shifting maze of social boundaries and interconnections, Annie experiences a minor crisis of identity—her own and others'. She does not know, in ways that might enable her projected social philanthropy, either the people of the local working classes or those with whom she shares now tenuous connections of class and girlhood personal acquaintance. This alienation from her community gives her a deepening, oppressive sense of "the difficulty of being helpful to anything or any one" (672) in the town she had felt sure would offer her ample opportunity to make herself useful to those outside her class. The townsfolk she sees from a distance "seemed terribly self-sufficing. They seemed occupied and prosperous, from her front parlour window; she did not see anybody going by who appeared to be in need of her; and she shrank from a more thorough exploration of the place" (672). The novel thus defines her initial failure to act as the result of insufficient knowledge: in effect, Annie Kilburn returns to her native Hatboro motivated by a powerful impulse toward sympathy but without the knowledge requisite to put her charitable impulses into action. She senses that action on behalf of the Other requires some real understanding of their lives and circumstances, but she is essentially a member of the community in name only, by way of family history, property, and class status rather than through a life integrated with the villagers.

The first break in what the novel later calls "the iron wall of uselessness" (748) within which Annie's generous impulses are imprisoned arrives on her doorstep in the form of a proposal to form a "Social Union" for the benefit of the village factory operatives. At first glance, the scheme appears to offer just the opportunity for which she has been wishing. The idea, as it is explained to Annie by Mr. Brandreth, who has been dispatched as an emissary from the South Hatboro colony to ask the help of her influence in supporting the project, is to raise money to establish a sort of clubhouse for the use of the mill-workers in their leisure hours, a gathering place where reading materials, beverages, and light refreshments would be available at cost to the factory hands. The proposal becomes the occasion for the novel's first line of critique of the upper classes' philanthropic impulse, for despite the fact that the Social Union is intended specifically for the benefit of the working people, the scheme increasingly appears to have much less to do with its ostensible beneficiaries than it does with the philanthropists themselves. Mr. Brandreth, for instance, spends most of his time with Annie explaining not the union itself but the plans for its fundraising event, an evening of amateur theatricals; as the scheme progresses, Annie repeatedly notes that "the Union always dropped out of the talk as soon as the theatricals were mentioned" (711). Brandreth also suggests, apparently without any awareness of the incongruity, that another primary motive of the event is to make an opportunity for "the old village families and the summer folks . . . to mingle more than they do" (669)—a social union not of the leisure classes with the working poor but of the upper classes of Old and South Hatboro. Brandreth thus comes to represent the upper class's well-meaning heedlessness of the real needs of the poor, an attitude that will become even more pronounced in the self-serving machinations of Mrs. Munger, the social leader of the South Hatboro colony and the motive force behind the Social Union theatricals. Annie recognizes in Brandreth and Mrs. Munger, dimly at first but with increasing clarity, precisely the condition that she herself is seeking to escape: a class-bound solipsism that thwarts the impulse toward either true knowledge of or sympathy with the working class in any other capacity than as an abstraction. (The lesson is powerfully confirmed later in the novel when Mrs. Savor's diseased baby, whom Annie has unsuccessfully attempted to aid, dies. Annie is astonished to find in the responses of her peers "an indifference and an incredulity concerning the feelings of people of lower station which could not be surpassed in another civilisation. Her concern for Mrs. Savor was treated as a great trial for Miss Kilburn; but the mother's bereavement was regarded as something those people were used to, and got over more easily than one could imagine" [752].)

Annie herself is not completely exempt from this critique. Brandreth's request has immediate appeal for her (despite the fact that she hates theatricals) primarily because "it gave definition to the vague intentions with which she had returned to Hatboro'; it might afford her a chance to make reparation for the figure on the soldiers' monument" (670). In other words, her initial attraction to the Social Union, as to the idea of philanthropy itself, proceeds as much from her own psychic neediness as from any substantive understanding of the project or its beneficiaries; it is based in her own vague feelings of goodwill toward the less well-off but without the knowledge that would give those feelings a mode of expression in constructive action. When Brandreth blithely explains that, while all the villagers would be invited to attend the theatricals, invitations for the postperformance supper would serve to "keep out the socially objectionable element—the shoe-shop hands and the straw-shop girls" (671–72), Annie is at first but vaguely troubled by the contradictions at the core of the idea:

"Oh," said Annie. "But isn't the—the Social Union for just that class?"

"Yes, it's *expressly* for them, and we intend to organise a system of entertainments—lectures, concerts, readings—for the winter, and keep them interested the whole year round in it. The object is to show them that the best people in the community have their interests at heart, and wish to get on common ground with them."

"Yes," said Annie, "the object is certainly very good." (672)

Annie is partly complicit in Brandreth's assumption of class superiority, the attitude of assured condescension, the obliviousness to the real needs of the factory workers, and the nonsensical assertion that the provision of entertainments to the poor by the rich somehow constitutes their meeting together on "common ground." But she does nevertheless sense at some lower register that something is amiss in the foundations of this philanthropic enterprise, and she expresses that awareness by her approval of the plan's object without embracing the proposed means. When Brandreth leaves her, Annie is more depressed and frustrated than ever with her inability to find a way to do some good.

It remains for Reverend Peck, the "very liberal" (681) Orthodox Congregational pastor whom Annie consults for his opinion about the projected Social Union, to articulate the novel's Tolstoyan critique of the fundamental contradictions at the heart of any proposal of wealthy philanthropy toward the poor in a class-divided society. Peck immediately identifies the flaw in the plan for the theatricals that indexes the fatal contradiction in the plan for the Social Union itself. "I could not join at all," he states, "with those who were willing to lay the foundations of a Social Union in a social disunion—in the exclusion of its beneficiaries from the society of their benefactors. . . . The point is whether a Social Union beginning in social exclusion could ever do any good" (682–83). Peck rightfully doubts whether "these ladies . . . intend to spend their evenings there, to associate on equal terms with the shoe-shop and straw-shop hands" (683), and Annie can answer only by lamely reiterating Mr. Brandreth's line about winter entertainments as a way of finding common ground between the rich and the poor. "They can never get on common ground with them in that way," continues Peck. "No doubt they think they want to do them good; but good is from the heart, and there is no heart in what they propose. The working people would know that at once" (683). Peck immediately discerns what Annie has already indistinctly sensed: that the impulse toward charity among the South Hatboro leisure class is at once too abstract and too self-absorbed to issue in any genuine sympathy across class boundaries. The Social Union scheme prevents true interclass solidarity by seeing the working class as a theoretical entity that might be improved by the judicious expenditure of money rather than as individuated people with whom it might be possible and desirable to establish interpersonal relationships as one would with members of one's own class. "Sympathy— common feeling—the sense of fraternity," Peck concludes, "can spring only from like experiences, like hopes, like fears. And money cannot buy these" (684).

Peck's critique of cross-class charity thus rests in part on the asser- tion that social reconciliation and constructive reform can proceed only where the emotional will exists to establish open and genuine interpersonal relationships between individuals on opposite sides of the class divide. Ironically, Peck himself not only is the vehicle but becomes the object of this line of the novel's critique. At the end of his interview with Annie, for instance, the novel undercuts his moral authority when he accidentally leaves behind his young daughter, who has been sitting in Annie's lap dur- ing their conversation. This is not the only time in the novel he makes the mistake. Lost in his own set of Tolstoyan ethical abstractions, he too is in danger of losing individual, interpersonal sympathy with his own flesh and blood. Annie, exasperated by her inability to dismiss Peck's radical ideas out of hand, will later turn his tendency toward absentmindedness into a point of attack, likening him to the philanthropist Hollingsworth in Haw- thorne's *Blithedale Romance,* in that "they are always ready to sacrifice the happiness and comfort of any one to the general good" (686). In context, the authority of Annie's comment is reduced by her personal and petty motive for uttering it, yet the comparison does point to an obstacle to meaningful social action inherent in Peck's character and his approach to the problem of poverty. As Ralph Putney, the town lawyer with the rapier wit and labor sympathies, explains to Dr. Morrell, the appearance of sen- timentality in Reverend Peck's Tolstoyan gospel of egalitarian love coexists with an almost mechanical rationalism in his thinking. "When you come to talk with Brother Peck," Putney says, "you find yourself sort of frozen out with a most unexpected, hard-headed cold-bloodedness. Brother Peck is plain common-sense itself. He seems to be a man without an illusion, without an emotion" (727). While the effect that Peck has on others is

primarily the product of his straight-shooting expressions of moral and social ideas, with which the novel as a whole generally accords, Peck's cold
demeanor effectively distances him from all his parishioners and townsfolk (not to mention his daughter) and thus proves an obstacle to the sort
of genuine sympathy for which his own ethical system calls. If Annie's
unrealized impulse toward sympathy is blocked in part by her insufficient
knowledge of the poor, Peck, the former farm boy and mill hand who has
risen into the professional class, has an insider's knowledge of the working
folk but is nevertheless handicapped in the execution of his own social
ideals by a lack of the "heart" that he himself proclaims as a necessary
prerequisite for true sympathetic understanding across class boundaries.

When Peck eventually resigns his pastorate, he confesses to Annie that
he is bedeviled by the same frustration that she feels. "I am less and less
confident that I have become anything useful to others," (836) he says;
"Now I feel sure of nothing, not even of what I've been saying here" (838).
As Sarah Daugherty notes (in the only substantial recent critical treatment
of *Annie Kilburn*), "Like Tolstoy, Howells dramatizes his characters' baffle-
ment; but unlike Tolstoy, he complicates the issues without resolving them"
(29).[5] Peck's diagnosis of what is wrong with the scheme of Social Union—
both as a particular project of the citizens of Hatboro and as a general goal
for postwar American society—leaves people like himself and Annie, along
with the readers that Howells addresses, with no satisfactory mode of
fulfilling their own best intentions. True sympathy is hampered by class-
induced ignorance of the working-class Other, and the acquisition of true
knowledge is hindered by lack of sympathy, but not even the closest human
approximations of some workable combination of these qualities seem capable of finding a way out of the impasse. Both Annie and Peck maintain
our sympathy by the fact of their earnest seeking of a fruitful course of
action to redress contemporary social fragmentation, but neither of them
has found the answers they are seeking when the novel ends. Peck, who as
Putney notes has an air of "being rather stumped by some of the truths he
finds out" (729), resigns his pastorate to pursue an alternative path toward
social change in a dubiously conceived notion of "a sort of co-operative
boarding-house" (845) for mill workers in Fall River. For her part, nearly
all Annie's efforts to find and act upon a sympathetic knowledge of the
working class of Hatboro appear to have come to naught by the end of the

novel. The evening of theatricals has ended in an awkward intermingling of a few of the factory hands with the village elites that only the oblivious Mrs. Munger is able to mistake for "the ideal of a Social Union figuratively accomplished in her own house" (774). The union itself remains stalled in the planning stages, bogged down in uncertainties about its real form and purpose. Annie, in search of the more direct connection to the needy that Peck's counsel points toward, has taken to feeding the tramps who apply for help at her door, but she knows even as she does so that she is motivated by "the superstition that in meeting them she was fulfilling a duty sacred in proportion to the disgust she felt in the encounter" (747). Applying to Dr. Morrell for a way to make herself useful among the town's sick, she leaps at the chance to send the families of children ill with respiratory disease to the coast to take the benefits of the sea air. But when one of these children dies there, she emerges from the experience with a renewed sense of her own uselessness and a "revulsion from the direct beneficence which had proved so dangerous" (752). Her final, desperate attempt to make herself useful consists in her proposing to join Peck in the mills in Fall River, a commitment against whose impracticality she almost immediately revolts before Peck's death effectively releases her from it.

The novel thus leaves Annie almost where she began except that she has acquired a deepened understanding of the problem she faces and an intensified sense of frustration at not being able to find a way to solve it. The second strand of Peck's critique of social-union-via-charity proves not to point the way out of the quandary that both Annie and the novel itself face but to lead right back to it. If the kind of true, sympathetic understanding of the working-class Other that might lead to productive action depends on "like experiences, like hopes, like fears" (684), and if the insuperability of cultural barriers in an increasingly class-riven society prevents that commonalty of feeling and experience from occurring, what then is to be done? "I seem to have lost my old point of view," Annie tells Dr. Morrell late in the novel, "or, rather, I don't find it satisfactory any more. I'm ashamed to think of the simple plans, or dreams, that I came home with. . . . Now I think a Lady Bountiful one of the most mischievous persons that could infest any community" (817–18). Annie has learned from Peck and from her own failures that the mending of deepening social rifts in a rapidly industrializing nation requires radical change at the level of social and economic systems rather than individual charity handed down from above, which has the paradoxical effect of destroying rather than fostering cross-class sympathy and solidarity. Under the new social conditions, she continues in terms that echo one of Reverend Peck's final sermons, charity must be replaced with justice: "Those who do most of the work in the world ought to share in its comforts as a right, and not be put off with what we idlers have a mind to give them from our superfluity as a grace" (818). But such systemic transformation, even though it is ultimately dependent on the actions of individuals, seems wholly beyond the power of any individual to effect. "But what till justice *is* done?" (818) Dr. Morrell asks. "'Oh, we must continue to do charity,' cried Annie, with self-contempt" (818). Annie and the novel both end with a fuller understanding of the depth of the contemporary social schism and with a deepened anxiety over what to do about it. In the final chapter, having accepted once and for all Peck's philosophy, Annie finds herself troubled "that Dr. Morrell, after admitting the force of her reasons, should be content to rest in a comfortable inconclusion as to his conduct, till one day she reflected that this was what she was herself doing, and that she differed from him only in the openness with which she proclaimed her opinions" (864).

The prevailing impression left by the end of the novel is essentially this sense of resigned anxiety over not having found a suitable response to the question Howells borrowed from Tolstoy. A Social Union, on more or less the plan outlined by Reverend Peck for Fall River, has been established in Hatboro using the money raised by the theatricals, and it becomes a destination for outsiders who "visit it as one of the possible solutions of one of the social problems" (863). In accordance with Peck's principles, both the money and the management of the union are placed in the hands of representatives of the working people, who operate it on their own terms as a cooperative rather than depending on the charity and direction of the village gentry. They eventually request Annie's help in managing its funds, for which services they pay her a nominal salary. "She is really of use" (862), the narrator informs us, even if the union's success and her part in it are imperfect. All in all, the novel presents these outcomes as truly positive but too limited and provisional to point the way past Tolstoy's question. The novel has faced the further questions implied by Howells's aesthetic antitheory, has probed the powerful obstacles to translating sympathetic knowledge into fruitful social action, and has failed to reach any but the most makeshift conclusions about how to proceed. Settling into the "inexorable centrifugality" (858) of her comfortable life as the adoptive mother of Reverend Peck's orphaned daughter and respected member of the community, Annie does achieve a measure of contentment with her life. But the novel that bears her name leaves its readers with the unsettling sense that it has merely re-presented its original problem and superadded a heightened angst: "I feel that something must be done," Annie complains, "but I don't know what" (820). In accordance with the social-ethical aesthetic Howells developed in the *Editor's Study*, Annie's experience suggests that sympathetic knowledge of the social Other is prerequisite for meaningful ethical action but also that such knowledge is insufficient under contemporary social arrangements, which render most individual actions, conceived on the traditional plan of charity, ineffective if not outright harmful. Systemic or institutional classism operates independently of and imperviously to the goodwill of individuals, yet the sympathetic goodwill of individuals is nonetheless necessary to keep alive the future possibility of changing the system. Only when Annie Kilburn resigns herself— at least provisionally—to accepting and working through the isolating effect of her class status do her efforts begin to bear some limited fruit. It would remain for Howells's final novel to make a less provisional peace with the limited capacity of the upper classes to understand and alter their relationships with the working-class Other.

The Vacation of the Kelwyns

Howells's posthumously published final novel, *The Vacation of the Kelwyns* (1920), has routinely been dismissed as a harmless but inconsequential exercise in nostalgia by a novelist long past his prime and out of touch with contemporary social realities. As of this writing, the novel had inspired a grand total of one critical article since 1963 (by James Doyle in 1979), in addition to an unpublished critical edition undertaken as a doctoral dissertation (by Don R. Smith, also in 1979). Biographer Kenneth Lynn pronounced the novel "a tired piece of work" (236) and found unaccountable

Richard Chase's high praise of it in *The American Novel and Its Tradition* (1957),[6] and even the usually sympathetic Edwin Cady found that "the novel slumped into tired failure" (*Realist* 255).

The novel's subtitle, "An Idyl of the Middle Eighteen-Seventies," aptly suggests the book's topic, setting, and mood: a middle-class, midsummer vacation somewhere in southern New Hampshire, the account of which Chase describes as "charming for its pervasive quality of reminiscence, calm wisdom, and idyllic pleasure in life" (177). But while the title's backward-looking chronological designation and pastoral setting seem to imply a cul-turally irrelevant nostalgia for an innocent bygone era (especially when considered from the vantage point of the novel's publication in the same year that Warren Harding was elected president by a landslide largely on the basis of a platform that was short on specifics but steeped in nostalgic longing for a lost, pre-Great War "normalcy"), the genesis of the book sug-gests otherwise. Howells began the novel (under the working title *The Chil-dren of the Summer*) during the mid-1870s in response to two discrete im-petuses. The first was the long and deep economic depression of 1873 to 1879, which threw large numbers of laborers out of work, significantly reduced wages for those who were able to keep their jobs, and led to a series of increasingly violent confrontations between labor and capital, the latter backed in most cases by the federal and various state governments. In his editorial duties at the *Atlantic* during these years, Howells not only was acutely aware of these disturbing contemporary economic events but also increasingly cognizant of their antidemocratic implications; the economic troubles of the seventies moved him into the first stages of the gradual radicalization of views that would gain momentum with his experience of Haymarket and Tolstoy in the next decade. One of the human faces that the seventies depression assumed for him was a series of unnerving encoun-ters during the Howellses' own summer vacations with representatives of the army of itinerant unemployed created by the economic crisis. In the novel, such manifestations of the depression present themselves in the re-curring presence (or threat thereof) of tramps, who are occasionally spot-ted on the roads and paths of the rural neighborhood in which the Kelwyns have leased their summer house and who are repeatedly suspected of vaguely conceived intent to harm the farmstead's inhabitants—or at least make off with their property. The Kelwyns' fear of tramps forms a pervasive undercurrent in their neighborhood wanderings and in their relations with the Kites, the farm family who have been retained to keep house for the vacationers. (The tramps are blamed, for instance, for stealing Mrs. Kite's pies, until it is revealed much later that in fact the Kites' son has been feeding the pies to an itinerant French-Canadian and his trained bear, who are recuperating from illness in a neighborhood shanty.)

The second impetus for the original conception of the novel also emerged from the Howellses' vacations, during which the family bore extended witness to the disconcerting but fascinating spectacle of extreme domestic strife between the already once-divorced landlord and landlady of their holiday rental. While the Kites in the published version of the novel do not suffer from marital discord, the convergence of economic with domestic crises in the novel's initial creative genesis stands at the center of the novel Howells created from the earlier drafts of *The Children of the Summer* after 1907.[7] Far from resting easy with complacent reminiscence about the good old days, *The Vacation of the Kelwyns* emerges from and addresses the personal and domestic implications of national economic catastrophe. Like Edith Wharton's *The Age of Innocence,* another novel published in 1920 and focused on the American 1870s, Howells's portrait of that bygone era is at once both affectionate and ironic, functioning simultaneously as a paean to a lost way of life and as a pointed criticism of the social *moeurs* and assumptions that made such a life possible. While the twentieth century's predisposition to see in Howells only the stuffy old dean of a (happily) dead and utterly irrelevant American-Victorian culture acts as a powerful block to our seeing it,[8] *The Vacation of the Kelwyns* is firmly rooted in persistent issues stemming from social class disparity and cross-cultural misunderstanding. The novel follows the Kelwyns' troubled efforts to come to terms with the rural working-class Other as represented by the Kite family.

While the consciousness of national economic trauma signified by the shadowy presence of the tramps is unremitting, the novel's primary venue for its engagement in cross-cultural mediation occurs on the domestic front, in the Kelwyns' ongoing confrontation with the economic other half in their everyday relations with Mr. and Mrs. Kite, who have been hired by the remnant Shaker community that owns the farm to perform the various household duties that no self-respecting middle-class family could think of performing for themselves. Specifically, the Kites have contracted to provide the Kelwyns with meals, housekeeping, routine maintenance, and transportation as needed. This arrangement is inherently destabilizing to established boundaries between the classes: the Kelwyns rent the house from the Shakers and pay the Kites for their board, but the Kelwyns deduct from their board the money the Kites would normally have paid to the Kelwyns for rent. In the meantime, the Shakers and the Kites have a share-cropping arrangement that obliges (or allows) the Kites to farm the Shakers' fields in exchange for a share of the profits from the harvested crops. The net result is that it is fundamentally unclear who has the ascendancy in economic matters, who are the landlords and who the tenants, who the householders and who the guests. Mrs. Kelwyn, for instance, wrestles with her class anxieties even before the Kelwyns' arrival on the farm, indulging "an obscure resentment" (24) of Mrs. Kite on the basis of her own tendency toward "feeling like a guest" (24) because of the Kites' prior habitation; she resolves, "though Mrs. Kite was not to be quite her servant," nevertheless to make her "realize distinctly that the house was Mrs. Kelwyn's, and that she was in it by Mrs. Kelwyn's favor" (24)—a resolution that would hardly be necessary were the class boundaries in their new situation clearly defined. This subtle destabilization of accustomed class roles is exacerbated by the Kelwyns' almost immediate discovery that the Kites are not only incompetent to provide the quality of service to which they believe they are entitled, but also unwilling, as the Kelwyns exasperatedly complain, to learn how. Class conflict thus becomes, quite literally, domestic conflict.

The novel reinforces this welding of issues of cultural division with the routines of middle-class domestic life in a number of ways, among which is Howells's selection of a moribund Shaker community as the novel's setting. The Shaker experiment was premised on a revolution in domestic arrangements that would lead progressively to a corresponding revolution in the earthly social order. The Shakers sought to establish an order governed by communal principles of equally shared work, hardship, and prosperity, and they adopted the family as both the primary model of their social organization and an object of their reform, adopting the familial principles of brotherly and sisterly love and mutual responsibility, but removing from their reconception of family life the elements of sexuality and reproduction, which they saw as the sources of deep discord not only in the lives of individual family units but also in the life of the society as a whole. ("Go through the graveyards," a visiting Shaker Brother preaches one Sunday, "and read the records on the tombstones of the delicate females, sometimes two or three, the wives of one husband, whose lives have been sacrificed. Look at the large families of children that wore their mothers out and grew up untrained and uneducated" [140].) While none of the novel's characters is even remotely tempted by the Shaker social solution of absolute celibacy, they nevertheless treat the Shakers' thinking with respect for its well-meaning sincerity, and Howells employs the setting of the Shakers' radical though fundamentally domestic experiment in social reform to enable ongoing counterpoint with the parallel social/domestic experiment unwillingly being enacted in the same place by the Kites and Kelwyns. Thus, for instance, the fact that the five members of the Kelwyn family inhabit alone a twenty-five room Shaker family house designed explicitly to promote and accommodate communal sharing of public and private space, while the Kites are relegated to the rooms adjoining the building's kitchen, stands as an ongoing, ironic reminder of the class divisions that mar the Kelwyns' relationship with the Kites and of their fitful attempts to deal constructively with the Kites across those divisions. Indeed, that the Kelwyns choose to summer at the Shaker farm in the first place results from the initiative of one of the Shaker Elders, who seeks Kelwyn out in his place of work "because of some account he had read of the kind of work he was doing in the university . . . [The elder] had thought he would be pleased, in his quality of lecturer on Historical Sociology, to know something of the social experiment of the Shakers" (7). Even though Kelwyn initially reacts "with amusement at the notion of his august science stooping to inquire into such a lowly experiment as that of those rustic communists" (7–8), the point has been made: the Shaker setting, in short, places the Kelwyn-Kite relationship—even if Kelwyn himself becomes only incompletely aware of it—within the broader historical context of longstanding American efforts at egalitarian social reform, encouraging readers to understand the Kelwyns' immediate domestic predicament in terms of broader and deeper social and ethical considerations.

Howells assigns to Elmer Kelwyn the profession of university lecturer in the nascent discipline of Historical Sociology, and his professional pursuits encourage readers, again, to see the domestic relations between the Kites and the Kelwyns as indicative of larger patterns of social relationship. Kelwyn's enthusiastic practice of his profession commits him to studying in history the patterns governing the social interactions of discrete groups of people within societies, but, as Howells pointedly interjects, Kelwyn initially has "no thought of applying his science to his own life or conduct" (2). Kelwyn, at least initially, embodies the liberal middle-class myopia that allows the gap between values and practices to stand conveniently unquestioned; he is comfortable dealing in the abstractions of history but feels no particular need to apply sociological principle to his own personal situation. It is primarily through his family's growing intimacy with Elihu Emerance, a young man of indeterminate class status and provisionally radical social ideals who also happens to be summering in the Shaker community, that Kelwyn reluctantly begins to see the Kelwyn-Kite relationship in terms of its social significance rather than merely its impact on the availability to his family of clean rooms and good meals. The brewing confrontation between the Kites and the Kelwyns, in other words, moves the issues of class and cultural difference that for Kelwyn have been wholly academic and abstract to the center of his own domestic establishment, where they remain for the rest of the novel. And the presence of Emerance, who is Kelwyn's intellectual equal if not precisely his class peer, keeps a subtle pressure on Kelwyn to continue thinking about—and discussing—the social-ethical implications of the ongoing Kite-Kelwyn fracas.

Elihu Emerance is the bridge or swing figure whose ambiguous social status and radical openness both to others' experiences and points of view and to new ways of understanding them Howells uses to challenge the middle-class verities of Kelwyn and of his own readership. The question that introduces Emerance into the novel is voiced by a suspicious Mrs. Kelwyn, who is grilling the Shaker women about the unknown young man's identity. "What *is* he?" she asks, in response to Sister Saranna's inability to give a satisfactorily clear sense of his origins or status (46). It gradually emerges that Emerance, like the Kelwyns, wishes to summer with the Shakers, but unlike them he wishes to pay his way by physical labor; he has neither the sunburn nor the work-roughened hands of a manual laborer, but he has been dressed "by the clothier rather than the tailor" (47); his walk, demeanor, and speech all seem to Mrs. Kelwyn to indicate some degree of cultivation and refinement, yet "he was still not what she would have called a gentleman" (49). Emerance's own attempt to answer her accidentally overheard queries about him hardly serves to clarify his social niche: "As for what I am, I *am* a laborer, in one sense. I am a teacher, or have been; but I was brought up on a farm, and I know about gardening. This is my vacation, and I like to work while I'm resting" (47). Mrs. Kelwyn's questions, as well as Emerance's responses to those questions and her reactions to them, all point to the ambiguity of his social status and suggest the unreliability of the external markers of class in indicating individual identity, an idea that the novel will develop further. Emerance's position betwixt and between easily defined sociocultural roles—a farmer's son with urban experience, a member of the working class refined by a gentlemanly education, an economically poor man with a highly developed personal culture, and so on—enables his eventual role as a mediatory figure between the Kelwyns and the Kites, a role that he plays, albeit in somewhat different ways, in both of the novel's major plotlines, and one that makes him a figure of the receptive, open-minded reader Howells must have hoped for when imagining his own audience.

The echo of Emerson in Emerance's name suggests the nature of his character and role in the novel. Like Emerson, Emerance's stance is that of a democratic idealist, looking for a social application of his ideals that will do justice to them and wrestling in the meantime with the contradictions between the ideal, democratic America and the class-riven reality of the United States as it actually existed in his time and in Howells's. This idealism in search of practical expression leads him to a life of what he calls "empiricism" or "experiment" (248); he is a man in search of a socially useful career, who has successively tried (or considered trying) teaching, philanthropy, cooking, law, the ministry, acting, and playwriting; indeed, the only common denominator among his various projected pursuits is the desire to make his work "more directly important to others" (169) and the resolution to "decide upon the future without so much loss of the present" (169). Emerance's experimental impulse leads to a certain heedlessness of class boundaries and toward the established valences of social meaning that attach to certain occupations and actions. He seems oblivious, for instance, to the middle-class sense of opprobrium (which his interlocutor, Mrs. Kelwyn's cousin Parthenope Brook, feels quite keenly) attached to his contemplation of a career as an actor, which is only marginally improved when he thinks that he may pursue instead an opportunity as a playwright. On one occasion early in the novel, he leaves the Kelwyns' table, where he is a dinner guest, and enters the kitchen in order to help Mrs. Kite with dinner preparation and cleanup, quite as if it were normal for the leisure class to help "the help." He undertakes this action on wholly practical grounds—Mrs. Kite hasn't managed to provide a satisfactory meal—without paying any mind to the social signification of his actions. Even the normally staid and proper Parthenope, caught up in the moment, appears happy to go along for the time being, but the Kelwyns are thoroughly flustered by Emerance's apparent disregard of class boundaries, and his consistent if mild tendency toward class-transgressive thinking and behavior keeps them, in their role in loco parentis for Parthenope's absent aunt, in a constant state of low-grade worry about the possibility of an attachment forming between Parthenope and Emerance. The developing relationship between these two young people constitutes the novel's second major plotline. In both strands of the novel, Emerance's irrepressible impulse toward democratic freethinking goads the others to question their own class-based assumptions, to seek a better understanding of the rural working-class Other embodied primarily in the persons of the Kites, and to grope for ways to act upon that understanding.

In Kelwyn's first extended conversation with Emerance, which Kelwyn retrospectively dubs "a sociological inquiry" (91), Kelwyn almost parenthetically identifies the key issue with which the Kites confront him and his family and with which the novel confronts its middle-class readership. The conversation they have just had, he says, "seemed a survival of the sort of question that vexed Emerson and Lowell in their turn. . . . They were perplexed by their relation to those who got [their supper] for them" (92, 93). The content of the comment is relatively insubstantial, and Kelwyn does his best in the surrounding passage to minimize its significance to his own situation not only by his flippant tone but also by his framing of it in terms of Emerance's eccentricity and the implication of the inherent triviality of domestic pursuits. But Kelwyn's words point nevertheless to the novel's main strategy of middle-class engagement with the rural underclass Other: in this novel, class contact and class conflict occur, as it were, in the kitchen. As the novel continues, the Kelwyns' encounters with Emerson and Lowell's problem progress beyond vague discomfort to delve into its more serious underlying causes: an inherent conceptual and ethical conflict between the democratic impulse to value individuals on their own merits and a hierarchical valuation of people based on their class membership, as measured for instance by economic status; level of education; occupation; regional and family background; and manners.

Kelwyn and Emerance's conversation begins with the former's confession that he feels himself degraded by his association with the Kites:

> It is odd . . . but it is true that under the regimen of Mrs. Kite I've had the sense of sinking lower and lower in my own opinion. I haven't been able to recognize myself as a gentleman. . . . There seems to have been some force in the environment that vulgarized— that surrounded me with the social atmosphere of a mechanics' boarding-house. There have been times when I rose from Mrs. Kite's table—I can't call it ours—with the feeling that I was not fit for society—that I ought to resign my position in the university. (87, 88)

The reference to the ownership of the table is telling, for it suggests that Kelwyn's feelings of degradation are not simply functions of the social "environment," as he at first claims, but of his need to assert his sense of possession and control over the human elements of that environment on the basis of superior class status. When Emerance asks, "If you had had these people serving you in your house at home you would not have felt degraded by the manner or make of their service?" (89), Kelwyn readily if uneasily assents. He would not—and indeed does not—feel degraded by the presence of servants in his own home, where customary relations between middle-class employer and working-class employee remain unquestioned; he is degraded only by the presence of servants who neither conduct themselves as nor consider themselves to be servants. In other words, Kelwyn feels degraded by his association with the Kites precisely because the unconventional nature of the business arrangement that governs their relationship challenges his class-authorized right to control its every term. The Kelwyns' ambiguous status as paying guests at "Mrs. Kite's table" in the house that both families have borrowed from the Shakers upsets Kelwyn's class-supported sense of self by throwing into question the established order of power between the urban genteel class and the rural working class.

Emerance follows up his query with a second line of questioning that proves no less disruptive of Kelwyn's assumptions regarding the social classes than the first:

> "If you put people who are used to simpler things than yourself in your place here, would they be humiliated by the environment?"
>
> "Yes, I think they would, if they were people of any refinement at all," Kelwyn had a sense of generous democracy in urging.
>
> "They might be people of another kind of refinement. They might not feel the woman's shiftlessness as much as you, and yet be grieved for her by it. . . . I'm trying to imagine the sort of religious—it isn't the word—spiritual culture which seems to have pretty well gone out of the world, if it was ever much in it, and which once considered the uncultivated on their own ground and not on that of their superiors. I'm not sure—yet—that this sort of culture didn't implicate a certain amount of sentimentality. I should like to ask your opinion."
>
> "Yes," Kelwyn said, after taking a moment for thought, "I should think it did. And I suppose we should agree that sentimentality is always to be avoided."
>
> "Why, I'm not sure—yet," the young man surprised him by answering. (88–89)

Emerance is working toward a system of personal valuation that disables class prejudices by attempting to imagine individuals independent of their social contexts. Kelwyn's sense of self—that class-specific self-respect that he feels has been violated in his interactions with Mr. and Mrs. Kite—is bound to his sense of class membership; for him, consideration of Mrs. Kite's supposed "shiftlessness" from some frame of reference other than his own, where not only might Mrs. Kite's actions not appear shiftless but also shiftlessness itself might cease to appear as egregious a sin as Kelwyn's class acculturation has taught him to regard it, threatens his valuation not only of Mrs. Kite but also of himself and the accepted middle-class truths by which he understands his life. A "religious" or "spiritual" mode of knowing other people, Emerance suggests, would require a continual disruption of one's social *moeurs* and class assumptions in favor of a radically egalitarian commitment to imagining others as they might see themselves, from within their own cultural frames of reference. Such a mode of cross-cultural knowledge would depend simultaneously on a rigorous awareness of cultural relativism and on a prior "sentimental" or emotional commitment to understanding the self of the Other on his or her own terms, no matter how upsetting to one's own self-actuating assumptions that commitment might prove.

Emerance drives his speculations home by rooting them in his own and Kelwyn's recent experience with the Kites:

> If we had all been at a picnic together, and I had offered to be your cook, as I did when I proposed going into Mrs. Kite's kitchen and getting your supper just now, we should have been remanded in common to the Golden Age, or at least to the Homeric epoch, and you would have found it poetic, primitive, delightful. But here we were not remanded to a period sufficiently remote—at least I wasn't. I only got back as far as the era of the sons of the farm-houses who have served you in the kitchen and helped wait on you at table, and it gave you a little start when I sat down with you. (89–90)

Emerance's fanciful imagination of alternative contexts for the evening's experience suggests the possibility of a basis for selfhood independent of, although conditioned by, acculturation. A true understanding of others' selfhood, he suggests, depends upon recognizing the cultural conditioning that colors our perceptions of other people, in order to remove—as far as possible—the class-specific identification of the Other that prevents understanding of individual others on their own terms. Emerance's reasoning both acknowledges how powerful the cultural environment is in forming the self and posits a second independent and unconditioned basis for selfhood that operates simultaneously. The "spiritual culture" he envisions is a means of understanding the lives of others across historically created cultural divisions via sympathetic imagination, despite historically conditioned, class-bound assumptions. Only this exercise of the sympathetic imagination can enable a genuine intersubjectivity across cultural boundaries. Paradoxically, then, a true understanding of people remote from one's own cultural background—that committed act of "sentimental" imagination that transforms the alien, monolithic Other into individual, knowable others—requires one to become more acutely cognizant, from a cultural-relativist perspective, both of one's own and of others' cultural identities, in order to move through class difference to recognition of individual identity and cross-cultural commonalty.

Emerance's mention of "the sons of the farmhouses" in his colloquy with Kelwyn accentuates in another way the arbitrary and precariously maintained boundaries separating one class from another. While Emerance's class status, as Mrs. Kelwyn worries, is more than a little problematic by virtue of his proximity to the very farmhouses he mentions here, Kelwyn's own background is only marginally more settled than Emerance's, as the narrative makes clear in the first chapter. Kelwyn himself is the son of a farmer turned "country merchant, who reserved him for an intellectual career" (3), which Kelwyn has pursued as diligently "as if he had been detached from the soil by generations of culture and affluence" (3). In other words, Kelwyn's middle-class status is a product of his father's will and his own studies, and he is but half a generation removed from the same class of Yankee farmers to which the Kites belong. "In America," Howells adds, "society does not insist that one shall be a gentleman by birth; that is generally impossible; but it insists that he shall be intelligent and refined, and have the right sort of social instincts; and then it yields him an acceptance which ignores any embarrassing facts in his origin, and asks nothing but that he shall ignore them too" (3). Kelwyn succeeds brilliantly at this achieved obliviousness to his own class history, which is made all the easier by the fortunate (in this respect) deaths of his parents and by the fact that he is an only child. His new class status ratified by marriage, "all his duties were to the present" (3); his utter disconnectedness from social history typifies a quintessentially American way of dealing—or not dealing—with history, and it intensifies his incentive for not acknowledging his spiritual kinship with the Kites and their like. The permeability of the boundaries between the classes in a society with a relatively large degree of upward mobility makes the task of maintaining those boundaries all the more anxious, but it also affords those who have moved upward a greater chance of imaginatively connecting with those they have left behind. The novel's juxtaposition of Kelwyn with Emerance reveals the fragility of the distinction between middle-class social respectability and the lower classes' lack thereof, and accounts for the mingled vehemence and uncertainty with which Kelwyn and his class must struggle in their efforts to keep intact a line of demarcation that can be blurred so easily. Under but slightly altered circumstances, Kelwyn's middle-class myopia might have developed instead as something like Emerance's culturally relativistic spiritual vision.

With this conversation between them, Kelwyn proceeds simultaneously in opposite directions, becoming more and more exasperated with the Kites and determined to rid himself of them, on the one hand, and on the other hand gaining, albeit fitfully, a grudging understanding and respect for them. The conflict between these dual impulses—one proceeding from his sense of middle-class entitlement and the other from Emerance's stirring up of his more democratic and egalitarian ideals—dominates Kelwyn's actions throughout the novel, even before the introduction of Emerance as a social-ethical gadfly. The Kelwyns' initial attitude toward the Kites and the class they represent is a mélange of self-justifying middle-class assumptions, but it includes, too, hints of an underlying susceptibility to sympathy and an ability to suspend judgment. Before meeting either of the Kites, the Kelwyns exercise their free reign to imagine them in terms that are wholly flattering to themselves. They picture the Kites as helpless recipients of their largesse and come to refer to them as "those poor little people" (14), figuring them "as of anxious and humble presence, fearful of losing the great chance of their lives" (14). They caution themselves, in Kelwyn's words, against "pretend[ing] that we are making the arrangement on their account. We are primarily doing it for ourselves" (13); whatever good proceeds to the Kites from the Kelwyns' actions is to be regarded as an "incidental" (13) advantage of a transaction that is "most distinctly a matter of business" (13) rather than charity. Kelwyn even takes the occasion to develop his little expression of self-interest into a sociological principle, asserting, "That is the way that most of the good in the world has come about. The history of civilization is that of certain people who wished to better their own condition, and made others wish to do the same by the spectacle of their success" (13–14). But this entire discussion proceeds from the Kelwyns' shared feeling of "a vague dissatisfaction" (13) with the adage that "charity begins at home" (13). "It struck me," Kelwyn says, "as rather a hollow-hearted saying; I don't know why. I never questioned it before" (13). That they are inclined to question it at all suggests that the Kelwyns, who do remain safely wrapped in their middle-class cocoon, are nonetheless subject to inklings that perhaps their habitual assumptions about their relations with the lower classes may after all be ethically suspect. Kelwyn begins his journey securely ensconced in the middle-class rhetoric of ethical self-congratulation, but he is not quite entirely comfortable there.

The real Kites, of course, pose an immediate challenge to the Kelwyns' prior imaginations of them. Mrs. Kite almost immediately proves incapable of fulfilling their culinary instructions, providing them with "cowy" milk, rancid butter, inedible salt-rising bread rather than their accustomed yeast bread, overcooked vegetables and over-brewed tea. The dining room table is thus transformed into the site of a power struggle, as Mrs. Kelwyn gives futile instruction to Mrs. Kite about what they require of her and how she should go about providing it. But amid these wrangles, Kelwyn suddenly becomes aware that at the root of the trouble is his own class-based inability to read the Kites with any assurance that his interpretations are correct. As Mrs. Kite receives Mrs. Kelwyn's instructions, "Kelwyn was taking involuntary notes of her, and he could not have said whether she was assenting willingly or unwillingly. She might have been meek or she might have been sly; she could have been pretty or plain, as you thought; her pale sandy hair might have been golden; her gray eyes blue. A neutrality which seemed the potentiality of better or worse things pervaded her" (30). The remarkable degree of equivocation in this passage reflects Kelwyn's dawning awareness that all his prior assumptions about the Kites' class tell him essentially nothing useful about the reality of the Kites themselves. With the facts staring him in the face, he is yet unable to make sense of them, his position as a class outsider having rendered the Kites hermeneutically opaque and himself incapable of knowing the meanings or motives of their actions. For the first time, Kelwyn becomes aware that his facile middle-class certitudes about the lives of the rural working class may be impediments to rather than guarantors of his understanding of people who are culturally different from himself.

After the advent of Emerance gives Kelwyn the beginnings of an intellectual framework for understanding his experiences with the Kites, his progress in the directions suggested by Emerance is anything but steady.

But his worries continue to rise from those two opposing sources: his middle-class sense of entitlement, which moves him to seek the Kites' dismissal, and his uncomfortable suspicions that the former impulse may not be ethically justifiable. Adding weight to those suspicions, for instance, is the "baffling anomaly" (41) that despite the numerous failings that the Kelwyns perceive in Mrs. Kite, she is the object of the "implicit deference and admiration" (41) of her family members and of the hired man, Raney. Likewise, Kite himself proves to have an unaccountable "standing in the neighborhood" (42), resting in part on his efforts to bring the drunken Tad Allson and his "slattern" (42) wife up to community standards of family life and public decorum. Too, Mrs. Kite routinely gives food to the itinerants whose presence consistently terrifies the city visitors, and Kelwyn is troubled by the further evidence of neighborly solicitude and levelheadedness displayed by Kite when he goes to the rescue of their elderly neighbor, Mrs. Ager, after the Kelwyn-Kite household is awakened one midnight by a scream of undetermined origin. "He seems to be the neighborhood moralist and philanthropist" (196), Emerance quips, only partially ironically. In short, the Kites' role in their community amounts finally to a sort of "social leadership" (43) that Kelwyn must acknowledge even though it comes nowhere near matching his own standards.

Meanwhile, Emerance's status as the swing figure between adjoining cultural identities has him serving the same catalytic function for Parthenope that he has served for Kelwyn; the progress of their relationship constitutes the second main plotline of the novel. As he does with Kelwyn, Emerance calls into question Parthenope's fixed assumptions about class, while serving too as a mediating figure between Parthenope's well-bred Bostonian gentility and the old New England uncouthness of the impoverished country folk with whom they together come into contact. She, along with the Kelwyns, undergoes the subtle disruption of her urban upper-class assumptions as Emerance's provisionally radical social speculations and freer modes of interaction with the local inhabitants open up other possible points of view toward the rural underclass. But the second, equally vital role of the Emerance-Parthenope plotline is to allow marriage itself gradually to accrue to itself the symbolic heft of Howells's project of cross-cultural communication.

From the first, the relationship between Emerance and Parthenope is presented as fraught with class implications. Mrs. Kelwyn's objections to Emerance as a (belatedly recognized) potential suitor for Parthenope are explicitly founded on his class inferiority. As we saw in her questioning of the Shaker women, Mrs. Kelwyn is already anxious about the shadowy nature of Emerance's background and identity well before the possibility of an alliance with her cousin presents itself to any significant degree. Her objections come to a head late in the novel, after the two young people have already spent significant stretches of time together both in and out of the Kelwyns' presence. Excusing her failure to intervene earlier—after, in fact, Emerance has already made one ineffectual (but recognizable by Parthenope) attempt to propose marriage—as due to "the confusion here, the perfect topsy-turviness of all our ideas" (212–13), Mrs. Kelwyn proceeds to warn Parthenope against Emerance: "You know yourself, Parthenope, that anything serious would be quite out of the question. The very fact that he was so different from ourselves in what Mr. Kelwyn calls his civilization had made me feel easier, but it doesn't excuse me. If he had been a young man of your own class I certainly should have objected to your being about with him so much at all hours . . . of the day and night" (213). The terms of her scolding are telling, based as they are on the presumption of a class solidarity between Parthenope and herself that has already ruled out any permanent attachment to the unsuitable Emerance on the basis of class difference; despite his acknowledged personal culture and education, his lesser degree of "civilization" makes him acceptable as a temporary companion but not as a suitor. The close juxtaposition of Mrs. Kelwyn's intervention in Parthenope's relationship with Emerance to the "topsy-turviness" of the Kelwyns' thinking about their own class relationship to the Kites makes the former essentially a continuation of the latter: Parthenope's association with Emerance is no less disruptive of the class assumptions upon which Mrs. Kelwyn relies in her conversation with her cousin than are Emerance's radical social speculations and the muddled state of the Kelwyn-Kite affiliation.

Parthenope's rejection of Emerance's proposal just a few pages later employs logic identical to Mrs. Kelwyn's. "We are too unlike . . . in our ideals" (235), Parthenope explains, and she immediately defines her use of the word in terms very much like those her cousin had earlier used: "We've been brought up in such different worlds we never should understand each other. I should always be unjust to you" (235). Emerance's response diminishes Parthenope's "different worlds" to mere differing "traditions" (235), which he subordinates in importance to their shared "principles" (235); to the democratic idealist, predictably, personal worth handily trumps class background, and an interpersonal communication that bridges learned cultural conventions is always eminently possible. The terms of the colloquy that follows, which unfolds largely as a debate between the values of idealism versus empiricism, tempt a reading that would follow the familiar Howellsian pattern perhaps most famously embodied in the Laphams' ethical struggles with questions of morality in *The Rise of Silas Lapham*: whether a true morality is determined by adherence to absolute a priori principle or by a calculation of the practical effects of a particular line of action on all concerned parties. But here the terms of the debate become curiously shuffled and increasingly muddled, amounting in the end to a new approach to the relation between Pragmatist and Idealist ethics.

Emerance claims Parthenope as the "ideal" that would redeem him from his aimless empiricism, but Parthenope refuses Emerance (somewhat self-contradictorily) both because he "live[s] in the ideal" and would be "clogged" by her and because he does not represent her a priori ideal of manhood and husband-hood. Emerance wishes to "reason" with Parthenope about her feeling for him, but Parthenope asserts that "if I could reason about it I'm sure I shouldn't have it" (236). Emerance, verging on the principle that will become the key to resolution of their debate, retorts that it seems "very strange . . . that reason can have nothing to do with the highest and humanest thing in the world" (236–37). But his comment brings the couple to an impasse, and Emerance resigns himself to Parthenope's rebuff. Meanwhile, the carriage that they have been riding in all the while has paused before the Shaker office, ostensibly from the horse's habit but symbolically to underscore the nature of the realization she is about to make: "the Shakers had got rid of love, and all that came of it. She had never meant to do that" (237). She "imagined his anguish from her own pain" (237), abandoning her construction of him as socially unsuitable, as not matching her prior ideal, and recognizes him instead for what his words and actions reveal him to be: "a man whose goodness she owned as greater than that of any man she had yet known; a generous spirit, full of ambition and the power that the future would turn into success" (238). She consents, therefore, as she had formerly refused, to "reason" with him about their feelings, and she outlines her ideal of manhood: in sum, a paragon of unswerving integrity and philanthropic purpose, a finished perfection rather than a work in progress. Emerance responds by redefining the notion of ideality, saying that he "would rather be an ideal which you would be willing to live for. I should like to be some faltering, imperfect creature that you could strengthen and straighten into the sort of man you would like him to be. I believe that you would be happier in that than in dying for somebody who didn't need you. How could you be of use to a man who didn't need you?" (240). Emerance's retort, which he believes to have been ineffective, constitutes a plea for Parthenope to temper her ideals by merging them with reality, with a man—himself—as he really is rather than a perfect imagination of a man. It also constitutes a suggestion that such a merger calls for her active engagement with him, in constructive defiance of all obstacles posed by birth and class acculturation.

Marriage thus becomes, in small, a figure of the kind of cross-cultural understanding and resultant action with which the whole novel has been concerned, one that is dependent on sympathetic feeling, on the imagination of an ideal state of relationship better than the reality, and on a commitment to the messy and inconclusive process of seeking the realization of that ideal despite the knowledge that it can never be completely realized. When Parthenope finally—after Emerance has given up his suit—accedes to his proposal, she does so by re-conceiving marriage as an ideal-informed "experiment," as the active effort to try the ideal in the real. Her realization of the lovelessness of the Shaker ideal and of the necessary imperfection of any interhuman relationship, marital or social, amounts to little less than a postmodern theological revelation, a quasi-mystical faith commitment to a new relationship comprised equally of love and rationality, ideal and experiment, romanticism and realism. (These qualities of the novel go far in accounting for Richard Chase's unwonted positive response, in terms of Shakespearean romance, to this of all Howells's novels.) Parthenope and Emerance's projected marriage models the last, experimental basis upon which Howells envisions whatever progress there is to be made in the project of sympathetic cross-cultural communication and concomitant action that he had launched four decades earlier.

Just as the novel employs the Emerance-Parthenope marriage as a sym-

bolic representation of the essential bases for successful cross-cultural understanding and action, it figures the demise of the Kelwyn-Kite relationship
in terms of divorce. The (temporary) demise of the relationship between
Kite and Kelwyn is caused by Kelwyn's choosing to privilege his class-
specific personal and legal rights over his sense of Kite as a knowable, living, feeling, human equal. The chronicle of their dysfunctional mutual
association climaxes in Kelwyn's imposition, as urban, professional-class
master, of his prerogatives over Kite, as rural, working-class servant. Kelwyn's intention is calmly to impose his rational justification of the Kites'
dismissal upon his employee; he assumes that the inherent unpleasantness
of the situation will be borne away by the impeccable logic of his case
against the Kites, fully authorized by his assumption of his own superiority
in social and legal terms over his quasi-tenant. But the show of rational
circumspection ends in a shouting match under a tree at the edge of the
meadow that Kite is mowing, both participants "wip[ing] the drops of
fury from their faces" (188). In the aftermath, Kelwyn feels ashamed and
suddenly doubtful about the certitudes upon which he had based his
argument—particularly since he senses a "moral gulf" (188) between him
and the Shaker, Brother Jasper, the sole witness of the dispute, who (Kelwyn suspects) disapproves of Kelwyn's action despite his reluctant acquiescence. The more concrete the break between Kites and Kelwyns becomes,
the less satisfied Kelwyn becomes with his own actions; his attempt to suppress the personal, emotional aspect of his relations with the Kites by acting upon his legal and social rights has failed, and he passes into second
thoughts and self-reproach. At length, he expresses his feelings to Emerance
(with Parthenope listening, unseen), suitably reframed as rational assertions:

It is strange how difficult it is to withdraw from any human relation,
no matter how provisional. There is always an unexpected wrench, a
rending of fibres, a pang of remorse. . . . I think that at the end of
every relation in life there is a sort of blind desire, unreasonable and
illogical, to have it on again. If it ends abruptly or inimically this is
especially the case. We go back of the cause of disagreement and find
potentialities of continued reciprocity. We see defects in ourselves
and excellences in our antagonist—if it has come to antagonism—

and we wish we could try it all over again. I am speaking abstractly, of course. (190, 192)

But Kelwyn is, of course, not speaking purely in the abstract but seeking to work out rationally his feelings in the wake of the breech in his relation to the Kites. Emerance furthers Kelwyn's idea by domesticating it even further: "I have often wondered how the parties to a divorce, people who had once cared for each other, really felt when it came to the point of severing. . . . I have wondered whether there wasn't always a touch of regret, a lingering kindness as they had when their outlook was the brightest" (191). Emerance's comments follow the path of his emotional preoccupation with Parthenope just as Kelwyn's have followed his feelings about the Kite melee. But both men's words place social and marital discord in the same context, suggesting negatively, as the Emerance-Parthenope relationship does positively, the thorough involvement of the emotional with the rational, the concrete with the abstract, the interpersonal with the sociological in every human relationship, from the domestic to the national.

The next morning, Kelwyn rises from bed "with as generous a resolution as ever filled the breast of a lecturer on historical sociology" (201), and he sets out for the Shaker Office to countermand his dismissal of the Kites and announce that the Kelwyns themselves will find new quarters instead. "You know the plain and logical view of the matter," he explains to Parthenope, "the legal position would be to stand upon our rights. Perhaps, in the interest of society, we should not enable the Kites to remain where they could impose upon other long suffering and unoffending people" (202). Thus far Kelwyn speaks from his position of class privilege and self-interest. "But," he continues, shifting from abstract consideration of class implications and toward the particularities of the Kites and their immediate situation, "we cannot bring ourselves to stand upon our rights. To put those people out would be to disgrace them before their neighbors, and cloud their future wherever the rumor of their disgrace followed them" (203). Thus the Kelwyns reach the furthest point of their progress away from fixed class assumptions about the relationships between themselves and the rural working-class Other toward sympathetic recognition of individual members of the lower class and accordant personal action in relation to them.

The Vacation of the Kelwyns, then, like its predecessors, is a novel about the comfortable classes' reluctance to seek and difficulty in gaining knowledge of the cultural Other, and about the problem of knowing what to do with that knowledge once it has been gained. The novel offers Emerance's egalitarian spiritual vision as its primary response to the antidemocratic tenor of post–Civil War social, economic, and political development, asserting more forcefully than had either *The Minister's Charge* or *Annie Kilburn* the sheer persistence, along with the fragility, of the impulse to recognize others across the obscuring barriers imposed by cultural difference and class training. Alone among the three novels, *The Kelwyns* ends with its characters having acted effectually, if limitedly, upon their newfound sympathy with the poor. But the novel remains, like the other two, less than completely optimistic about the willingness or the ability of the upper classes to achieve and to follow through on such a vision; in his search for a mode of constructive, ideal-infused engagement with the persistent problem of cultural discord, Howells never abandons his Realist commitment to representing the situation as it really, in his assessment, existed. The Kelwyns do, in the end, act magnanimously toward the Kites, not only abandoning their attempt to evict the Kites but also leaving the house to them entirely—a decision that Kelwyn makes before he knows (as Emerance does already) that another suitable house in the neighborhood has become available for the remainder of the summer. But the Kelwyns' action on behalf of the Kites is mitigated by the narrowness of its scope, as well as by the mixed motives from which it proceeds: along with their altruism, the Kelwyns are motivated by the simple desire to escape what has become a thoroughly uncomfortable situation.

Similarly, Emerance and Parthenope's projected marriage, whose symbolism suggests the bridging of learned class differences via interpersonal emotional commitment, yet embodies only a limited victory over Parthenope's class-based myopia and Emerance's lingering inability to translate egalitarian ideals into a committed course of action. Parthenope transgresses class boundaries by committing herself to Emerance, but she does so without a fully conscious revolution in her social ideals; Emerance continues to speak from his egalitarian principles but remains susceptible to his tendency toward uncommitted experimentalism in his actions. All the major characters make genuine progress toward the modes of feeling, thought, and action hoped for and projected by Howells's literary theory, but that progress is no less limited than it is genuine.

The experiences of Emerance, Parthenope, and Kelwyn, finally, enact the only response to class issues that Howells seems to have been able to reconcile to the facts of middle-class America during the decades following the Civil War. Optimistic about the persistence of the impulse toward a truer valuation of individuals despite the acculturation of the more privileged classes in values that tend to render the Other opaque, the novel remains doubtful about the extent of people's willingness and ability to translate that impulse into concrete and meaningful action and yet sympathetic toward the psychological and emotional trials of those who would try. The novel's "insistence on the virtual equality in any person of the good and the bad, or of the interesting and the dull" (to borrow from Lionel Trilling, the other major dissenting voice in nearly universal critical dismissal of *The Kelwyns*) comprises a kind of "loving wonder at the fact that persons of the most mediocre sort somehow manage to make a society" ("Howells" 210). *The Vacation of the Kelwyns* criticizes the minor and equivocal progress that Howells saw as possible in a nation simultaneously more prosperous, more class-riven, and more deeply entrenched in an obfuscating ideology of middle-class normalcy than ever before, but the novel nevertheless maintains a sympathetic patience with its characters and its readers. This, Howells implies, is perhaps the most a socially conscientious artist can hope for from readers who are fundamentally like his characters: an imperfectly achieved knowledge of the cultural Other that allows a degree of sympathetic insight that just might, on given occasions, issue in constructive interaction between members of different classes. The novel, committed to the imagination of ameliorative social action but also to imagining those possibilities within the boundaries of probability (as Howells saw it), offers no political program for making the class problem (broadly defined) disappear. Instead, it shows characters engaged in a difficult process of social and self-reevaluation that is no less radical for not being revolutionary. That this process leads to but limited ameliorative actions, performed primarily on the small stage of the domestic sphere, may make the novel's address of class issues seem singularly inconsequential to those of us who wish for more comprehensive and momentous change in our social arrangements. But the novel suggests that such actions, despite their modesty, are no less valuable in and of themselves and offer the advantage of being achievable by anyone without waiting for the onset of a revolution that may never come. From a Marxist perspective this may look like quiescence and despair, but from Howells's liberal and Realist perspective, it constitutes instead a pragmatic idealism, an attempt to assess honestly the prospects for people like his own readers to imagine and enact a more egalitarian, more democratic reality in a United States that seemed during Howells's lifetime to be moving ever farther away from its own founding principles.

At one point in *The Vacation of the Kelwyns,* Emerance notes in response to Parthenope's puncturing of his fantasy of escaping the troubles of his present existence by assuming a happy life as a rural day laborer, "The world is here, as it is everywhere, and it is always the same old world" (162). Howells's practice of his social-ethical aesthetic in his fiction is based on this recognition that for most of us, most of the time, engagement with the pervasive social ills of society at large, if it is to occur at all, must occur primarily in the routine and chance interactions with the social Other that happen in the normal course of daily life. It is on this scale and in this quotidian setting, for Howells, that the responsible novelist, his characters, and his readers most profitably engage the pressing question of what to do in response to the age's apparent social disintegration. Howells's explorations in fiction of the implications of his own aesthetic of social-ethical responsibility reveal to us characters who struggle both to gain the kind of sympathetic cross-cultural knowledge that (to Howells's mind) all literature worthy of the name should aim to produce and to know what to do with that knowledge once it has been gained. As we have seen, his characters have a decidedly mixed record of success, on both counts. Learning to realize and act toward the Other as fully human and individuated persons rather than as representatives of an antagonistic class, Howells suggests, is a process that is only incompletely and sporadically possible but is no less valuable or necessary thereby. If Howells's fiction seems more pessimistic regarding the possibilities for substantive social-ethical transformation on the basis of a sympathetically mimetic literature than did his enthusiastic critical pronouncements in the *Editor's Study,* the fiction nonetheless demonstrates the seriousness and consistency of the author's commitment to those values. The impossibility of achieving final, comprehensive, and productive knowledge—whether in literature or in life—across the myriad cultural divisions in American society is for Howells the index of the urgent necessity of trying to do so, however limited the prospects for success.

3
"Unwritable Things"
Sarah Orne Jewett's Dual Aesthetic in *Deephaven* and *The Country of the Pointed Firs*

When Sarah Orne Jewett entered into correspondence with the *Atlantic Monthly* regarding prospective publication of the sketches that later became her first book, *Deephaven* (1877), it was W. D. Howells with whom she communicated. Howells, then in transition from assistant to chief editor, was already guiding the *Atlantic*'s editorial policies in accordance with the nascent conception of literature's social-ethical mandate that would gain full expression a decade later in the *Editor's Study*. The American regionalism that came into vogue during the postwar decades and of which Jewett's work was an example was well suited to Howellsian literary purposes, situating itself as it did along the boundaries between the urban centers of a newly nationalizing economy and the local, small-town, and rural realities of what still constituted a near-majority of the country's population. On the grounds of his social-ethical aesthetic Howells accepted for publication Jewett's early sketches of life along the southern Maine coast and later encouraged her to revise them into book form.

Jewett's unique variant of the Howellsian social-ethical agenda for American literature is clearly implemented in both *Deephaven* and *The Country of the Pointed Firs* (1896), but while the latter is acclaimed almost universally as Jewett's most successful work, the earlier book usually has been considered as a promising but uneven apprentice work. *The Country of the Pointed Firs* immerses its readers in an effectively realized local culture, detailing the living network of everyday events, objects, places, and relationships that comprises the commonplace life of a Maine coastal village. But at the same time, the vivid impression of regionalist authenticity, along with the powerfully evoked sense of readerly communion with narrator and narrated to which generations of readers and critics have responded, derive in large measure from the book's evocation of further dimensions of these realities: the sense that mundane social life resonates with an intuited spiritual immanence that both transcends and informs everyday existence. In *Country*, these tendencies exist within an aesthetic fusion (to borrow a term from Elizabeth Ammons) "that is so subtle and complex as to appear quite simple" (45) and that leaves readers with a vital sense not only of persons and places but also of what Jewett elsewhere terms the "unwritable things" (*Letters* 112) that slip the traces of linguistic specification but constitute the "heart" (*Letters* 112) of the story and its internal webs of interrelationship. In *Deephaven*, however, this fusion is only fitfully successful; despite the narrator's dogged attempts to do justice to both the mundane and the unwritable aspects of her local subjects, she is apt to vacillate from one agenda to the other, her narrative mode lurching awkwardly back and forth between the two in search of the voice that will enable readers fluid access to both facets of her subject matter and both aspects of her literary purpose simultaneously.

Perhaps because of this disparity in achievement between otherwise analogous fictions, *Deephaven* reveals the process by which Jewett arrived, in *The Country of the Pointed Firs*, at the seamless narrative union between ethically purposeful literary communication of local social realities and the almost mystical evocation of the "unwritable things" that bring the local fully to life. Rereading Jewett through the lens of a Howellsian conception of literary purpose allows one to discern some of the sources of this disparity and reveals how Jewett reshaped the literary-ethical imperative she shared with her editor, adapting it to her own conceptions of both the nature of commonplace experience and the literary mode best suited to communicating it. *The Country of the Pointed Firs* is the result of Jewett's adoption and extension of Howells's model of ethically purposive social fiction to include a suprasocial, spiritual dimension of commonplace reality without which, she felt, any real knowledge of the cultural Other was impossible. *Deephaven* reveals the process by which its author learned to transform linear Howellsian literary mediation into a more evocative, reader-participatory narrative mode that was able fully to grapple with Jewett's spiritualized sense of temporal social realities. The earlier novel's very incompletion in achieving these goals allows one more easily to understand the terms of Jewett's later success.

"To Make Them Acquainted with One Another": The Dual Aesthetic of *Deephaven*

Critical Bifurcation and Social-Ethical Mediation

Over the decades, critical evaluation of Sarah Orne Jewett's two primary works of regionalism has vacillated between privileging their function as social documentation and emphasizing their supposedly extra-Realist preoccupation with the intangible, emotionally and tonally suggestive qualities of their narrations of village life. Critics almost unanimously agree, for example, that *The Country of the Pointed Firs* is Jewett's highest achievement, but the grounds for this judgment, critic by critic, shift emphasis from one pole of the spectrum to the other. Consider for example the essays collected in Richard Cary's early *Appreciation of Sarah Orne Jewett* in 1973, an important precursor to Jewett's full reincorporation into the canon(s) of American literature during and beyond the 1980s.[1] In that volume, Warner Berthoff asserts that Jewett's primary authorial interest is "sociological" and "historical" (158), Mary Ellen Chase terms Jewett a "social historian" (182), and Cary himself calls her "the most illustrious depicter of Maine life" (vii). But Francis Fike claims that Jewett's "interest is not sociological" (172), Hyatt Waggoner finds not social realism but "a unity emerging from symbolic texture and structure and partaking of the quality of a vision of life" (162), and Jean Boggio-Sola discovers, rather than "a social document," writing that "radiates a deeper realism akin to that of poetry" (202). This critical concern to settle the relationship between the social-documentary and the evocative aspects of Jewett's literary project continues through the largely feminist revaluation of *The Country of the Pointed Firs* during the eighties (see for example criticisms by Judith Fetterley, Marjorie Pryse, Sandra Zagarell, Elizabeth Ammons, Marilyn Sanders Mobley, and Marcia McClintock Folsom, among many others) and in the impassioned and illuminating debate ongoing between critics who see

Jewett's regionalism as an act of cultural imperialism and those who continue to read Jewett (in June Howard's formulation) "as an empathetic artist of local life" (377). Feminist reappraisals shift the terms of discussion away from older New Critical preoccupations with form versus content toward new understandings of Jewett's evocativeness, interpreted in terms of the natural and mythic solidarities that comprise and define relationships within communities of women. And the more recent debate substitutes for a relatively unproblematized assumption of Realist textual mimesis a fuller awareness of the texts' complex ideological investments in other kinds of ongoing cultural discourses. But each phase of the critical conversation continues to call attention to the fact that something in these texts simultaneously enables both sociohistorical readings that privilege the works' mimetic functions and "expressionistic" interpretations founded upon the books' more indefinable qualities of intersubjective, communal, affective—even mystical—experience. The tendency in these criticisms is to emphasize, respectively, either the works' representations of social realities or their narrative evocations of communities that somehow seem to include not only the narrated subjects but also narrators, author, and reader; these two emphases correspond to the two aspects of Jewett's aesthetic project, and the best of these criticisms begin to put the two in dialogue with each other, as this chapter aims to do.

Jewett implements her version of the Howellsian social-ethical agenda from the first pages of *Deephaven,* launching a narrative that has all the earmarks of a regionalism aimed at mediating the cultural differences between the lives of the narrated and those of the audience. Jewett deftly introduces the enabling situation: the narrator, Helen Denis, and her friend Kate Lancaster, will spend their summer vacation in the vacant mansion of Kate's deceased grand-aunt Brandon, in the sleepy coastal village called Deephaven. While Kate and Helen's family members summer at more usual holiday destinations (the Berkshires, Newport, Lake Superior, Britain), the two young Bostonians (accompanied by Kate's house servants) will join the postwar vogue for roughing it in quaint, rural backwaters. The first chapter of *Deephaven* allies its readers with Kate and Helen, as educated, upper-middle-class, urban outsiders eager to experience the local culture; the regionalist narrative, in a process that Richard Brodhead contextualizes in terms of the rise of tourism, thus enables an audience comprised chiefly of people who more closely resemble the narrators than the narrated to share vicariously in Kate and Helen's vacation.[2] Before Kate, Helen, and Jewett's readers have even arrived in Deephaven, we have already met our first authentic local character: Mrs. Kew, the lighthouse keeper's wife. Jewett has her narrators travel by train from their native Boston to an outlying station—the last outpost of their civilization—whence they share a coach ride to Deephaven with Mrs. Kew. The travel arrangements themselves serve to emphasize the cultural distance between Deephaven and the world of its narrators and readers.[3]

Subsequent chapters are devoted, in regionalist fashion, to the tourists' fascinated observations of provincial life, focusing on the details that most clearly mark Deephaven, its residents, and their way of life as "Other." Helen makes passing mention of city visitors whom the young women periodically receive, but even these visits serve primarily to provide occasions for Deephaven-based storytelling. Pages are devoted to detailed descriptions of the Brandon mansion and its furnishings, presented as harbingers of a lost eighteenth-century heritage. Frequent calls upon Mrs. Kew give Jewett's narrators opportunity for close observation and description of the lives and accoutrements of those quintessential shore dwellers, the lighthouse keeper and his wife. Another local denizen, Mrs. Patton, an old friend of the deceased Aunt Brandon, grants Kate and Helen free entrance into the homes and domestic histories of other Deephaven citizens. Kate and Helen, as sympathetic outsiders who yet win their way into the confidence and intimacy of the natives, provide us readerly access to a wealth of local experience, mediating between two different cultural worlds.

Toward this end, the narrators assume a relatively objective yet clearly appreciative stance toward the subjects of their narration, rendering culturally representative characters, events, and objects in transparently mimetic prose readily amenable to regionalist social documentation. The account of Kate and Helen's visit with Mrs. Patton in chapter three, for instance, faithfully transcribes the old woman's Down-East dialect and uses it to reveal local culture through the memories associated with quotidian household objects. "She had all genealogy and relationship at her tongue's end" (31) and "had either seen everything that had happened in Deephaven for a long time, or had received the particulars from reliable witnesses" (32), Helen Denis writes; via Mrs. Patton, Helen communicates family and community history through the stories that attach themselves to the implements of everyday life in the village. Thus the appearance of a battered earthenware mug that Kate and Mrs. Patton had once used for picking currants becomes the occasion for rehearsing the social history of the mug itself: its various owners, the uses it has served, the emotional associations it has acquired through decades of service. Likewise, the rediscovery of a quilt buried in a forgotten trunk leads to a rehearsal of the history of the watered-silk gown from which it was made, complete with the personal drama of local history memorially annexed to it. When Mrs. Patton serves the young women some cake, she includes with it a complete oral history of the recipe and the circumstances of its transmission from England to her hand. Thus Jewett mines the artifacts of the local culture for what Bill Brown, writing about *The Country of the Pointed Firs,* calls "the narrativity of physical objects" (209), their capacity to reveal the histories of the lives and interrelationships of their possessors, past and present.

Deephaven's union of local cultural content with a literary form ideally equipped for close description of that content testifies to Jewett's social-documentary purposes. Despite her public disavowals of any actual prototypes for her Maine village, Deephaven (and later, Dunnet Landing) derives from the features Jewett would have observed during her own summer vacations in York and Wells on the southern Maine coast during the years of *Deephaven*'s genesis in the late 1860s and early 1870s but even more pervasively from her lived experiences in and around her hometown of South Berwick, a village on the Piscataqua River a mere ten miles from the coast and sharing in large measure a common culture with the shoreline villages.[4] The narrative adopts a literary form well suited to the documentation of local realities and calculated to establish an impression of their authenticity. Formally, the book proceeds as a series of sketches, linked primarily by locale and narrative voice rather than by elaborate plotting. Howells's suggestion to Jewett that she try to write something more lengthy led the two eventually to agree, in their correspondence concerning *Deephaven,* that the open-endedness and descriptive flexibility of the sketch form made it ideal for Jewett's gifts and purposes—a realization that may have been aided, on Howells's part, by his analogous experiments in *Suburban Sketches* (1871).[5] To make literature from "the every-day life" of such "a quiet old-fashioned country town" as Deephaven, Helen asserts in a

directly narratorial comment anticipating the *Editor's Study's* pronouncements on the literary value of the commonplace, "one must care to study
life and character, and must find pleasure in thought and observation of
simple things, and have an instinctive, delicious interest in what to other
eyes is unflavored dulness" (37).

If Helen's comments place a Realist premium upon the interest to be
found in observation and representation of commonplace social life, Jewett
aligns her narration of the culturally normative aspects of commonplace
coastal Maine life as well with a Howellsian vision of social-ethical literary
purpose. Her 1894 preface to a newly illustrated edition of *Deephaven*
comments explicitly on the origin of the sketches in an ethical imperative
for literary mediation of postbellum social divisions. The sketches, she
writes, responded to new national conditions; urbanization, increased prosperity, and expanded rail service "brought together in new association and
dependence upon each other" rural districts and "crowded towns," making
possible "a new and national circulation of vitality" (2). But "the young
writer of these Deephaven sketches was possessed by a dark fear that
townspeople and country people would never understand one another, or
learn to profit by their new relationship" (3). Significantly, Jewett's preface
frames the momentous upheavals of the post–Civil War era both as threats
to social cohesion and as opportunities for better cross-sectional understanding. To bridge the social chasm between town and country became
the informing goal of her writing.

The basis for this mediation, Jewett explains, consists of an underlying
human commonality that may form a new foundation for community in
a time of social schism. In words that distinctly anticipate one of Howells's
most pointed statements of literature's ethical raison d'être in the *Editor's
Study,* Jewett writes in her preface that "Human nature is the same the
world over" (6) despite the myriad of potentially alienating differences
among various local cultural practices and forms. In terms of nascent national identity, Jewett writes, "There is a noble saying of Plato that the best
thing that can be done for the people of a state is to make them acquainted
with one another" (3). This goal, she continues, can be achieved only when
literature abandons the malicious impulses inherent in caricature and dedi-
cates itself to the accurate representation of the lives and circumstances of
the Other; "the caricatured Yankee" (3) of conventional fiction must be

replaced with "a more true and sympathetic rendering" (qtd. in Cary, *Letters* 84) drawn from life rather than literature.[6] Once faithfully represented in literature, Jewett writes elsewhere, "The people in books are apt to make us understand 'real' people better, and to know why they do things, and so we learn to have sympathy and patience and enthusiasm for those we live with, and can try to help them in what they are doing, instead of being half suspicious and finding fault" (qtd. in Blanchard 230). As Josephine Donovan asserts, Jewett's literary purposes are thus closely "related to her view of literature as a form of moral teaching" designed in part "to rescue rural Mainers who are the subjects of her fiction from preconceived touristy prejudices held by the urban upper classes" ("Reply" 405).[7] Jewett aims to enable her readership of largely middle-class outsiders (from Deephaven's point of view) to feel their kinship with the lives of the natives by allowing full imaginative entry into their peculiar cultural forms, to enable cross-cultural sympathies without erasing local differences and thus to issue in concrete changes in their social interactions with each other.

Jewett's linkage of mimetic literary representation of socially alien people to the generation of sympathy among her readers and resultant changes in their ethical behavior is remarkably consonant with the social-ethical aesthetic that Howells would develop fully a decade later but that was already guiding his editorial work at the *Atlantic* during the 1870s. "Men are more like than unlike one another," Howells would write in September 1887; the writer's task, therefore, is to "make them know one another better" (96) in order that they might act differently toward each other.[8] Jewett, in full accordance with Howellsian literary imperatives, ties her literary practice, through its potential for real ethical effects on an audience conceived not as a collective abstraction but as individual readers, to a specific conception of the social uses to which literature should be harnessed. The Howellsian model of literature's ethical use-value assigns primary importance to fiction's mediation between an audience and subjects in some way alien to that audience. Fiction promotes the readerly sense of belonging to a common culture with the represented Other by incorporating the Other into the audience's enlarged sense of its own group identity. Socially alien subjects thereby come to appear to readers as recognizable, if still distant, kin. Jewett and Howells both place their faith in the notion that the literary promotion of cross-cultural sympathies will lead not only to an audience's feeling and thinking differently, but also to their acting differently. Jewett's adoption of a Realist mimetic mode of depicting people and places in all their local detail rather than by adhering to preexistent literary models is thus an instrument for moving a society of readers toward a more sympathetic understanding of the rural Other and a concomitant ethical action—behaving differently toward the provincial outlanders with whom they were more and more brought into contact by the very forces of historical change that simultaneously were exacerbating the long-standing cultural divisions between them.

In *Deephaven,* Jewett subordinates choices of form and style—in ways by now familiar to us from the *Editor's Study*—to this ethical formulation of literature's socially mediatory purposes, fostering readers' imaginative access to local lives by insisting that fiction's value as truthful social communication should be the primary determinant of aesthetic choices. Thus, for instance, Jewett's adoption of the sketch, as we have already seen, derives from its relative lack of prescribed form: its formal characteristics would arise on an ad hoc basis directly from the requirements of the social "materials" the fiction seeks to document. Likewise, Jewett's deployment of a transparently referential language subordinates literary style to clear communication of mundane experience. "Don't try to write *about* people and things," her father, Theodore Jewett, had counseled her, "tell them just as they are!" (qtd. in Cary, *Letters* 19).[9] If the informing goal of literature is to make the Other known to an actual readership, then "literary" concerns must efface themselves in the interests of unimpeded reference.

Deephaven's enactment of a socially mediatory ethical agenda also leads Jewett to her book's particular configuration of its narrators, Kate and Helen. In order to communicate provincial realities successfully to an audience of cultural outsiders, Kate and Helen must somehow simultaneously claim membership in both the narrated culture and the culture of their audience; accordingly, Jewett places the "girls" (as she consistently refers to them) in a "double insider/outsider positioning" in relation to the local culture that, as Francesco Loriggio points out, "regionalist writing unavoidably generates" (11). Jewett's narrative arrangements foreground Kate and Helen's status as dual-credentialed narrators in order to foster their mediatory role, first by choosing a first-person narrative voice and then by carefully specifying Kate and Helen's claims to dual cultural citizenship.

The narrative begins in the city, emphasizing the girls' solidarity of outlook with their educated, urban audience, thereby staking a claim to narrative reliability on the basis of social kinship with their readers. Having arrived in Deephaven, Jewett uses the girls' natural sympathies and, more prominently, Kate Lancaster's local family connections to grant the narrators plausible access to the "inside knowledge" of the life of the local culture. Anxious to capitalize on *Deephaven*'s mediatory capacities, Jewett goes out of her way to establish her narrators' double credentials.

This line of argument, it will be seen, runs counter to the tenor of much recent discussion of Jewett's regionalism, whose tendency has been to emphasize the ways in which it is complicit with the emerging postwar cultural hegemony of the urban middle classes over the increasingly marginalized rural peripheries within the new, national consumer economy. The debate centers in various ways on the tensions created by the inevitable participation of Jewett's texts in Loriggio's "double insider/outsider positioning."[10] Much of the discussion stems from the work of Richard Brodhead (142–76) and Amy Kaplan ("Nation" 250–54) and has been extended by several essays in the edited volume entitled *New Essays on The Country of the Pointed Firs*. Brodhead sees the literary regionalism of Jewett and others as an act of cultural imperialism, designed to satisfy the urban consumer classes' Veblenian urge toward "'serviceable evidence' of a socially differentiating freedom from need" (126). "This fiction," Brodhead argues, "produced the foreign only to master it in imaginary terms" (137) as a proof of urban middle-class cultural hegemony. Related lines of argument have been forwarded by Amy Kaplan ("Nation"), Elizabeth Ammons (who reads *The Country of the Pointed Firs* as a celebration of "white colonial settlement and dominance" ["Material" 97]), and Sandra Zagarell (see "Country's Portrayal of Community and the Exclusion of Difference"; see also "Troubling Regionalism," where Zagarell reads *Deephaven,* in contrast to *The Country of the Pointed Firs,* as a "self-questioning regionalism" that "places the cosmopolitan and the native in conspicuous tension" [641]).

While the arguments of these works differ significantly from each other, they share versions of a basic assertion that part of Jewett's regionalist project is to impose an urban, middle-class, nationalist, and imperialist cultural hegemony upon the rural Others that are the subjects of her literary representation—or, as Josephine Donovan summarizes their claims in order to refute them, that Jewett's "work was racist, classist, pro-imperialist—even 'proto-fascist'" ("Reply" 403). Donovan has, I think, definitively countered these lines of thinking in their major outlines ("Reply" 403–16), taking them to task for being "simplistic and distortive," founded upon "slim" and "ahistorically misinterpreted" evidence (403). These arguments also suppress regionalism's innate potential for productive resistance to social and cultural hierarchization afforded by the genre's "low" subject matter, its modest requirements for authorial competence (which Brodhead, ironically, dwells upon pejoratively at some length), and its Howellsian capacity for producing genuine and constructive understanding across cultural boundaries. As Kaplan notes (before charging regionalism with effacing the "more explosive conflicts of class, race, and gender made contiguous by urban life" by replacing them with more easily containable regional differences), "regionalist fiction expands the boundaries of the imagined community and democratizes access to literary representation" (251). Brodhead's argument also relies on the questionable assertion that Jewett, who maintained lifelong dual citizenship not only in Boston but also in her provincial hometown of South Berwick, Maine, writes unequivocally from and for the ideological perspective of a cosmopolitan elite and through an unambiguously elitist high-cultural literary medium.[11] In short, Brodhead reduces what Howells and Jewett understood as a class-mediatory, communicative literary transaction to a one-way, aristocratic imposition of cultural meaning upon the rural masses from above.

Marjorie Pryse counterargues:

Brodhead accurately depicts Jewett's narrator as belonging to a different world—a different socioeconomic class—than Mrs. Todd; what he fails to give Jewett credit for, however, is her resistance to such categories as 'urban world' and 'social class' and her fiction's struggle to remain always on the borders that create barriers within such categories. . . . Kaplan's and Brodhead's readings do not distinguish between those outsiders to rural life who come to gawk and those whose perspective alters to take in the lives of rural people. ("Sex" 48)

June Howard, too, decries the binary nature of the divide between "strongly opposed current views of Jewett as an empathetic artist of local life or as a literary tourist" (377), arguing that while there is truth in charges of regionalist cultural hierarchization in Jewett's work, "we need . . . a complementary acknowledgment that for Jewett a radically different order simultaneously occupies the same space. . . . Jewett's work for many readers sustains a sense that the center of the world is not the site of social dominance but the site of consciousness; it is potentially everywhere and anywhere" (377–78). If Jewett's regionalism inevitably participates in cultural hierarchies of class and race, revealing the traces of its inflection by the prior assumptions and values of its participant-observer, surely the project of both *Deephaven* and *The Country of the Pointed Firs* is to expand both the narrator's and her readers' understanding of the Other beyond and against such powerful determinants of perception. Critiques like Brodhead's presuppose a corrective, objective knowledge of places like Deephaven posited as readily available to the critic but always unavailable to the class-blinded author/narrator. But Jewett's writing debunks any such notion of objective, outsiders' knowledge by insisting on the necessity, in any quest for a true knowledge of the rural Other, of inside experience, of immersion in the local, of empathy with the individuals therein, and ultimately (as we shall see presently) of acceptance of the mysteries of the spiritual. Approaching Jewett through Howells's particular sense of literary use-value accentuates the mediatory and hence democratic aspects of Jewett's regionalism without, I hope, erasing the multiform tensions between dominant and subdominant cultures that inform all regionalist writing.

Representing the Unrepresentable

What first meets the eye in *Deephaven*, then—in Jewett's choices about narrative stance, subject matter, language, form, and style—is a text dedicated to sympathetic documentation of regional cultural realities, allied with a Howellsian program of ethically purposeful social mediation. Gradually, though, it becomes clear that *Deephaven* aims at significantly more than this socially mediatory agenda. The narrative begins to focus on elements of the local culture and character whose signification is not only mundane and social but simultaneously spiritual and suprasocial. As *Deephaven* turns its attention to such occult concerns as telepathy, madness, and death, the book reveals Jewett's struggle to enact, in Josephine Donovan's words, "a theory that erases the divide between spiritual and material, seeing the transcendent as incarnate in the physical" ("Swedenborg" 732). *Deephaven* increasingly works to "evoke, suggest, hint at the existence of a higher realm, a transcendent realm, by means of earthly objects, characters, and relationships" (Donovan, *New England* 100) whose full significance can be apprehended only through these mystical connections. Jewett's book begins to expand the basis of regionalist representation from the Howellsian field of social-ethical relationship to a less easily specifiable realm of spiritual signification. Only by taking account of both these dimensions of reality, Jewett maintains, can her book truly communicate the essence of Deephaven lives and thus fulfill its social-ethical undertaking.

More than any other influence, Jewett's encounters with an Americanized version of Swedenborgianism during the writing and revision of *Deephaven* served simultaneously to strengthen her solidarity with Howellsian literary goals and to push her beyond its temporal social boundaries. As Josephine Donovan has established, Jewett's involvements with the Swedenborgian spokesperson Theophilus Parsons, whom Jewett had met at Wells Beach in 1872 and with whom she corresponded over the next decade, played several important roles in the formation of her aesthetic. The Swedenborgian "doctrine of uses" reinforced Howellsian Realist ethics by enabling Jewett to see literature as an ethically useful instrument for social amelioration; at the same time, it situated the origins of ethical obligation in a realm that both transcended and informed temporal human relationships. The "doctrine of correspondences" likewise strengthened Jewett's sense that "the spiritual interpenetrates the material," but Jewett replaced Swedenborg's elaborate system of allegorical correlations with "a theory that erases the divide between spiritual and material, seeing the transcendent as incarnate in the physical" (Donovan, "Swedenborg" 732). Significantly, those passages of *Deephaven* that most conspicuously employ occult materials—the Captain Sands chapters among them—date from after Jewett's introduction to Swedenborg during her revision of the original *Atlantic* sketches into book form. Parsons's variety of Swedenborgianism, modified further by Jewett herself (and shared in part by Howells), thus gave Jewett both a further incentive to enact a Howellsian model of literary enterprise and a basis for expanding its range of representation.[12]

Helen's Howellsian narratorial comment—that the regionalist "must care to study life and character, and must find pleasure in thought and observation of simple things, and have an instinctive, delicious interest in what to other eyes is unflavored dulness" (37)—arises from a visit to the village churchyard, symbol of a realm of existence that is intimately integrated with, yet simultaneously transcendent of, the everyday life of the community. Here Helen and Kate begin to piece together the interwoven stories of Deephaven's past, soon to be further embroidered by the memories of the village's still-living residents; here they receive early intimations "that an external reality hitherto objectively perceived and transparently visible can blur and dissolve, that the firm, knowable texture of a familiar world can be shaken and lost" (Bader 176), revealing other possibilities of meaning beyond.[13] On one level, the graveyard is but another detail of authentic local culture, but it stands also as a subtle indicator that Jewett seeks the full significance of commonplace social life on a plane that transcends social signification. The graveyard is an apt metaphor both for the Howellsian regionalist's documentation of quotidian social realities and for Jewett's dawning sense that such realities are thoroughly suffused with a mysterious, spiritual immanence.

Deephaven's first extended foray into the realm of the supernatural occurs in Kate and Helen's encounters with Captain Sands, a "peculiar and somewhat visionary" (64) retired seafarer with an endless supply of true tales of mental telepathy. In accordance with her Howellsian social-ethical agenda, Jewett narrates the Captain's appearance, personal history, possessions, and conversation as further examples of authentic local culture. But the content of Captain Sands's conversation, the recurring themes of which are telepathy and death, points to a further level of significance in the Captain's experiences. The girls' interaction with Sands culminates in an experience that pointedly demonstrates Jewett's mystical interests.

The Captain and his two guests are fishing on the bay when the Captain unexpectedly turns the boat toward shore and announces the onset of a storm, no sign of which is yet visible to any of the boat's occupants. Safely landed, he explains: "Folks may say what they have a mind to; I did n't see that shower coming up, and I know as well as I want to that my wife did, and impressed it on my mind. Our house sets high, and she watches the sky and is al'ays a worrying when I go out fishing" (93). Encouraged by Kate and Helen, the Captain continues his ruminations, citing several other instances of "one person's having something to do with another any distance off" (96) and culminating with a brief disquisition on the metaphysical implications of such experiences:

> "It's the thinking that does it," says I, "and we've got some faculty or other that we don't know much about. We've got some way of sending our thought like a bullet goes out of a gun and it hits. We don't know nothing except what we see. And some folks is scared, and some more thinks it is all nonsense and laughs. But there's something we have n't got the hang of." . . . I guess we shall turn these fac'lties to account some time or 'nother. Seems to me, though, that we might depend on 'em now more than we do. (96–97)

Through Helen, Jewett acknowledges that such ideas are usually considered eccentric "by even a Deephaven audience, to whom the marvellous was of every-day occurrence" (93). But as the Captain goes on to cite his evidence, anecdote after anecdote about people's having sure knowledge of the lives of relatives and close friends separated from them by immense physical distances, it becomes increasingly difficult not to accept this evidence with as much respect and sympathy as Kate and Helen do. Jewett carefully distinguishes such occurrences from the "dream-books" and "spirit-rappings" (172) of crass, commercialized spiritualism, which Sands himself regards as superstitious foolishness, and Helen's narrative interpolations encourage us to suspend our skepticism. "It loses a great deal in being written," Helen writes (in a comment that predicts narrative difficulties that I shall discuss presently), but "it was impossible not to be sure that he knew more than people usually do about these mysteries in which he delighted" (174).

By the end of the chapter it is clear that Jewett intends the Captain Sands episode as much more than another regionally representative description of a provincial character. While it is certainly that, the content of the Captain's conversation pushes Jewett's readers to take seriously further dimensions of commonplace reality and to accept them, along with our more mundane knowledge of local realities, as a further basis for cross-cultural sympathy and understanding. The primary difference between Sands's tales and the spirit-rappings and dream-books that the text disparages is, as the Captain himself notes, that "You don't get no good by" (96) the latter, while the former signify a supernatural order wholly congruent with ordinary village life and potentially with the lives of an urban readership as well. The spiritual, Jewett maintains, permeates the normal, everyday social interactions that constitute the life of the village; any account of local realities that neglects this dimension of the communal life fails to do full justice to its subject and neglects an essential common ground with its readers. The Captain Sands chapters comprise Jewett's first extended effort to move her regionalist social-ethical project onto a new plane, one concerned not only with the social aspects of the quotidian but with their metaphysical connections as well.

Helen and Kate, as the figures of the Howellsian narrative mediator, faithfully translate the meaning of Sands's stories into terms more amenable to a cosmopolitan audience. Jewett uses their speculations to steer her readers toward a sense of spiritual interconnection that informs the web of social and ethical relationship more usual to Howellsian literary purposes and gives readers an enlarged basis for sympathetic understanding of the rural Other. Kate transposes the Captain's theory of undeveloped mental capacities into Greek mythological terms, citing the myth of Demeter and Persephone to amplify the meaning of Sands's experience:

> I was just thinking that it may be that we all have given to us more or less of another nature, as the child had whom Demeter wished to make like the gods. I believe old Captain Sands is right, and we have these instincts which defy all our wisdom and for which we never can frame any laws. We may laugh at them, but we are always meeting them, and one cannot help knowing that it has been the same through all history. They are powers which are imperfectly developed in this life, but one cannot help the thought that the mystery of this world may be the commonplace of the next. (103)[14]

Helen in her turn extends the thought beyond the human, to include a sense of the spiritual animation of all physical nature. Deephaven folks' readiness to believe in "supernatural causes," she speculates, arises not from provincial ignorance but from proximity to natural facts that are fully saturated with supernatural energies. "The more one lives out of doors," she continues,

> the more personality there seems to be in what we call inanimate things. The strength of the hills and the voice of the waves are no longer only grand poetical sentences, but an expression of something real, and more and more one finds God himself in the world, and believes that we may read the thoughts that He writes for us in the book of Nature. (104)

Such narrative asides make it very clear that Jewett intends in *Deephaven* not only a narration of provincial culture for Howellsian social-ethical ends but also a widening of readerly sympathies beyond the realm of social reality to include the perception of an all-pervasive metaphysical order, which includes the social and the material but is not limited to it. The sympathy that Jewett's Howellsian regionalism seeks to promote between wealthy city reader and poor country subject seeks its basis in an all-inclusive spiritual interconnection.

But the ends of this expanded agenda in *Deephaven* are hampered by Jewett's choice to enact her mediatory regionalist project by foregrounding the role of the narrator, a decision that has the unintended effect of distancing her readers from narrated experiences that require a more intimate mode of reader involvement to convey their full significance.[15] Writing under a Howellsian model of literary purpose that emphasized literature's role as a mediator between divided subcultures, Jewett chooses to incorporate in *Deephaven* a first-person narrator, whose overt presence *as a mediator* would presumably help forward the process to which Jewett's text is devoted. But by making literature's mediatory function so conspicuously a feature of the book's narrative configuration—in other words, by embodying it in a first-person narrator who relies on linear narration of provincial social, material, and spiritual reality—Jewett unintentionally obstructs her readers' ability to interface fully with those spiritual aspects of local reality that both inform its real life and constitute the most promising ground for encouraging readers' full sympathetic investment in that life. Put another way, when it comes to representing the essentially metaphysical aspects of

Deephaven lives, the deliberately linear "objective" narrative of local life obstructs its own primary goals.

Jewett signals her partial awareness of this problem in an incident that occurs during one of Helen and Kate's frequent visits to Mrs. Kew's lighthouse. When a boatload of city visitors arrives to tour the premises, just as Kate and Helen themselves have done earlier, they mistakenly assume that Kate is a local denizen, a family member of the lighthouse keeper. Kate plays along with the visitors' mistake, consenting to guide them on their tour. She reveals her true identity only when one of the visitors, who clearly occupies a lower social stratum than does Kate, innocently offers to provide Kate with a reference for employment in a Boston department store. The incident simultaneously establishes both the degree to which Helen and Kate fit in with the local culture and the degree to which, as figures of the regionalist narrator, they remain separate from and above it. Their role in Deephaven society grants them the appearance (at least to other outsiders) of belonging wholly to the provincial culture. But Kate's willingness, as Ann Romines puts it, to invoke "'superior' class or sophistication or erudition to stave off Deephaven, when it comes too close" (209) points to the problematic in-but-not-of status of the regionalist narrator that both enables and complicates Jewett's social-ethical task.[16] Successful mediation of regional realities depends on Kate and Helen's dual membership in two different subcultures, but the first-person narrative arrangement that arises from it reemphasizes the very divisions it is intended to bridge.[17]

Similarly, Helen's attempts to mediate between Captain Sands's reality and that of her audience result in a narrative, as Romines points out, that "vacillates between admitting the possible influence of such uncontrollable powers in [the women's] own lives, and placing them at a safe and interesting distance" (211). Since we rely for our access to Deephaven directly on Kate and Helen as first-person narrators whose cultural solidarity with their audience enables their narrative mediation, their vacillation is recapitulated in our readerly relationship to *Deephaven*'s characters and events. Experiences like those of Captain Sands, when narrated from and for the perspective of educated outsiders, can hardly avoid retaining a hint of the ludicrous no matter how strenuously the narrator may explicitly endorse their validity. The thematic content of the Captain's storytelling signals Jewett's expanded literary intentions, but because she has not yet learned sufficiently to manipulate the regionalist narrator's ambiguous status, they remain "trapped" within the objective reporting of Sands's character, circumstances, and speech; the spiritual truths into which the Captain's stories open a window are stranded in a linear narration instead of gaining an evocative, emotionally involving reality of their own. Consequently, the narrators are forced to rely on a series of narrative asides that explain the metaphysical significance of these occult materials without allowing us full access to them as lived experience. As readers, we are left, along with Kate and Helen, as sympathetic outsiders observing someone else's spiritually suggestive experiences rather than participating in them in our own right.

Ensuing chapters continue this pattern: the mediatory logic of linear narration interferes with the metaphysical half of Jewett's aesthetic agenda. The chapter entitled "Miss Chauncey" attempts to use yet another Deephaven native both to communicate the nature of the local culture and to suggest further transcendental dimensions of that reality, and the terms of that use once again point to Jewett's difficulty in harmonizing the two aspects of her project. Miss Sally Chauncey and her house, both of them relics from an age of seafaring mercantile prosperity, comprise a treasure trove of provincial history that the girls are eager to exploit. So eager are they, in fact, that they take advantage of Miss Chauncey's deafness to steal a self-guided tour of her mansion—this after having been thwarted in an earlier attempt to break into the house, thinking it uninhabited. Jewett emphasizes the voyeuristic, culturally appropriative aspects of the regionalist project by establishing the girls' initial involvement with Miss Chauncey on the basis of their insatiable appetite for authentic, "collectible" specimens of the local culture.[18]

Gradually, as the girls establish a personal relationship with their hostess, this narrative voyeurism gives way to a more sympathetic identification with the old woman's experience as opposed to her material possessions, which enables Jewett to deploy Miss Chauncey's precarious mental state as a thematic doorway—analogous to Captain Sands's almost obsessive interest in telepathy—into the realm of metaphysical transcendence that comprises Jewett's expansion of the Howellsian project. Miss Chauncey's madness, on one level, is of a piece with her value as a regionalist resource: it results from the emotional impact of the violent deaths and partial insanities of her father and her brothers, victims of the precipitous nineteenth-century decline of Maine's coastal economy. But the nature of her madness suggests the existence of a realm of transcendental significance beyond her value as a record of local history. Miss Chauncey's present, quite literally, is her past. She sees around her the undimmed splendor of the familial estate of genteel and prosperous seafarers, despite the fact that the house is actually in a state of advanced dilapidation. In her visitors she sees contemporaries of her own bygone youth; she asks Kate and Helen for news of long-dead Boston acquaintances as though they still enjoyed a healthy middle age. The very idea of death is alien to her: "Ah, they say every one is 'dead,' nowadays. I do not comprehend the silly idea!" (129). In her insanity, Miss Chauncey lives in an eternal, historically transcendent present that utterly obliterates the everyday boundaries of time and space.

As it was in Kate and Helen's narration of Captain Sands's tales, Miss Chauncey's thematic significance as a symbol of transcendent spiritual realities is at odds with her status as a regionalist exhibit. Miss Chauncey functions both as a sign of eternal realities and as a picturesque local eccentric. The narrators' moments of intimacy with her seek to draw us into participation with her expanded sense of reality, but the mediatory logic of the narration will not let us forget either the limited nature of their relationship to Miss Chauncey or the plain fact that the woman is mentally incompetent. Once again, by the chapter's end the narrator is reduced to making abstract pronouncements about the spiritual significance of her subject, in lieu of full readerly participation in that experience.

Jewett's struggle to fuse her complementary aesthetic goals is even more evident in the chapter entitled "In Shadow." Kate and Helen's narration of their acquaintance with a severely impoverished farm family makes a pitch for our sympathetic identification with these living examples of rural privation; the girls' excursion to the rock-bound, exhausted soils of a failing coastal farm offers an opportunity to describe yet another phase of local life and culture. The sudden deaths of the farmer and his wife, killed by years of fruitless struggle with the rocky soil, provide the perfect occasion for a union of socially mediatory description with a more evocative, metaphysically symbolic narrative mode. Death—at once absolutely mundane yet undeniably mysterious—becomes the nexus for Jewett's attempted fusion of aesthetic goals. On the one hand, the farmstead funeral is an opportunity for sympathetic observation of a central rite of local culture; on the other hand, the proximity of death brings near a realm of occult signification that pervades and transcends commonplace social realities.

At their best, Helen's funeral observations effectively couple social and natural description, in a prose highly evocative of the enigmatic presence of death:

> The minister and some others fell into line, and the procession went slowly down the slope; a strange shadow had fallen over everything. It was like a November day, for the air felt cold and bleak. There were some great sea-fowl high in the air, fighting their way toward the sea against the wind, and giving now and then a wild, far-off ringing cry. We could hear the dull sound of the sea, and at a little distance from the land the waves were leaping high, and breaking in white foam over the isolated ledges. (122–23)

Descriptive detail here is so thoroughly invested with the emotional and spiritual significance of the event that we cannot help experiencing natural facts as metaphysically charged entities; Jewett blends natural and human to evoke our emotional participation with the mourners in response to the presence of death. But the mood is shattered when Helen abruptly reverts to a more linear narration, reminding us that she is observing the scene from the perspective of an outsider and reporting it for other outsiders: "We had never seen what the people called 'walking funerals' until we came to Deephaven," she interrupts herself. Representative details of Deephaven's "rigid funeral etiquette" (122) follow, narrated as a parcel of interesting items in a touristic travelogue, interfering with the attempt to evoke the mystical dimensions of the experience of death.

No matter how fully the narrator may wish to participate in all dimensions—metaphysical included—of the local reality transpiring before her, no matter how clearly Jewett's social-ethical aesthetic aims to incorporate the spiritual as part and parcel of the social and as the surest road to a full and sympathetic knowledge of the Other, the text's self-conscious foregrounding of the act of narratorial mediation thwarts those intentions. Kate can assert the "sudden consciousness of the mystery and inevitableness of death" (123) among the funeral participants, she can speculate on the power of the occasion to make her feel "how close to this familiar, every-day world might be the other" (123), but her own presence as the figure of Howellsian narrative mediation effectively precludes—except in fits and starts—our feeling as though we are immersed, to the extent Jewett so clearly wishes us to be, in the fullness of local lives. Helen's careful descriptions of the funeral rites have the unintended effect of distancing the reader from the narrated experience, leaving us with Kate and Helen on a hillside neighboring the farmstead, uninvited guests, observing the rites from a respectful distance.

Social Supernaturalism in *The Country of the Pointed Firs*

Deephaven reveals an author struggling to find the narrative means to enact an expanded set of aesthetic ends necessitated by an alternative vision of the reality that literature must seek to represent in its pursuit of Howellsian social-ethical ends. The central inclusion of occult materials and themes expresses Jewett's extension of purposes in writing about Maine coast people and places beyond Howellsian mediation of a fundamentally social and ethical reality to evocation of a metaphysical realm both transcendent and inclusive of commonplace social reality. Jewett's mysticized sense of human commonality necessitates an expanded aesthetic agenda for her work, which in turn calls for a new narrative mode of engaging readers in represented reality: one that will replace the distancing effect of linear, socially mediatory documentation undertaken on the Howellsian plan with a more evocative, symbolic, reader-participatory reading experience. As Josephine Donovan puts it, since every "'thing' is animated with a spiritual presence," language must move beyond the mimetic and mediatory to "directly express this unmediated spiritual reality" ("Swedenborg" 744). Howellsian mediatory narration must give way to a narrative mode that enables more direct reader participation in orders of reality that by their very nature defy linguistic specification. *Deephaven* moves experimentally toward this mode, but Jewett would fully discover the aesthetic means to unify her social-ethical purposes with a spiritualized understanding of local realities two decades later in *The Country of the Pointed Firs*. The result is a book that, while roughly homologous in form and intent to *Deephaven*, manages to fuse a powerful evocation of the spiritual with a definitively descriptive regionalism, transforming the earlier book's disruptive tensions into a new narrative unity and fulfilling Howellsian social-ethical purposes via an expanded aesthetic. The discussion that follows concentrates on the author's handling of the two areas of narrative art that had posed the most serious challenges to the union of her adopted Howellsian goals with a more mystical, reader-participatory mode of writing in *Deephaven:* the positioning of the narrator and the narration of the spiritual.

A pair of literary advices that Jewett received during the writing of *Deephaven* pointed the way toward realization of the new narrative mode that *Deephaven* itself would achieve only sporadically. In an 1871 diary entry, Jewett again quotes her father: "A story should be managed so that it should *suggest* interesting things to the *reader* instead of the author's doing all the thinking for him, and setting it before him in black and white" (qtd. in Donovan, *New England* 100). The tendency of the advice was reinforced by an excerpt from Flaubert, which Jewett pinned above her writing desk in South Berwick: "Ce n'est pas de faire rire, ni de faire pleurer, ni de vous mettre à fureur, mais d'agir à la façon de la nature, c'est à dire de faire rêver. (It is not to provoke laughter, nor tears, nor rage, but to act as nature does, that is, to provoke dreaming.)" (qtd. in Blanchard 84). In both cases, the author moves her attention away from the content of literary representation, away from close observation and specification of material and social realities, and toward the quality of readers' imaginative experience of those realities as embodied in their literary representation. Where Howells in the *Editor's Study* would aim at readerly immersion in the experience of the text through mimetically faithful representation of commonplace social life, Jewett's emerging aesthetic relies more heavily on a process of co-creative readerly concretion of literary experience. This "imaginative realism" (as Donovan, borrowing from Jewett's letter to a young artist, has named it,)[19] aspires to employ the literary documentation of the quotidian not only to further Howellsian social-ethical mediation but also to evoke full readerly emotional involvement in the spiritual underpinnings of commonplace experience. Writers' lack of understanding of "those unwritable things" and the necessity of making them palpable to readers, Jewett asserts in her letter to Sarah Whitman, cause them to "confuse our scaffoldings with our buildings" (qtd. in Jewett, *Letters* 112) and thus lose "the true soul" (112) of the story.

Like *Deephaven, The Country of the Pointed Firs* prominently includes a regionalist participant-observer who, in order to fulfill the socially mediatory purposes inherent in the Howellsian facets of Jewett's aims, must belong simultaneously both to the subculture of her readers and to that of her represented subjects. But Jewett's handling of the narrator in the latter work indicates from its first sentence how markedly her approach to regionalist mediation has become subordinated to her quest for readerly evocation of her story's "true soul." Where the earlier work employs its opening chapter to introduce readers to the narrators preliminary to their (and our) Deephaven visit, explicitly documenting Kate and Helen's personal and cultural backgrounds, their relationship to each other, and the circumstances that lead to their vacation, the first chapter of *Country* places us with the unnamed narrator directly in medias res, involving us immediately in an already-proceeding relationship with the ongoing life of Dunnet Landing. The chapter title itself, "The Return," indicates that the description of place that follows is something already known, already experienced. Significantly, the text does not unequivocally specify to whose "return" the title refers; the narrator, as Sarah Way Sherman points out, "appears only as the implied member of a generalization" (203), her presence blurred and effaced in order to promote a more direct readerly experience of that which is narrated. The weak construction of the opening sentence—"There was something about the coast town of Dunnet which made it seem more attractive than other maritime villages of eastern Maine" (377)—amplified by subsequent, similar third-person constructions, encourages us to see Dunnet Landing from some unspecified, vaguely collective perspective while calling our attention away from the existence of the unspecified yet undeniably present narrator whose perspective it is. The narrator's prior acquaintance with the town becomes, more indefinitely, "the simple fact of acquaintance," again unattributed to any definite center of perception, and she repeatedly presents the details of the town as "seeming" to be this or that directly *to us* as much as to herself. As the implied and effaced narrator approaches the village from seaward, the "houses made the most of their seaward view," their windows "like knowing eyes that watched the harbor and the far sea-line beyond," in effect reversing the regionalist's quasi-touristic gaze as the village itself looks at its readers, apparently free of any narrator's mediation. Not until the second paragraph does the narrative, still in the third person, refer to its narrator and then no more definitely than as "a lover of Dunnet Landing," "a single passenger" (377) returning to a place already known. The net effect of the first chapter is to establish a narrative pattern that suffuses each of the parties to the text's communicative transaction—reader, narrator, and local subjects—with the others to create the sense of a shared participation in a shared reality, an interpersonalization of the objective, material world.

Not until halfway through the second chapter does the narrative voice emerge into an identifiable, first-person subject, the still-nameless "I" who boards at Almira Todd's, writes in the empty schoolhouse, and shares the lives of Dunnet Landing's citizens, and throughout the book she remains, as Melissa Homestead points out, both a seductive and "an elusive figure" (76). Homestead argues persuasively that Jewett's handling of the narrator represents a strategic manipulation of shifting audience conceptions of the relations between authors and readers, from earlier imaginations of "novel reading as an immediate, personal communication with the author" (77) toward a (putatively) Realist "withdrawal" of the figure of the author from the text (82). Exploiting the ambiguous distinction between fiction and nonfiction in her chosen form, Homestead continues, Jewett used both models of authorship simultaneously, to gain for her text both the representational authority over social reality granted by the Realist model and the intimate, interpersonal, domestic relationality between author and reader afforded by the older model. The narrator's self-revelation occurs unobtrusively, buried in the middle of a paragraph devoted to Mrs. Todd's herb-gathering, and it encourages us to see ourselves as participating familiarly with her in the experiences she narrates. Thereafter, the text's disclosure of the narrator as character remains minimal and indirect, emphasizing her relatedness to Dunnet Landing's communal life rather than her function as a mediator of that life for an audience of outsiders and relying on the implied reader-author relationship to guarantee her representation of local experience. We never learn, for instance, where she is from, only that Dunnet Landing is not her home; she never tells us about her occupation but leaves us to surmise from her rental and use of the schoolhouse that she is a professional author; and despite the intimate relationship she establishes with Almira Todd, we never hear the older woman speak her visitor's name. The first-person narrator is the means of our achieving intimacy with the inner life of the village, not (as in *Deephaven*) on the model of a socially reportorial mediator, who flits from one locally representative scene to another in search of authentic episodes to document, but as an experiential medium for our passage into a more direct experience of that life.[20]

The narrative mode of *The Country of the Pointed Firs* thus subsumes a Howellsian conception of social-ethical mediation within a spherical narrative model that produces the effect of a merging of the reader with both the narrator and the narrated. Jewett uses the collective subjectivity provided by her effaced first-person narrator as a portal for readers into a local world that we experience "always in the context of [the narrator's]"—and our own—"coming to know it" (Sherman 225). The insider/outsider tension inherent in regionalist narration cannot and does not entirely disappear; for Jewett's national, middle-class readership, there still exists an "alien" subculture into which the dual-cultured narrator provides entry. But Jewett's new narrative mode achieves its social documentary purposes by allowing us to experience alien cultural objects, practices, and people as a multidimensional, intersubjective experience, knowable only through our immersion in processes that precede and extend beyond the boundaries of the narrated reality. Jewett's transmutation of the narrator's linear mediatory function into a more participatory, relationally evocative reading experience allows via alternative means the kind of sympathetic access to the lived textures of local life at which Howells's social-ethical aesthetic aimed. *The Country of the Pointed Firs* achieves all that Jewett had hoped for in her adoption of Howellsian literary mediation by abandoning mediation in favor of a spherical, reader-participatory narrative mode.[21]

Jewett includes in *The Country of the Pointed Firs* a pair of episodes that seem designed to mark her awareness of the narratorial sea change that has occurred between her two Maine-coast books. In the chapters entitled "Captain Littlepage" and "The Waiting Place," Jewett introduces us to the Dunnet Landing analogue of *Deephaven's* Miss Chauncey, the village eccentric whose lunacy marks Jewett's early attempt to harness the power of the spiritual to her socially and ethically mediatory narration of local realities. The narrator's encounters with Littlepage recall *Deephaven's* unsuccessful attempts to capture the transcendent by means of linear narration. The Captain's bizarre tales of an otherworldly ghost town hidden in the almost inaccessible reaches of the Arctic Ocean represent precisely the sort of interface between the material and the mystical worlds that the earlier book figures in Miss Chauncey's time-transcendent madness and Captain Sands's telepathic stories. Josephine Donovan identifies the Littlepage episode as the first in a series of "referents" to the occult realm that became familiar to Jewett through Theophilus Parsons ("Swedenborg" 745), and it is via American Swedenborgianism's union of mystical symbolism with ethical purpose that the Littlepage chapters become germane to Jewett's expanded sense of Howellsian aesthetics. In short, Jewett uses the episode simultaneously to mark (once again) the supernatural as part of the reality she wishes to narrate and to signal her new awareness of the kind of narration that is called for in order to represent that expanded reality successfully. The Littlepage chapters, in other words, serve as a sort of metacommentary on the narrative mode that the narrator and Jewett herself must adopt in order to convey the mystically invested nature of the reality they wish their text to represent.

Jewett flags Littlepage's tale, as Elizabeth Ammons notes, "as an exemplum of the kind of story . . . that the narrator, like the narrative, must leave behind" (*Conflicting* 48).[22] Significantly, the episode occurs immediately after the narrator, having prematurely excused herself from a village funeral procession in order to get some writing done, realizes—in sharp contrast to Kate and Helen's aloof spectatorship in *Deephaven*'s funeral scene—that by exercising her professional duties she has unintentionally marked herself as an outsider and distanced herself from the life of the community. The episode constitutes a symbolic recognition that regionalist narration on a conventional, linearly mediatory plan—that which predominates in *Deephaven*—is aesthetically counterproductive because of the distancing effect it inadvertently produces. Jewett amplifies this recognition by parodically framing Littlepage's account of the "waiting place," which he undertakes on that same distancing, reportorial narrative plan, within not one but three distinct narrative filters: our reception of the tale depends not only on the narrator's reporting of Captain Littlepage's words but also on the Captain's account of the words of Gaffett, the shipwrecked sailor who experienced it firsthand. By the time this narrative token of spiritual transcendence reaches its readers, it has been too thoroughly disconnected from the shared world of narrator and readers by its attenuated

linear transmission—a tale within a tale within a tale—to have any appre-
ciable emotional impact. The narrator, like Helen Denis before her, is reduced to informing us in an aside that "all this moving tale had such an
air of truth that I could not argue with Captain Littlepage" (399). Neither
linear narration, Jewett suggests, nor tales of the occult—however significant of Swedenborgian truths—can produce the kind of immediate readerly experience of a simultaneously social, material, and metaphysical reality upon which real readerly involvement with the lives of folk like
Littlepage depends.

The chapters that immediately follow the Littlepage episode signal
Jewett's relocation of her mystical aims from the plane of the occult back
into the world of commonplace social interactions, where the intangible
elements of communal interrelationship and emotion express spiritual
truths. The chapter titles of "The Outer Island" and "Green Island" iden-
tify a single place by two names, replacing an abstract spatial designation
with a word suggestive of a range of interrelated values, from peace and
quiet to natural profusion to human culture. The shift in titles mirrors a
shift in the narrator's and our relationship to the content of the narration.
The transition begins in "The Outer Island," a short chapter divided evenly
between the end of the narrator's encounter with Captain Littlepage and
the beginning of her intimacy with the inhabitants of the outermost island
in the bay: Almira Todd's mother, Mrs. Blackett, and her brother, William.
Jewett links by juxtaposition the Captain's thrice-removed account of another world with the narrator's more earthly vision of a similarly spiritually
invested reality. The narrator and Mrs. Todd are standing on the shore
amid a gray and cloudy dusk when, looking across the bay, they watch as
"a gleam of golden sunshine struck the outer islands, and one of them
shone out clear in the light, and revealed itself in a compelling way to our
eyes" (400). The narrator is quick to note the spiritual significance of the
sight, which is "like a sudden revelation of the world beyond this" (400).
Her intuition is symbolically akin to Littlepage's "waiting place"; both are
locales that somehow participate in two orders of reality at the same time,
and both are named according to a literalistic, spatial conception of the
relation between the worldly and the spiritual, analogous to conceptions of
heaven and hell that locate them as physically upward and downward. But
unlike the alienating effect of the Captain's story, the narrator's vision of

the outer island brings the realm of spiritual signification one step closer to ordinary experience by moving it from a supernatural plane onto a natural and symbolic one. Taken as natural facts, the outer isles are "outer" only because they are the most remote from shore, and the narrator's "revelation of the world beyond" is merely a shaft of sunlight penetrating the clouds. But these natural facts have their existence only in the shared subjectivity of the narrator, Mrs. Todd, and us, and they gain thence symbolic implications that integrate the spiritual with the mundane. The outer island exists both as a geographical place, an unremarkable feature of the landscape surrounded by the sea, and as a shared experience of something that is at once a natural, a social, and a spiritual geography. The island's narration naturalizes and subjectivizes what Littlepage's yarn can only report as a set of remarkable facts. The island is illumined not only by a stray sunbeam but by the narrator's and our own subjective willingness to experience natural reality as spiritually invested occurrence.

Jewett interweaves the narrator's intuition of transcendent meaning even more tightly with the mundane and allies it with the narrative aim of generating sympathetic knowledge of local realities through Almira Todd. As the two women witness the illumination of the outer island, they both feel a certain awe at the grandeur of the sight, but Mrs. Todd watches with an added expression of "affection and interest" (400). The reason, as she informs her companion immediately after their shared island vision, is that the Outer Island was her girlhood home and continues to be her mother's home. With the addition of this communal and familial relationship to the cumulative symbolic associations of the island vision, Jewett brings the mystical realm even more squarely into the realm of the social. When the narrator and Mrs. Todd journey to Mrs. Blackett's home in the next chapter, their visit transforms "The Outer Island" into "Green Island," investing the natural supernaturalism of the former chapter with a social supernaturalism, as well. The journey begins with the propitious conjunction of an intuition and a natural fact: Almira Todd "waked up early thinkin'" of her mother, and the season, wind, and tide all favor a sailing trip to the island and home again. Through sheer immersion in emotionally charged homey detail, Jewett involves her readers in the shared experience of the journey. Where *Deephaven* shuttled its narrators abruptly from one locally representative scene to the next, "Green Island" allows its narrator and its readers to share in the particulars and the texture of the voyage itself. While the narrator does ask typical touristic questions about the names of the islands and the meaning of the island's herring flag, these signs of her mediatorship are submerged within our collective participation in the process of the experience. When they reach the island, Jewett deftly establishes the spiritual interconnections that are subjectively accessible through the quotidian and uses her narrator to pull her readers directly into the experience. Having arrived at the landing, the narrator writes, "I looked, and could see a tiny flutter in the doorway, but a quicker signal had made its way from the heart on shore to the heart on the sea" (405). The interchange represents a domesticized equivalent of Captain Sands's telepathic communication with his wife but is allowed here to remain a matter of mysterious emotional affinity rather than become the subject for a disquisition on the occult. "How do you suppose she knows it's me?" (405) asks a smiling Mrs. Todd. Her rhetorical question confirms the narrator's intuition and, with it, their sympathetic intimacy with each other and with us. The remainder of the chapter, and the three ensuing Green Island chapters that follow it, chart the steady progress of the narrator's closeness with Almira and William Todd and their mother. The narrator, and we with her, participate firsthand in the household routines—from dinner preparation, to herb-gathering, to singing—all fully invested with intangible yet emotionally perceptible interpersonal significance. Just before the visitors return to Dunnet Landing, Mrs. Blackett invites the narrator to sit in the old woman's rocking chair—"the real home, the heart of the old house on Green Island!" (420). The visit culminates in an emblematic moment of narratorial union with the subjects of her narration. "I looked up," she writes, "and we understood each other without speaking" (420). Near the end of the Green Island sequence of chapters, Mrs. Blackett's final words point once again to the webs of relation that bind people to each other through the medium of local experience but also, through sympathy and memory, beyond the limits of time and place: " 'I shall like to think o' your settin' here to-day,' said Mrs. Blackett. 'I want you to come again' " (420).

This reading does not, it will have been noted, significantly alter feminist critics' appraisals of how Jewett's narrative produces for many readers such a powerful sense of participation in the Dunnet Landing community in all its aspects—natural, material, human, and spiritual. But implicit in this argument has been the assertion that Jewett's creation of a community that seems to reach beyond the boundaries of the text to include its readers is much less exclusively feminine than the largely feminist critical recovery of Jewett in the eighties and nineties would have it, and that it is possible and profitable to understand her literary creation of community in terms of an aesthetic that she shared with Howells and that she developed to include an expanded and spiritualized sense of what the real nature of local realities was—both those that her regionalist writing sought to communicate and those inhabited by regionalism's far-flung readers. The Green Island chapters, as Elizabeth Ammons (in *Conflicting Stories*) and others have noted, form a core of *The Country of the Pointed Firs* in part because they mark the narrator's fullest achievement of participation in the lives of her hosts, but also because they mark a high point in Jewett's narrative ability to evoke all the dimensions of local reality—natural, material, familial, spiritual—at once, to suffuse each with the qualities of the others, and to induce in receptive readers precisely the sense of sympathetic knowledge of provincial Others necessary to enact the purposes of a Howellsian social-ethical aesthetic. Ammons has more recently called into question her identification of these central chapters as "the most intense part of the book, its dramatic climax" ("Material" 96). She now finds in the book, especially in the succeeding chapters devoted to the Bowden family reunion, "subtle but clear protofascist implications" (96–97), asserting "that the communion at the end of *The Country of the Pointed Firs* is about colonialism" (97). But the reunion chapters, rather than endorsing fascistic social values, maintain the empathetic aura of the Green Island chapters while tempering it with the social frictions of everyday local life. Jewett thus reintroduces the relatively limited, familial, sequestered Green Island figurations of communal interrelationship onto a more broadly social plane. Despite the fact that "constant interest and intercourse . . . had linked the far island and these scattered farms into a golden chain of love and dependence" (452), the world of this expanded community is characterized also by the same disagreements, dislikes, misunderstandings, and conflicts that exist in any culture. Thus Mrs. Caplin speaks "scornfully" of Sant Bowden's "stim'late"-induced uselessness (463); Alma Todd denounces Mari' Harris as a "sordid creatur" (464), "dreads seeing some o' the folks that I don't like" (464), and questions the family credentials of one reunion reveler; "old feuds" have been "overlooked" (469) but only temporarily, and the less than uniformly rosy texture of everyday social interactions will resume the next day. The reunion serves as an oblique reminder to the narrator and to her readers of the necessity for Howellsian literary mediation, for the literary analogue of the community-building through storytelling, memory, and recognition of mutual interdependence and spiritual kinship that Dunnet Landing's inhabitants enact as the dialectical antidote to the community's entropic tendencies.

Jewett's narratorial adjustments between *Deephaven* and *The Country of the Pointed Firs* achieve everything that her reconception of a Howellsian sense of these literary social-ethical purposes requires: the book makes Dunnet Landing, its people, and their local folkways vividly, sympathetically known to its readers. Jewett collapses the distances that separated readers from narrator and narrated subjects in *Deephaven,* subsuming that book's predominantly linear, mediatory narration within a more spherical narrative mode. The new narrative not only reinforces Howellsian literary ends but allows Jewett's fiction to incorporate more effectively the metaphysical dimensions of reality that she sees as incarnate in the material and social worlds, and therefore absolutely necessary to our understanding of regional realities. Jewett transforms our readerly interaction with Dunnet Landing from sympathetic curiosity to something much more akin, as Marcia McClintock Folsom has written, to the empathy that characterizes the narrator's relationships—both lived and written—with her narrated subjects.

4

Charles W. Chesnutt and the Limits of Literary Mediation

As thoroughly as that of any other figure in American literature, Charles W. Chesnutt's writing career proceeded from a prior commitment to a particular set of social and political goals. Chesnutt's fiction, from his first conjure tale in 1887 to his last published novel in 1905, and including his three recent, posthumously published novels, persistently sought to alter prevailing white racist conceptions of contemporary African-American life, deploying fiction as a tool against the intensifying post-Reconstruction trend toward civil re-enslavement of black freedmen and women. During Chesnutt's first forays into the literary world, this strong sense of vocation received powerful confirmation from the deeply congruent conception of literary purposes contemporaneously developed in W. D. Howells's social-ethical aesthetic in the *Editor's Study*. As the productions of a writer who embarked on a literary career for the express purpose of using his fiction as a tool for the social-ethical transformation of his audience, Chesnutt's works seem to embody perfectly a number of the pragmatic aesthetic principles at the core of Howells's thought. Like Sarah Orne Jewett's, however, Chesnutt's adoption of a Howellsian prescription for the new American literature's purposeful engagement with its society entailed significant adaptation as well. Despite Chesnutt's adherence throughout his writing career to a Howellsian principle of literature's social-ethical use as an instrument of reform, his writing also comprises an ongoing critique of that same notion. The course of Chesnutt's career demonstrates the depth of his commitment to his writing as an instrument of Progressive racial reform; however, as others have noted, his movement toward polemic and, ultimately, away from a primary commitment to fiction as the path to reform testifies to Chesnutt's deepening doubts about the efficacy of literature to create the social and ethical transformations at which he aimed.[1] Chesnutt's enactment, revision, and critique of Howellsian aesthetic principles in his literary representations of African-American life and culture constitute a complex questioning of the efficacy of a Howellsian literary mediation of that most divisive and intransigent cultural division in American life: race.

This chapter investigates works that constitute the beginning and end of Chesnutt's career as a published fiction writer: the conjure tales of the 1880s and 1890s, collected as *The Conjure Woman* in 1899, and the last of Chesnutt's published novels, *The Colonel's Dream* (1905). Both works adopt the Howellsian agenda, seeking to promote social and political reform by communicating Southern black cultural realities to a predominantly white audience. But they do so, paradoxically, while interrogating the ability of literature to communicate effectively across the deeper cultural divisions at all, much less achieve the comprehensive social-ethical transformation of its audience. *The Conjure Woman* appropriates the white Southern regionalist conventions of plantation-dialect fiction for racially progressive purposes, reforming generic conventions to serve a Howellsian purpose of cross-cultural mediation across the racial divide. Chesnutt deploys the characters in the frames of the conjure tales, however, to explore the limitations of cross-racial literary mediation on the Howells plan imposed by readers steeped in overdetermined generic conventions and racial stereotypes. *The Colonel's Dream* adopts a more conventionally Realist literary form to further its parallel social-ethical goals but ends by dramatically enacting Chesnutt's mounting pessimism about the possibility of achieving meaningful Southern reform by any means—literary or otherwise—during the long post-Reconstruction period of hardening racist attitudes, politics, and laws. The novel's forceful statement of its case against the white South demonstrates Chesnutt's continued commitment to the socially ameliorative project of using literature to communicate the truth across the racial and regional divide, but the novel's focus on the failure of its reformer-hero focuses attention on the nearly impossibly rigorous psychoemotional demands placed on those individuals who would dedicate themselves to the reform effort. Chesnutt's last published novel thus continues *The Conjure Woman*'s critique of the Howellsian aesthetic by interrogating the problematic relationship between the individual reformer—literary or otherwise—and the apparently intransigent facts of contemporary Southern social reality.

"High, Holy Purpose": Chesnutt's Aesthetic of Social Reform

Rarely has a literary figure specified so minutely, before the fact, his purposes in undertaking a literary career as did Charles W. Chesnutt. In 1880, resolving in his journal to "write a book" (139) for the first time in his life, Chesnutt describes the "high, holy purpose" to which he would devote his fiction:

> The object of my writings would be not so much the elevation of the colored people as the elevation of the whites,—for I consider the unjust spirit of caste which is so insidious as to pervade a whole nation, and so powerful as to subject a whole race and all connected with it to scorn and social ostracism—I consider this a barrier to the moral progress of the American people: and I would be one of the first to head a determined, organized crusade against it. (139–40)

Chesnutt fuses his aesthetic ambitions with a moral and democratic vision of literary purposes in ways that are remarkably consonant with the social-ethical aesthetic that Howells would develop in the *Editor's Study*. He conceives of the literary enterprise as an essentially moral and communicative project whose goal is to transform the attitudes and ideas of an audience—conceived as individual members of the body politic—in order to persuade them to alter their personal, social, and political behavior toward their fellow (African-American) citizens.

In ways that would determine the course of his subsequent literary career, Chesnutt here defines literature in terms that exceed entertainment, commodity, or high-cultural art, aiming instead at transforming the deep-seated prejudices that block a white readership's recognition of human and democratic commonalty with their African-American neighbors. Literature's function in making them know one another better will serve the purposes not only of African-American empowerment but also of the "moral progress" of the entire citizenry, reconstituted on a more humane and inclusive basis. Chesnutt's initiating vision of a socially and ethically purposive literature, without specifying any particular aesthetic mode for its fulfillment, espouses a remarkably Howellsian sense of literature's social-ethical purposes. Having outlined his objectives, Chesnutt goes on in the same journal entry to describe the literary mode best suited to achieving these goals. Again, his thinking coincides significantly with a Howellsian vision: "The negro's part is to prepare himself for social recognition and equality; and it is the province of literature to open the way for him to get it—to accustom the public mind to the idea; and while amusing them to lead them on imperceptibly, unconsciously step by step to the desired state of feeling" (140). The business of promoting social reform for blacks through literature involves effecting a "moral revolution" (140) in the hearts of white Americans by enlarging the boundaries of their sympathies through truthful literary documentation of African-American life and experience on its own terms. But where race is concerned, Chesnutt asserts, a fiction dedicated to these ends must work by stealth, translating African-American realities into white literary forms so subtly that an audience will not fully realize that its sense of group identity is being expanded to include the black Other. Thus Chesnutt's initial decision to become a writer of fiction is predicated upon a remarkably Howellsian conception not only of literature's social-ethical use-value but also of the narrative and representational strategies necessary to accomplish his declared goals. Chesnutt's nascent aesthetic derives from a prior set of social goals, accomplishment of which constitutes literature's raison d'être; in defining his art, Chesnutt conceived of literature as a fully engaged participant in the public life of contemporary society, as a vehicle "driven by the engine of social reform" (Lauter 63) and aimed at "making readers like, or, more to the point, find interest in matters and people quite outside their experience" (Lauter 69) rather than as a private, high-cultural aesthetic entertainment.[2] On virtually all points, Chesnutt's self-prescription for the fiction he would write during the next decades fits the Howellsian bill for the new American literature while seeking to accommodate a social-ethical aesthetic to the unique exigencies of the nation's "race problem."

For an aspiring writer in the decades immediately following the Civil War, there was ample precedent for such a project, not only in the ever more ubiquitous apologetics and editorial influences of Howells but also in overtly activist works by writers whose direct influence upon Chesnutt is documented elsewhere in his journal. Most importantly, Chesnutt read and admired both *Uncle Tom's Cabin* and Albion W. Tourgée's pro-Reconstruction best-seller, *A Fool's Errand*. Both novels had successfully targeted a vast and influential white readership with overtly polemical fictive treatments of the race problem, inspiring Chesnutt with parallel hopes of reaching a politically powerful Northern white audience with fictions designed to salvage white sympathies for African Americans from the accelerating deterioration of post-Reconstruction race relations. In modeling his projected activist fiction upon these antecedents, Chesnutt was assuming not only a particular sense of literary use-value but also a concomitant conception of mimetic literary representation as the most efficacious way of fulfilling that use-value. He understood the success of both writers' books in terms of their close observation and description of Southern social life and character, based on firsthand regional experience and designed to make "alien" lifeways comprehensible to an outside audience. In her "Concluding Remarks" and in the accompanying *Key* to *Uncle Tom's Cabin,* Stowe had insisted upon the veracity of her accounts of social arrangements in the slaveholding South as a crucial element in her book's moral and political argument; for contemporary readers, the book's impact derived at least as much from its powerfully documentary qualities as from its sentimental appeal. Similarly, Chesnutt attributes Tourgée's "interesting descriptions" and "vivid pictures of Southern life and character" to his "faculty of observation" of the "men and things" of the South, exercised during the author's decade-long sojourn in postwar North Carolina (*Journals* 125). "Judge Tourgee's book is about the south," Chesnutt wrote in his journal, "—the manners, customs, modes of thought, etc., which are prevalent in this section of the country" (124). Just as Stowe and Tourgée had done, Chesnutt would represent in writing his own knowledge of the post-Reconstruction South, derived from firsthand regional experience, careful observation, and historical research, to make white audiences better acquainted with black social and cultural realities and thus to build the case for reform. In his journal, Chesnutt counts among his chief advantages "a fund of experience, a supply of material" born of "fifteen years of life in the South, in one of the most eventful eras of its history" (139). So equipped, he asks, "Why could not . . . a [colored] man, if he possessed the same ability, write a far better book about the South than Judge Tourgée or Mrs. Stowe has written?" (125).[3]

Chesnutt astutely noted that the object of his efforts required different literary tactics for handling the representation of Southern realities from those employed by Stowe and other Northern abolitionist writers. They had "stirred up public opinion in behalf of the slave, by appealing in trumpet tones to those principles of justice and humanity which were only lying dormant in the northern heart" (140). Abolitionist writing had mounted a direct attack upon the institution of slavery, and abolition itself had been accomplished, finally, by radical political action expressed as military force directed against a readily identifiable economic, political, and social institution. The post-War racial situation, on the other hand, was "something that force can but slightly affect" (140); "the subtle almost indefinable feeling of repulsion toward the negro, which is common to most Americans . . . cannot be stormed and taken by assault" (140) but must be ameliorated gradually by winning white readers unobtrusively toward sympathetic understanding of black citizens as worthy of full civil, social, and political equality. Chesnutt aimed at altering deeply rooted cultural assumptions impervious to purely legislative or political remedies and held by Northern as well as Southern whites. He looked to literature, in its capacity to engage a mass audience at the level of their emotional investments in cultural norms, as the most suitable medium for softening white racist defenses against acceptance of African Americans. Chesnutt's sense of literary vocation thus prescribed the Howellsian literary mode in which he would work: his fiction would enable white audiences to experience the lives of culturally alien black Others, subtly mediating across deeply inscribed racial boundaries on the assumption that sympathetic literary representation would lead to constructive social and ethical transformation. Decades later, writing about *The Marrow of Tradition* in the year of publication of *The Colonel's Dream,* Chesnutt reconfirmed the literary purposes he had espoused in his youth: "The book was written, as all my books have been, with a purpose—the hope that it might create sympathy for the colored people of the South in the very difficult position which they occupy" (*Author* 234).

In short, Chesnutt's project lent itself to precisely the sort of fiction writing for which Howells argued in the *Editor's Study* as Chesnutt began to enact his literary career plan. If Chesnutt's primary symbols for a fiction of social activism at the time of his vocational decision in 1880 were Stowe and Tourgée, his literary ambitions and nascent aesthetic were to receive a powerful seconding from the chief figure in the new American literature of social and ethical purpose as Chesnutt began writing the conjure tales during the 1880s and 1890s. As a writer who served his literary apprenticeship during decades in which Howells's presence as writer, editor, and public intellectual was ubiquitous, Chesnutt could hardly have avoided his influence. Nor did he, as Howells's reviews of Chesnutt's work, along with the two writers' incompletely surviving correspondence, indicate. Howells met Chesnutt early in 1900 and shortly thereafter published in the *Atlantic* a highly favorable review of Chesnutt's first two story collections, *The Conjure Woman* (1899) and *The Wife of His Youth* (1899).[4] Therein, Howells assessed Chesnutt's work on the basis of his social-ethical aesthetic canons, which, as William L. Andrews notes, consistently "judged literature on the basis of its probable social and moral as well as aesthetic effect on the American reader" and accordingly evaluated "black writing ultimately from the standpoint of its contribution to race reconciliation" ("Howells" 333).

These reviews led to a correspondence in which Howells acted on behalf of the Harper Brothers to solicit from Chesnutt (apparently unsuccessfully) a new novel. Howells reviewed Chesnutt's second novel, *The Marrow of Tradition* (1901), in the December 1901 *North American Review,* in an essay which (again in Andrews's words) "with ambivalence, ambiguity, and contradiction . . . condemn[ed] as 'bitter' a novel which he nevertheless acknowledged was courageous, powerful, and just" ("Howells" 335) in its depiction and assessment of Southern social conditions.[5] For his part, Chesnutt was an enthusiastic, respectful, but self-assertive recipient of Howells's praise and advice, considering him "my friend" even as he denied Howells's charges of literary bitterness and his overly optimistic claims that there was "no color line in literature" (qtd. in Helen M. Chesnutt 178). There exists no extant evidence that their personal communication continued after Howells's review of *Marrow,* but Chesnutt continued to respect Howells's work, repeatedly expressing for instance his admiration for Howells's 1891 miscegenation novel, *An Imperative Duty.*[6] Joseph McElrath finds in the two men's aborted personal relationship evidence of Chesnutt's refusal to acknowledge "the strategic blunder in his campaign to win the hearts and minds of readers like Howells" (256) by foregoing subtle persuasion in favor of "literary invective" (257), and of Howells's low "tolerance" for "the 'novel with a purpose' subgenre" (257). But while it is true that Howells consistently saw polemic as an obstacle rather than a boon to literature's successful promotion of cross-cultural understanding, Chesnutt's writing, even in its latter, more polemical manifestations, is nonetheless firmly rooted in the sense of literature's social-ethical use-value that he shared with Howells. Andrews (like McElrath) suggests that Chesnutt's problem in communicating with Howells was identical to the problem he faced in his fiction in relation to a white audience: "how to get a hearing for an increasingly vigorous expression of protest from a white reading audience, which, if listening at all, was already attuned to the more soothing message of Booker T. Washington" ("Howells" 328). Chesnutt's awareness of this problem, as this chapter will demonstrate, predates his turn to polemic in *The Marrow of Tradition* and *The Colonel's Dream.* In *The Conjure Woman,* Chesnutt adapted regionalist Realism in its plantation-dialect fiction variant both to further his Howellsian purposes and to question their efficacy in reaching and moving their predominantly white audience to constructive social action.[7]

The Conjure Woman and Plantation-Dialect Fiction

Generically, the plantation-dialect tradition constituted the tool nearest to hand for Chesnutt's attempted racial mediation. As William L. Andrews notes, the conjure tales were "designed at least ostensibly to conform [to] the tradition of dialect-local color writing about plantation life in the Old South" (41) while modernizing its subject matter to "[satisfy] the curiosity of northern readers about social idiosyncrasies and economic conditions in the New South" (42). To the stock formulas of leading practitioners such as Joel Chandler Harris and Thomas Nelson Page, Chesnutt added a contemporary frame, within which a white Ohioan businessman reports his and his wife's interactions with the black residents of their newly acquired North Carolina plantation. John and Annie experience this interaction primarily through the medium of the freedman Uncle Julius McAdoo and the "authentic" black conjure tales he tells them. This framing of Julius's tales establishes, as Andrews points out, "a bridge of acceptance and understanding between the Yankee observer and his newly adopted southern home" (43); more importantly for Chesnutt's Howellsian purposes, the frame enables Chesnutt to cultivate a parallel sympathetic dynamic between his audience, for whom the frame narrator and his wife act as proxies, and the exotic content of black lives and culture in North Carolina's Cape Fear region.[8]

Having chosen a literary genre with an inherent capacity for cross-cultural mediation, Chesnutt had next to confront the genre's prior saturation with white racist ideologies. The plantation fictions of Harris, Page (especially), and other white Southern writers use black folktales or their facsimiles as tools to further a white, conservative, "reconciliationist" (Andrews, *Career* 43) agenda, such that their ostensibly sympathetic narration of black life and character reflects primarily white fantasies of interracial relationship, reconfirming white cultural norms and racial ideologies rather than confronting them with black self-representations of African-American experience.[9] The white narrator in Page's "Marse Chan," for instance, offers a tale told by a former slave as proof positive of the idyllic social harmony of Tidewater Virginia under antebellum white rule, implicitly calling for Northern acquiescence in the post-Reconstruction reestablishment of white hegemony in the New South. Even this least-promising feature of the genre, however, may have seemed to Chesnutt to present an opening for his literary project: quintessential plantation fictions like those in Page's *In Ole Virginia* tended toward a relatively mild and beneficent white paternalism over the putative black child-race rather than the pathologically violent race-hatred of a novelist like Thomas Dixon. Even the susceptibility to racism of Chesnutt's chosen genre, based as it was on a species of apparent goodwill toward the people and culture he set out to re-represent, may have seemed amenable to his avowed literary intentions. Chesnutt's task was to employ one facet of his white audience's generic expectations against another: to exploit plantation-dialect regionalism's capacity for cultural mediation while turning its permeation with white racist presumptions back on itself.

The primary site for pursuing this project is in the interplay between the "black" representational content of Uncle Julius's conjure tales and the responses to that content of an internally figured white audience (comprised of John and Annie) in the tales' frames. If regionalism itself, as Brodhead has argued, carries with it the danger of a metropolitan imposition of a sort of literary cultural imperialism upon local subcultures, it affords as well an opportunity for self-representation by the "subject" subculture. Brodhead grants to Chesnutt's writing what he refuses to Jewett's: the possibility of a genuinely bicultural perspective. In Chesnutt's work, "racial difference . . . becomes not the distant object of someone else's literary attention but a property of the author himself" (Brodhead, *Cultures* 177). Where Page, for instance, employs his African-American oral narrators to demonstrate his unstated thesis of white racial superiority and servile black contentment, Chesnutt appropriates generic conventions to represent African-American culture in ways more closely approaching its own terms. Like Jewett's replacement of the "caricatured Yankee" with a truer and more sympathetic representation of Maine country people as she had observed them, Chesnutt's fiction aims to alter stock literary representations of blacks, thereby making a bid to change a white readership's attitudes by guiding them gently toward a more genuinely Other-centered attention to local African-American society, culture, and people.

Other critics (Robert Bone and Raymond Hedin, for example) have noted Chesnutt's manipulations of plantation-dialect framing conventions as a distinguishing feature of his conjure tales without, it seems, fully recognizing Chesnutt's use of them to call attention to the relationships among author, audience, and social reality upon which the success of this culturally mediatory literary project depends.[10] Chesnutt's primary departure from his white antetypes consists in the virtually unprecedented attention he grants to the frame characters who constitute Julius's, and represent Chesnutt's, audience. By constructing John and Annie not as neutral, transparent markers of an invisible whiteness but as differentiated representations of types of real-world white readers, Chesnutt self-consciously foregrounds the crucial role played *by readers* in determining the success or failure of any literary attempt at Howellsian literary mediation. In so doing, he not only initiates the conjure tales' signal revision of the plantation-dialect genre but also grants himself a mode of inquiry into the real potential and limitations of an audience-dependent literary genre for productive cross-cultural communication. Chesnutt's adoption of the plantation-dialect genre for purposes of Howellsian literary mediation thus entails not only a revised representation of African Americans but also a deliberate investigation of the ways literature might communicate such representations to its audience—or fail to do so.

Superficially, the conjure tales seem to follow a standard plantation-dialect formal pattern. A white, cosmopolitan outsider introduces us to picturesque local scenes and interesting folkways, and records the vernacular storytelling of an African-American ex-slave about old times on the antebellum plantation. John's voice, as he introduces the tales of his resident ex-slave, is the literary voice of the metropolis, translating alien cultural realities for consumption by a readership eager for details of "other" Americas just beyond their urban-industrial doorsteps. Like such plantation-dialect staples as Page's *In Ole Virginia,* Chesnutt's tales rely on a genteel white literary narrator to transcribe the words of an uneducated black oral narrator, narrated as an authentic representation of local black culture. Page's narrator remains virtually invisible, functioning solely as an instrument for promoting an unequivocal identification between narrator and audience that ensures both that the (racist, nostalgic) representation of black culture will remain firmly under white control and that questions about readerly interface with black realities will go unasked. By contrast, Chesnutt's John, Annie, and Julius are remarkably individuated, calling attention to their own status as figures of narrator, author, and—especially— audience and thereby opening up the possibility of productive questioning of those roles and their relationship to the content of literary representation.[11] Devoting much more space than was usual in the genre to describing interchanges between Julius and his listeners, Chesnutt employs John and Annie to explore the possibilities and limitations of his own readership. If John constitutes, on the one hand, a figure of the plantation-dialect author, he functions simultaneously as a figure of the audience for the fictions he tells, at one remove, to us. Annie, whose understanding of Julius's tales more often than not counters her husband's, provides an alternative assessment of the same audience. Chesnutt designs the interplay between frames and tales to call attention to the nexus of relationships among author, audience, and represented cultural subject matter; he deploys figures of the plantation-dialect fictionist's available audiences in order to test the possibilities for success of a cross-racially mediatory fiction undertaken on the Howellsian aesthetic plan.

White Readers and Black Realities: The Racial Limits of Audience

"The Goophered Grapevine," the first published conjure tale (1887) and the opening story in *The Conjure Woman,* emphasizes John's typicality as a member of the plantation-dialect audience. John is an outsider in terms of both class and region but (as is characteristic of regionalist narrators and readers alike) his interest in the local culture, which he approaches as a resource for rest, relaxation, and entertainment as well as an economic opportunity, are fundamentally sympathetic. He willingly succumbs to the "sabbatic . . . restfulness" and charm of the "quaint old town" (32) of Patesville and its rural Cape Fear environs, and his attention consistently gravitates toward just those details of local landscape and culture most likely to appeal to the interests of an urban vacationer in quest of the picturesque: the antebellum buildings and seemingly pre-industrial lack of bustle, the scenic disrepair of abandoned plantations, the charm of unpaved roads through forests of pine and scrub oak, and the romance of "a little negro girl . . . walking straight as an arrow, with a piggin full of water on her head" (33) in an authentic display of local customs. John's whole demeanor and angle of interest in his adopted Southern home establish him as a figure who is consonant with Chesnutt's white regionalist readership, eager to soak up the local culture for their own enrichment.

No less prominent than John's position as a sympathetic outsider is his occupation as a bourgeois capitalist. As a Northern businessman intent on gaining a return on his new investment in Southern agriculture, John shows a marked tendency to understand everything he sees and hears in terms of economic self-interest. This most prominent individualizing characteristic colors his entire narration of local reality and of Julius's tales. If Patesville is somnolent and restful, it is also (somewhat contradictorily) "one of the principal towns in North Carolina, [with] a considerable trade in cotton and naval stores" and "all the appurtenances of a county seat and a commercial emporium" (32). Similarly, if the old McAdoo plantation is a romantic ruin, it is simultaneously—and more importantly—a business opportunity, a chance to undo years of "shiftless cultivation [which] had well-nigh exhausted the soil" (32–33) and profit from a reinvigorated grape-growing enterprise. Although John cites his wife's precarious health as the ostensible reason for their abandonment of the Great Lakes in favor of the South, he consistently emphasizes economic rather than medical motives for their move.

John's first encounters with Julius underscore the limitations of character that will prevent his full responsiveness to Julius, his tales, and the black culture that they express. Ever the entrepreneur, John has an unshakable disposition to interpret the black man's storytelling through a lens of economic self-interest that he assumes is universal and definitive. On their first meeting, John is quick to assert a "shrewdness in [Julius'] eyes . . . indicative of a corresponding shrewdness of character" (34) that he understands in economic terms. Julius does eventually confess to telling his tale, in part, in order to prevent John's purchase of the vineyard which, since the wartime demise of the plantation's former owners, has been Julius's private preserve and the source of a tidy subsistence income for him. But the tale itself—in a pattern amplified in succeeding conjure stories—includes a much wider range of significance than John's mercenary presumptions about the black man's motives can grant. Julius's tale concerns white exploitation of property—in both land and slaves—and its human costs in the lives of African Americans. In his relentless pursuit of profits, Mars Dugal' McAdoo not only invokes the death penalty against any slave caught sampling the grapes they themselves have grown but also cheats his neighbors and overworks both soil and slave until both are destroyed. In terms equally applicable to both the tale's antebellum and postwar contexts, the story thus warns against the dire consequences of white greed, protests against the destructive exercise of the authority of white owners over black laborers, and pleads for recognition of black rights to the fruits of their own labor. McAdoo's brutal mistreatment of his slaves for economic gain makes Julius's legitimate interest in the paltry profits from the vineyard—to whose cultivation he has devoted his life but in whose profits he has never shared—pale by comparison. But despite the fact that John's purchase of the vineyard represents the recapitulation in post-Reconstruction terms of the original sins of the antebellum proprietor, John fails utterly to hear the tale's potential application to himself, perceiving only Julius's desire to preserve "a respectable revenue from the product of the neglected grapevines" (43). The tale expresses Julius's deep and multifaceted involvement with the cultural history of the plantation, but John can credit him only with what his own self-interest as an agricultural businessman makes visible to him; the full resonance of the tale simply exceeds its audience's limiting assumptions.[12]

While the primary focus here is upon *The Conjure Woman*'s investigation of audience, it is worth noting that Chesnutt's delineation of John as a figure of the regionalist reader occurs concurrently with his establishment as a figure of the regionalist author/narrator. His characterization as a rather shallow, economically self-interested, and consequently insensitive register of African-American cultural experience suggests that, from Chesnutt's perspective, the motives of the average white regionalist author may be considerably less admirable than the Howellsian desire to make citizens in various corners of the republic understand each other better. The fact that Chesnutt deploys his internal narrator, Uncle Julius, as a competing, black, insider narrator whose storytelling is infinitely more multivalent and self-aware than John's narrative "filtering" of it reemphasizes the potentially serious shortcomings of the white regionalist's authorial stance, at least when it comes to representing black lives. Significantly, the text encourages us to hearken to Julius's tales rather than to John's unidimensional interpretations of their meaning; reversing the established generic pattern, Julius's narration is authoritative while John's narration becomes primarily a register of his failure as a listener and interpreter of local experience—a failure of his functions as both narrator and audience.

John's failure as an audience for Julius's tales proceeds in part from the nature of the plantation-dialect genre itself and thus serves as a caution to Chesnutt's readers not to be blinded by their own generic preconceptions. Like Chesnutt's readership, John experiences reality through prevailing cultural myths, primary expressions of which are literary generic conventions; as Craig Werner suggests, John's perception of the "signified" in his narration, Julius himself, conforms the man to antecedent literary signifiers

(355), so that genre itself becomes an obstacle rather than an aid to John's sympathetic understanding of the represented racial Other.[13] But despite readers' dependence on John for access to Julius's tales, Chesnutt gives his readers all the clues they need to develop a critical suspicion of the biases and cultural conditioning that so severely limit John's responses. In fact, the ever-present framing of Julius's powerful storytelling by John's imperceptive commentary serves to call readers' attention to the obstacles posed by their dependence upon John's white narration, with all its attendant prejudices and blind spots, to their gaining even the most rudimentary access to the experience of the black Other through this literary medium. Unwary readers—particularly a contemporary audience of casual readers willing and eager to submit to accustomed generic routines—would be highly likely to privilege the literate, standard-English prose of John's frame over the putatively inferior dialect offered by Julius. For the careful reader, however, Chesnutt's manipulation of the dual-author arrangement calls attention to its own generic status and the hindrances the genre itself poses for truthful communication of black experience. The interplay between John's and Julius's narrations simultaneously inscribes both the possibility and the severe limitations—multiplied to the point of improbability—of cross-cultural mediation through the plantation-dialect variety of literary regionalism, identifying readers and their interpretive limitations as the primary determinant of success or failure for the Howellsian social-ethical project.[14]

If John registers Chesnutt's fears (as Raymond Hedin has argued) about his actual audience's incapacity to understand the antiracist essence of his tales, he also serves as a conduit to a more capable, imagined readership: his wife, Annie. This second, more promising, alternative figuration of audience inhabits the frames of the conjure tales solely as a solicitor of and respondent to Julius's stories; her exclusive function, unlike her husband's, is to serve as an audience.[15] Her responses to Julius's stories constitute a distinct set of positive possibilities—and potential new obstacles—to the Howellsian practice of literature as ethically motivated cultural mediation. In "The Goophered Grapevine," for instance, where John confesses only to being "somewhat interested" (35) in Julius's tale, Annie is by contrast "evidently much impressed" (35), as she will continue to be throughout the tales. When Julius has finished his tale, Annie asks him "doubtfully, but seriously" whether his story is "true" (43). Annie clearly does not intend the remark (as her husband believes) to express a literal belief in the magical elements of the tale she has just heard; her culture and education preclude the sort of thinking that would lend credence to a literal belief in "conjure." Rather, Annie understands the tale figuratively and empathetically, as revelatory of truths about African-American life under slavery that go well beyond either the literal facts of the folktale or bare historical facts about the workings of the slavery system. Annie's apprehension of these truths can be achieved only via her full sympathetic, emotional investment in Julius's tales on their own terms—a set of readerly capacities John is totally lacking and upon which the success of the Howells aesthetic depends utterly.

"Po' Sandy" further clarifies the divergence between the tales' two figures of audience. John reintroduces his wife as a woman "of a very sympathetic turn of mind" (45), "who takes a deep interest in the stories of plantation life which she hears from the lips of the older colored people" (46). John is sufficiently attuned to Julius's tales—or at least to his wife's responses to them—to acknowledge, along with their "quaintly humorous" and "wildly extravagant" (46) qualities, their capacity when "poured freely into the sympathetic ear of a Northern-bred woman, [to] disclose many a tragic incident of the darker side of slavery" (46). But this recognition is undermined by its tone of tolerant contempt for the womanly audience who would take such disclosures seriously, as well as by the twin assumptions—common to post-Reconstruction white reconciliationist thinking—that the dark side of the peculiar institution constituted an aberration rather than its distinguishing feature and that all such barbarous practices were now safely buried in the past.

Annie, on the other hand, is sympathetically attuned not only to the tale's portrayal of black life under slavery but also to the tale's teller and, through him, to contemporary African-American plantation life. The mournful sound of a sawmill blade passing laboriously through a pine log prompts Julius to remember the tragic tale of the slave Sandy, and his expression of sympathy moves Annie to reciprocate by asking to hear Sandy's story. The tale itself, like "The Goophered Grapevine," is centrally concerned with white exploitation of plantation resources—physical and human—for white profit, to the detriment of the slaveholders' African-American "possessions." Sandy, a slave so popular with all the adult children of his owner that he is ceaselessly rotated from household to household, seeks respite by asking his wife, Tenie, to turn him into a pine tree; when she complies, their master sends Tenie away to fill her missing husband's place, and she is therefore unable to prevent Sandy, still in tree form, from being felled and sawn into lumber for a new kitchen outbuilding, causing Tenie to go mad with grief. The tale thus recounts the horrific consequences of the absolute lack of autonomy and home stability inflicted upon people who do not own even their own bodies; both Sandy and Tenie are casualties of the white exploitation of black "property."

The question of who should get the benefit of plantation resources constitutes the primary link between the antebellum content of Julius's tale and its resonance for the Reconstruction reality of the tale's frame. The lumber that in the conjure tale symbolically represents the use-value of Sandy's body for his white masters is, not coincidentally, the same lumber that Annie and John wish to reclaim for their own use in the story's frame. Mars Marrabo having exploited his slave's body to build a new kitchen for his wife, the material has since found its way into the walls of a schoolhouse, now abandoned. John seeks to reappropriate it in order to build, at Annie's request, a new kitchen outbuilding, both literally and figuratively recapitulating the original abuse of Sandy. As the second part of the frame reveals, Julius and his peers wish to use the schoolhouse for their church meetings. At issue in the present, as in the past, is a conflict over the question of whether plantation resources should be dedicated to African-American communal purposes or to white expedience.

As a figure of the plantation fictionist's audience, Annie demonstrates a much deeper and more sympathetic understanding of the tale and of its ethical implications for herself than does her husband. The fact of Julius's church meetings gives the permanently disgruntled John all the basis he thinks he needs for correct interpretation of the tale's motive. Annie, by contrast, having listened to Julius "with strained attention" (53), exclaims: "What a system it was . . . under which such things were possible!" (53), immediately cutting to the heart of the tale's historical meaning. Her vehement and sympathetic response testifies to the high degree of emotional involvement Julius's narration of African-American experience has succeeded in evoking from her. John, on the other hand, can comprehend only with the greatest difficulty that the truths to which Annie is so responsive are figurative and moral rather than literal, that she does not think that a slave named Sandy was once literally transformed into a pine tree. Annie's readerly response, however, does not end with her emotional participation in the tale's antebellum significance. Instead, her sympathetic comprehension of the tale's implications for its contemporary context leads her to accept a measure of responsibility and to undertake ethically principled action. Not only does she cancel plans to build her new kitchen, thus sparing the schoolhouse, but she convinces John to grant to Julius's "Sandy Run Colored Baptist Church" (54) the right to hold their meetings there, and she offers a subscription for the church's upkeep. Thus, as Henry Wonham notes, she "implicitly refuses to perpetuate the dehumanizing economics of slavery into the postwar era" (*Study* 22) on the basis of her deep recognition that the tale's representation of African-American realities calls for socially ameliorative action in the present.

Chesnutt's exploration of audience in "Po' Sandy" demonstrates a degree of optimism about the possibilities for cross-cultural literary mediation resulting in social reform in this genre of regionalism. Literature may indeed result in sympathetic understanding of the racial Other by at least one sector of its white audience: a cadre of white, women readers steeped in the conventions of sentimental romance and its undergirding moral philosophy. Chesnutt's construction of Annie draws heavily upon cultural assumptions concerning superior feminine morality, emotionality, and empathy—values that Stowe had effectively put to use in *Uncle Tom's Cabin* to move a mass audience to decisive moral and political action. Given an audience of Annies, this tale urges, literature might indeed transform readerly sympathies into concrete ethical actions outside the pages of the book, even in the post-Reconstruction era.

Other tales in *The Conjure Woman* repeat and amplify the portrait of Annie as an almost ideally responsive reader for a racially mediatory fiction, further delineating the terms of the tales' successful emotional connection with their audience for socially ameliorative purposes. "Sis' Becky's Pickaninny," for example, Julius's tale of an infant separated from his slave mother by their master's horse trade, plays on the full range of culturally approved domestic and womanly pieties to win Annie's emotional participation. For the childless, ill, and chronically depressed Annie, a tale of thwarted and restored motherhood strikes a chord not only with deeply ingrained cultural values but also with her personal experiences and desires. The tale, which elicits from John only his habitual objections to its fantastic elements, leads Annie to acknowledge the "essential" human and historical truth within the "mere ornamental details" (92) of conjure: "The story is true to nature, and might have happened half a hundred times, and no doubt did happen, in those horrid days before the war" (92). Annie's response indicates that once again Julius has succeeded in employing fiction to bridge the cultural gap between white North and black South, to enlist his listener's sympathies toward African Americans. The tale underscores, however, the extent to which Annie's responses depend upon the consonance of her own education and experience with the content of the tale Julius tells; the resonance of a story like "Sis' Becky's Pickaninny" for a Northern, Protestant white woman is almost a given, requiring virtually no stretching of her preexistent sympathies and biases to comprehend the lives of people inhabiting a culture different from her own.

In sharp contrast, "The Conjurer's Revenge" marks out the boundaries of a white audience's sympathies and the concomitant limits of the genre's capability to communicate across racial boundaries. The tale's frame reemphasizes and further defines John's inadequacies as a reader. In one of the few instances when John actively solicits a story from Julius, Chesnutt uses the circumstances of this request to critique and dismiss the readerly motives of the average, casual reader of fiction. John frames the tale in terms of leisure-class reading habits that Brodhead in *Cultures of Letters* identifies as a primary basis for literary regionalism. John comments that "Sunday was sometimes a rather dull day at our place" (70) and proceeds to recite a laundry list of middle-class pastimes that he and Annie have successively rejected on a particularly boring Sunday afternoon. When Julius appears in the yard, John engages his storytelling services as a substitute for the newspaper, the magazine, the missionary report, and "the impossible career of the blonde heroine of a rudimentary novel" that he has just "thrown . . . aside in disgust" (70). John thereby reduces Julius's tale to what Chesnutt may have feared *his* writing was for a majority of readers: just another item in an endless series of casual and disposable leisure-time diversions. While more attentive readers might be expected to see through John's biases, his definitional limitation of literature as nothing more than a light entertainment preemptively disables his receptivity to the forthcoming tale's more serious social intentions even more decisively than had his accustomed businessman's myopia in previous instances.

Readers expect better of Annie, as Chesnutt's other major embodiment of his audience, and nothing in the first half of the frame leads us to expect anything different here. The yarn that Julius spins superficially resembles the others, arising from Julius's advice to his employer (this time concerning whether or not he should buy a mule) and incorporating folk magic to recount antebellum plantation history. But when Julius has finished narrating his tale of crime, revenge, and repentance, John unexpectedly informs us that Annie "had listened to Julius' recital with only a mild interest" (79). She proceeds to reject his offering in no uncertain terms: "That story does not appeal to me, Uncle Julius, and is not up to your usual mark. It isn't pathetic, it has no moral that I can discover, and I can't see why you should tell it. In fact, it seems to me like nonsense" (79). Annie's unwonted response, proceeding from the mouth of the character who to this point has acted as Chesnutt's representative of the best-case scenario for his audience, forces a search for ways to account for this complete failure of reception. "The Conjurer's Revenge" figures a failure on the part of the audience—even in its most sympathetic, well-intentioned, and sensitive incarnation—to read beyond its self-imposed racial, cultural, and class-based limitations. Annie herself gives us the terms of Chesnutt's critique when she lists the tale's alleged failures to produce pathos, instill a moral, and serve a clearly defined purpose. Tellingly, the elements that Annie finds missing are precisely those that heretofore have made her an attentive and receptive audience for Julius: the pathos of the tale evokes her emotional involvement in the lives of Julius's black characters, and this sympathetic imaginative connection with African-American realities enables her to understand the tales' contemporary significance, leading her to alter accordingly her actions toward her black neighbors. But here the mechanisms of reader response that Julius's fictions have so far been able to employ to their advantage suddenly become obstacles to fictive communication, and Annie—Chesnutt's ideal reader—simply refuses to receive Julius's communication. What is it about "The Conjurer's Revenge" that causes this sudden failure of audience reception?

The tale begins with the slave Primus's theft and consumption of a shoat belonging to a black conjure man, who, learning the identity of the thief, turns him into a mule and sells him into a life of hard labor. Feeling his own death approaching, the conjure man repents of his vengefulness and endeavors from his deathbed to change Primus back to a man. Externally, the tale is intended as an explanation of the lameness of the still-living Primus, who constitutes the only direct link between the world "inside" the tale and the contemporary world of John and Annie's plantation. Internally, however, the tale is a rather sensationalistic account of crime, vengeance, violence, and sexual jealousy (Primus the mule violently intervenes in another slave's attempt to seduce his woman), all of which transpires wholly within the plantation's African-American community. In short, Julius (and Chesnutt) reach the limits of their primary audience's interpretive sympathies when they deliver a narrative predicated—in its subject matter, emotional range, and generic components—upon African-American culture without reference to the surrounding white culture. White folk simply do not figure sufficiently in this tale, either as characters or as a projected audience, to win their sympathetic involvement in the black lives the tale represents. The tale-to-frame connection of Primus's misfortune, shot through with violent emotions alien to genteel generic conditioning, gives Annie no purchase for her emotional grasp of the tale's significance for her own understanding of and relationship to African-American life. The tale insists on black sexuality, a marker of African Americans' full humanity but for Annie a shocking reminder of the difference between black vernacular storytelling and polite white literature. Julius's tale virtually guarantees its unacceptability for its immediate audience: a genteel, American-Victorian lady.

The limits of literature's capacity to communicate black culture to a white audience, Chesnutt shows, are defined by white culture's demarcations of the acceptable range of black-white interaction. Where other tales appeal to Annie's sympathies through emotionally safe channels, based on appeals to a universal and color-blind notion of justice and reinforced by familiar generic conventions of both plantation-dialect and midcentury sentimental fiction, "The Conjurer's Revenge" narrates a range of black experience that exceeds the affective limits allowed to a white, female reader by her culture and its concomitant literary genres. Annie can find no "moral" or "pathos" in a tale that threatens to burst through generic boundaries with a too exuberantly direct representation of African-American agency, particularly in the realm of sexuality. A plantation tale that forgets the limits of white taste, Chesnutt concludes, risks losing an audience of even the most liberal sympathies. For Annie and the readership she represents, the black world disappears where its contact with her own world ends; African-American culture matters for whites only insofar as it provides a foil and an object for the exercise of white cultural values, safely contained within white literary forms.

Julius's response to Annie's rejection reinforces the terms of Chesnutt's critique. The storyteller is "puzzled as well as pained" (79) by the failure of his tale to reach its normally sympathetic audience: "He had not pleased the lady, and he did not seem to understand why" (79), John informs us. Seeming to apologize for his own failure, Julius covertly casts the blame upon his audience, proceeding to offer a point-by-point refutation of the terms of Annie's readerly rejection. "'I'm sorry, ma'm,' he said *reproachfully*, 'ef *you doan lack* dat tale'" (79, emphasis mine). Countering Annie's charge that the tale is morally purposeless "nonsense" (79), Julius defends his tale on the basis of its truth, once again assigning responsibility for the tale's failure to the listener rather than to the teller: "I'm tellin' nuffin but de truf. . . . Dey's so many things a body knows is lies, dat dey ain' no use gwine roun' findin' fault wid tales dat mought des ez well be so ez not" (79). If Annie cannot find the truth of his tale, Julius implies, the fault belongs to her own interpretive inadequacy; if she insists on "gwine roun' findin' fault" instead of searching for the tale's truth on the tale's own terms, then the failure of communication belongs to the audience, not to the author. True to his "let-them-who-have-ears" narrative strategy, Chesnutt leaves it to his readers to corroborate the suggestive accusations Julius makes against them or, alternatively, to accept Annie's assessment and move on unreflectively to the next story. To the extent to which a white plantation-dialect audience adopts Annie's posture, readers recapitulate her interpretive failures and are likewise damned by Chesnutt's critique.

Julius's defense of "de truf" of his tale launches a figurative exploration of the culturally perspectival nature of truth itself, suggesting a further reason for Annie's interpretive breakdown. Julius proceeds by offering a contrasting exemplum of untruth:

F'instance, dey's a young nigger gwine ter school in town, en he come out heah de yuther day en 'lowed dat de sun stood still en de yeath turnt roun' eve'y day on a kinder axletree. I tol' dat young nigger ef he didn' take hisse'f 'way wid dem lies, I'd take a buggy-trace ter 'im; fer I sees de yeath stan'in' still all de time, en I sees de sun gwine roun' it, en ef a man can't b'lieve w'at 'e sees, I can't see no use in libbin'— mought 's well die en be whar we can't see nuffin. (79)

The comic effect of this comment arises from the fact that what Julius in his ignorance denounces as a lie, his white audience accepts as fact. Annie, John, and the members of Chesnutt's elite, educated white readership invest with truth the scientific proposition that the earth turns on its axis while the sun remains stationary. But for Julius, such "truth" is, at best, irrelevant (as in fact it is for most of us in the course of our daily routines); within the very different context of his own daily life, such astronomical facts signify nothing. The truth, rather, consists of what one "sees," of how one uses and relies upon the practical effects of the sun in everyday life. The pragmatic truth of Julius's conjure tale derives from its quotidian use-value: a sort of truth better expressed in this case in the communally rooted figurative extravagances of the conjure tale than in the more staid conventions of genteel white literature.

Annie's failure to comprehend the truth of Julius's tale, like Julius's inability to accept the earth's rotation on its axis, depends on the conceptual contexts that comprise individuals' and cultural groups' knowledge of the world. Julius's commentary on truth calls attention to the severely limited possibility of understanding anything outside the conceptual fields that constitute one's own culture. The failure of "The Conjurer's Revenge" to mediate successfully across such cultural boundaries marks the limits beyond which Chesnutt's cross-cultural literary mediation seems unable to proceed. When the cultural contexts of the audience and the literary subject are as widely divided as they are here, Chesnutt asserts, the success of literature's Howellsian racial mediation depends entirely on the audience's willingness to recognize and transcend the blindnesses imposed by their own cultural chauvinism. Chesnutt's diagnosis of his audience in "The Conjurer's Revenge" displays a deepening skepticism about his readers' disposition to move beyond the kinds of culturally imposed interpretive limitations under which even Annie, the best audience Chesnutt can posit, falters.

If "Po' Sandy" and "The Conjurer's Revenge" demarcate the outer limits (positive and negative, respectively) of a white readership's capacity for sympathetic participation in African-American experience through literature, "Hot-Foot Hannibal"—another conjure tale with a carefully developed frame narrative—explores one possible strategy for undermining the cultural and generic conditioning of audience that leads to interpretive failure. Like "The Conjurer's Revenge," "Hot-Foot Hannibal" primarily concerns African-American community relationships only obliquely related to the surrounding white society, and it assumes black agency in those relationships—a recipe for failure if "The Conjurer's Revenge" is any indication. But this tale is constructed, as well, upon a conventional love plot thoroughly familiar to any reader reared on nineteenth-century sentimental romance, complete with true lovers thwarted by the treachery of a jealous interloper, a suicide committed from the grief of lost love, and a ghost who patiently awaits the return of her lover. Such a romantic tale of love won, thwarted, and irrevocably lost is calculated to appeal to Julius's (and Chesnutt's) best imaginable audience, and Annie and her visiting sister do in fact respond accordingly. "There was silence when the old man had finished," John tells us, "and I am sure I saw a tear in my wife's eye, and more than one in Mabel's" (118). By employing a familiar generic plot pattern based on the putatively universal emotional magnet of romantic love, Julius succeeds in winning a receptive white audience to a sympathetic hearing, even for a predominantly black tale. "Hot-Foot Hannibal" thus outlines the terms under which the literary representation of black agency may be expected to succeed in its bid for white reception. Unlike "The Conjurer's Revenge," which recounts black experience with no direct reference to white cultural values, "Hot-Foot Hannibal" appeals directly to an established emotional-generic pathway to make its cross-cultural connection.

The answer to the problem of audience posed by "The Conjurer's Revenge" lies in authorial conformity to white generic expectations, which may to a certain extent be made to serve the purposes of racial mediation. But while "Hot-Foot Hannibal" does indeed manage to make emotional contact across the racial divide, the social-ethical stakes for which the other tales play are sacrificed as the price of generic conformity; the real-world effects of this tale are strictly limited to the white world—they do not issue in socially ameliorative action undertaken across the racial divide. The occasion for Julius's tale is the breaking of a marriage engagement between Mabel and her lover, Murchison. Like Chloe in the inner tale, Mabel has sent her lover away in a moment of pique, an action that threatens to destroy their relationship permanently. Julius tells his story while he and his white listeners wait in John's carriage for the supposed ghost of Chloe to allow the balking mare who pulls the carriage to continue her journey. But the saga of Chloe and Jeff convinces Annie and Mabel to change their course, and Julius seizes the opportunity to put Mabel in the way of meeting and reconciling with Murchison. The frame story mirrors the conjure tale, except that the sentimental heroine, learning from Julius's exemplum, is happily reunited with her lover.

Julius's tale proves highly effective in moving his audience not just to sympathy with its characters but (in accord with Howells's hopes) to action in the real world based upon that sympathy, but the primary reason for that success is that Annie and Mabel are vitally self-interested in the frame situation that the conjure tale inversely reflects. Julius's success in reaching his listeners is at best a Pyrrhic victory: he has succeeded in making his white audience see *themselves* in the black protagonists' lives, but the limited terms of that identification do virtually nothing to expand their sense of group identity to include the more alien aspects of black culture—those aspects that define it as Other and necessitate literature's cross-cultural mediation in the first place. While Julius, as a figure of the black author, seems willing and content that his tale has a positive impact on the lives of his listeners, the inner tale's success in moving its audience to altered feeling and action is severely circumscribed by readerly attitudes and expectations that the tale seems unable to alter. The black storyteller, Chesnutt suggests once again, may indeed expect a sympathetic hearing among white audience members, and one that leads to constructive action in their lives, but only within certain strictly maintained racial parameters. Julius's generosity in devoting his services to Mabel and Annie, while it redounds to his moral credit and indicates his keen understanding of white cultural codes and *moeurs,* does not translate into a success for the Howellsian project of cultural mediation. Black appropriation of white generic conventions may sometimes prove affecting to a white audience, but the response to which it leads does nothing to further the social-ethical end of cross-cultural communication that Chesnutt seeks. The particular solution to the problem of audience presented by "Hot-Foot Hannibal," then, represents at best a superficially satisfactory compromise between authorial social-ethical purposes and audience recalcitrance.[16]

The Conjure Woman, fundamentally, is a book about how its own readers might be expected to read. Presenting the consumption of literary fiction as a socially and ethically charged act upon which the success of Chesnutt's Howellsian project depended, the conjure tales appropriate generically overdetermined conventions and subtly manipulate them to interrogate the genre's potential to reach its audience—or, more precisely, to gauge that audience's potential for responding constructively to the genre's representation of black Southern culture. Whatever social and ethical results can be expected from literary representation of African Americans by African Americans, the tales suggest, are thoroughly circumscribed by the limited capacity of a white readership to interact imaginatively with a culture perceived and defined—not least by literary generic conventions themselves—as wholly Other. As Chesnutt runs through the array of possibilities for audience response to plantation-dialect fiction, he consistently throws primary responsibility for the quality and consequences of that response back upon his audience. As a black author dedicated to wielding literature as a tool for social and ethical amelioration, Chesnutt uses his conjure tales to challenge his audience to a more sympathetic, more just reading of the African-American cultural plight represented in Julius's tales. Even as he courts his white readers' moral transformation, however, Chesnutt maneuvers the complex relations among his social subject matter and his internal figurations of audience to throw into question the notion that a real audience in the late-nineteenth-century United States could ever sufficiently overcome its collective prejudices to see through cultural (and literary) myths to the reality of African-American experience and to act constructively upon that knowledge. The conjure tales seek to harness whatever power may inhere in literature to mediate across the most deeply inscribed cultural boundary of all—race—while simultaneously questioning literature's capacity to enact the kind of cross-cultural communication envisioned in Howells's social-ethical aesthetic. *The Conjure Woman* constitutes a simultaneous enactment and critique of the Howellsian ideal of literature as a socially and ethically transformative instrument in American public life.

Chesnutt's (Im)possible Dream of Reform: *The Colonel's Dream*

Unlike *The Conjure Woman,* whose complex narrative self-reflection has encouraged frequent and ongoing critical attention in recent years (because contemporary critics love no narrative better than a narrative about narrative), Chesnutt's final published novel, *The Colonel's Dream* (1905), has been so completely overlooked that it has become a sort of tradition to begin discussions of it by noting the fact: Susan Blake, for instance, calls the novel "strangely neglected" (49), while Gary Scharnhorst terms it "virtually ignored" (271). In addition to these two essays, Chesnutt's novel has inspired just three chapter-length considerations and one shorter discussion, in monographs by William L. Andrews, Ernestine Pickens, Dean McWilliams, and Frances R. Keller. As with any such absence, its causes must remain necessarily speculative, but one reason for the relative critical silence may be the novel's "whiteness" relative to the rest of Chesnutt's canon. Among the published novels (including the posthumously published *Mandy Oxendine, The Quarry,* and *Paul Marchand, F.M.C.*), *The Colonel's Dream* remains the only work whose protagonist and major characters are white and whose polemic program, while it inevitably includes issues of race because of the novel's Southern topic, is not explicitly racial but instead comprises a more broadly Progressive critique of Southern institutions and attitudes. Too, the novel's peculiar formal qualities and its denouement in an abrupt and less-than-spectacular defeat for the single-handed reform crusade of its protagonist, coupled with its equally lackluster status as a publishing event,[17] may make *The Colonel's Dream* seem simply anticlimactic in comparison with Chesnutt's earlier productions and, particularly, with the panoramic cast and climactic race riot of its predecessor, *The Marrow of Tradition* (1901).[18]

Except for Scharnhorst, who approaches the novel through its manipulations of formal conventions, and more recently McWilliams, who investigates the book's investments in and critique of notions of aristocracy, all other approaches to the novel share a disposition to understand it in relation to Chesnutt's reform commitments, his increasing (and professionally fatal) tendency toward literary polemic, and the book's status as its author's last hurrah as a professional literary author. This discussion refocuses that approach in order to see Chesnutt's use of literature for reform purposes as undertaken in large measure in response to Howells's model of a socially and ethically purposive aesthetic—one that Chesnutt increasingly found (as the first part of this chapter argued) problematic when fiction was called upon to communicate across the racial divide. Just as *The Conjure Woman* may be read as a text that both employs literature as a medium for ethically purposeful cross-cultural communication and interrogates the real-world possibilities for the success of that project, *The Colonel's Dream* both enacts the ideal of literature as an instrument of reform and questions the viability of its self-assigned task. But where the earlier work focused its attention on the "weak link" in the Howellsian aesthetic model—its dependence on the individual and collective predispositions of actual readers to read and respond justly to literary representations of social reality— *The Colonel's Dream* addresses the role of the reformer/author in realizing Howellsian social-ethical goals. Others have noted the symbolic connection between Chesnutt and his failed reformer-hero, Colonel French.[19] This chapter pursues such insights by reading Colonel French as a figure not of authorship per se but of the author, Chesnutt himself. In *The Colonel's Dream,* Chesnutt constructs French as an embodiment of idealistic reform impulses and the personal qualities of character that compel both author and character to act upon them. French thus becomes a venue for Chesnutt to diagnose the reform temperament itself in relation to the project that he shares with his protagonist, and the novel explores the interaction of the reformer's motivating ethical idealism with seemingly intransigent sociocultural realities. French becomes a vehicle not merely for expression of the author's despair about his literary reform project, but more importantly for a critical reconsideration of the irreducible role of the individual reformer's temperament to any reform effort, and ultimately for rededication to social transformation that neither Chesnutt nor his literary protagonist can fulfill. *The Colonel's Dream* thus confronts a central paradox of reform itself and of Chesnutt's own ethically purposeful literary career: its success depends on an absolute dedication to objectives that may never be fully realized.

Chesnutt's approach to the topic of reform in *The Colonel's Dream* indicates both his continued allegiance to the Howellsian program and his on-going critical interrogation about its efficacy. By the time *The Colonel's Dream* was published, Chesnutt had long since turned from plantation-dialect fiction, whose conventions had proven fatally overdetermined by the need of an upper-middle-class readership to erase both African-American culture and the "Negro Problem" it posed for white society, to the novel genre and a more directly polemical approach, which in Howellsian terms represented what McElrath calls "the strategic blunder in [Chesnutt's] campaign to win the hearts and minds of readers like Howells" (256). Howells's affirmative responses to both *The Conjure Woman* and *The Wife of His Youth,* for instance, recognized both books' value as sympathetic documentation of African-American social realities but failed to acknowl-edge the implicit critique of the interracial applicability of Howellsian principles of literary mediation. In fact, Howells's *Atlantic* review claims that "In [literature] there is, happily, no color line" (701), an assertion that misses the idea of *The Conjure Woman* and that Chesnutt eventually came to regard with disdain.[20] Public response to the conjure tales and their suc-cessors seemed to confirm Chesnutt's asseverations in *The Conjure Woman* about the limitations of his audience and to furnish some justification for his adoption of a more militant literary approach. *The Colonel's Dream* remains true to Howellsian initiating principles by courting readers' sym-pathies and support for Colonel French's reforms, but it critically scruti-nizes the reformer's—and thence all reformers'—actuating motives and dispositions. As centrally concerned as the novel is with the ominous and potentially violent social currents underlying the tranquil surface of the Southern scenes it depicts, the book's window on these realities is the per-sonal history of one reformer. In short, Chesnutt uses his novel to affirm Howellsian goals while skeptically analyzing their enactors, himself in-cluded.

The oft-noted parallels between the author and his protagonist, which critics have noticed without fully investigating, are numerous: both are born Southerners who have achieved business success in the urban North; both are educated, liberal members of the rising, postwar professional classes; both return to the South after prolonged absence, committing themselves to the effort to reform the social ills they discover there; both meet with insurmountable opposition and return to the North in apparent defeat. The significant differences between Chesnutt and his main character—racially black versus white, middle-class versus wealthy, small businessman versus industrial capitalist, Northern noncombatant versus Confederate war hero—substantially qualify the correlations; the novel is certainly not autobiographical. Nevertheless, the suggestive parallelism between author and character on the basis of their shared status as reformers constitutes a significant indicator of Chesnutt's intentions. While Andrews, Pickens, Blake, and others have all recognized that *The Colonel's Dream* is vitally concerned with the critique of reformist strategies,[21] the more elusive author-protagonist connection suggests a specific focus upon the qualities of the reformer himself. The novel's concern with French's personal moral and emotional development as he unsuccessfully pursues his reform ambitions holds the key to resolving what has seemed to many readers a self-contradiction: the book's relentlessly pessimistic documentation of seemingly unreformable social facts on the one hand and on the other its status as a polemic clearly aimed at promoting the very reforms whose defeat it depicts.

Chesnutt works hard to establish his readers' identification with Colonel French from the novel's first pages, and the colonel's reformist cause is simultaneously a means and an object of that association; bonding with French is equivalent to bonding with his Progressivism. Before the novel makes its more sentimental appeal to readers on the basis of French's personal status as a widower and a devoted father to his motherless son, Phil, it introduces us to the colonel in his public status as a wealthy industrial capitalist with a fully developed social conscience. As the colonel and his business partner anxiously await word in the offices of French and Company, Limited, about the success or failure of their unwilling offer to sell their company to a newly established "bagging trust" (5), the narrator allies the novel's hero with the workers and consumers who will be victimized by the trust:

> The principal reason for the trust's existence was economy of administration; this was stated, most convincingly, in the prospectus. There was no suggestion, in that model document, that competition would be crushed, or that, monopoly once established, labour must sweat and the public groan in order that a few captains, or chevaliers,

of industry, might double their dividends. Mr. French may have known it, or guessed it, but he was between the devil and the deep sea—a victim rather than an accessory—he must take what he could get, or lose what he had. (5)

French's actions, furthermore, protect not only his own interests but those of a silent partner, a woman whom the colonel has chivalrously protected from knowledge of the catastrophe that would result from the trust's rejection of the company's sale. Chesnutt thus paints the colonel as a romanticized representative of an older, genteel brand of honest custom, victimized by Gilded Age robber barons in a lawless economy that recognizes no values but those that conduce to larger profits. Having successfully concluded his business, and stressed to the point of a physical breakdown calculated once again to generate readerly sympathy for him, French prepares to recuperate with Phil in the Southern town of his boyhood, Clarendon. The narrator takes the occasion to harness our growing sympathetic alignment with French to the Southern reform campaign that, unbeknownst to him, will occupy him through the remainder of the book. By constructing French as a white man with black sympathies, an industrious Northern businessman with Southern aristocratic roots, a wealthy capitalist with a social conscience, a Confederate war hero yet a living example of the benefits of Northern-style business and North-South reconciliation, Chesnutt constructs his main character to make as broad an appeal to all sectors of his potential audience as possible. Before the reform hero even arrives upon the field of battle, Chesnutt has made a strong bid for readerly emotional allegiance not only to the colonel himself but to the social ideals he will come ever more fully to embody. As Colonel French prepares himself for what he believes will be a short visit to the South, the narrator, leaping ahead, discloses that Colonel French "was to look back upon his business career as a mere period of preparation for the real end and purpose of his earthly existence" (14). The remainder of the book taps as a single resource the individual appeal of Colonel French and that of the reform project he undertakes; French embodies the Progressive spirit, and the novel stands or falls on its ability to win us to the man and his mission as a single entity.

As soon as Chesnutt moves his hero southward, he begins employing the emotional capital that has already accrued to the colonel in the opening chapters to enlist our support for his nascent reform efforts. The arrest of Old Peter, French's rediscovered boyhood "retainer" (32), becomes the occasion for the colonel's (and the novel's) attack on the convict-lease system, whereby Southern African Americans could be judicially remanded to a state of virtual slavery in order to satisfy white landowners' labor needs. French's intervention rapidly escalates from buying his former slave's prison term from the justice of the peace to searching for more effective and permanent ways to disrupt the convict-lease system itself, first by moral suasion, then by legal and ultimately legislative action. His efforts rapidly become allied to a comprehensive vision of Southern social transformation:

> Evidently Clarendon needed new light and leading. Men, even black men, with something to live for, and with work at living wages, would scarcely prefer an enforced servitude in ropes and chains. And the punishment had scarcely seemed to fit the crime. He had observed no great zeal for work among the white people since he came to town; such work as he had seen done was mostly performed by Negroes. If idleness were a crime, the Negroes surely had no monopoly of it. (69–70)

As French broadens his focus from Old Peter's particular predicament to its root social causes in Southern attitudes toward labor and race, the effort to help an old acquaintance becomes a more comprehensive diagnosis of the cherished (white) regional attitudes and assumptions that seem to French to constitute powerful preventives to Southern social and economic progress. In short order, French has repurchased his ancestral home and turned his vacation into a permanent commitment to Clarendon's future. He gradually takes on not only the reform of convict-lease but also the establishment of an institution for industrial education for blacks, the construction of a public library, and the rebuilding of the town's war-destroyed cotton mill using locally manufactured brick and well-paid local laborers of both races. As the colonel progressively commits himself more and more irrevocably to the remaking of Clarendon, the town's residents increasingly find his efforts distastefully radical, and local opposition to his extremist schemes—particularly those that threaten the scrupulously maintained color line—mounts steadily. Nevertheless, the novel seeks to discredit such responses as symptomatic of the social and moral ills that French strives to remedy and to maintain our twin allegiances to the colonel and to his reforms.

Despite this alliance of reform goals and principles with their human agent, however, Chesnutt increasingly portrays his protagonist in terms that should warn readers away from an uncritical acceptance of his motives. As French rediscovers long-forgotten scenes and acquaintances from his childhood, he loses himself in a haze of idealized antebellum associations that have the effect of calling into question the practicability of reform work thus founded. In addition to his purchase of the ancestral home and his resumption of the master-servant relationship (albeit on an altered legal footing) with Peter, French immerses himself in a new romance with the genteelly impoverished Laura Treadwell, a boyhood friend whom he eventually asks to marry him. Chesnutt pointedly and repeatedly reminds us that French's commitment to Clarendon is in part a surrender to nostalgia for his lost youth, of which the colonel himself remains only partially aware. "It is delightful here, Laura," he tells his friend. "I seem to have renewed my youth. I yield myself a willing victim to the charm of the old place, the old ways, the old friends" (50). Laura, for whom Clarendon represents the tedium of daily life rather than idealized reminiscences of childhood, tries to warn French against his tendency to romanticize what any successful reform will require him to see with rational clarity: "You see our best side, Henry. . . . You see us through a haze of tender memories. When you have been here a week, the town will seem dull, and narrow, and sluggish. You will find us ignorant and backward, worshipping our old idols, and setting up no new ones; our young men leaving us, and none coming to take their place" (50). Her assessment is one that French will come to share as he becomes more closely acquainted with Clarendon's deep-seated social pathologies, and yet he never arrives at a full recognition of the degree to which his feeling for Clarendon—and for his projected reforms—remains rooted in his fantasy about a Clarendon that "is like a scene from a play, over which one sighs to see the curtain fall—all enchantment, all light, all happiness" (50). Even when Colonel French begins to work more consciously and with increasing purposefulness to expose and alter the mechanisms of this dysfunctional society, he continues to indulge himself in such romantic reveries. When he repurchases the family home he acts as much under the influence of "ancestral feeling" (81) as with the fully formed intention of taking up permanent residence, and when he proposes to Laura Treadwell he does so unaware of his motives in nostalgia for the town and in the face of plain evidence that she does not fully share his reform attitudes and ambitions. The colonel's inherently romantic temperament, that which makes possible his sensitivity to others' suffering and fuels his passionate commitment to change for their benefit, prevents him from accurately gauging either the number and magnitude of the problems he seeks to redress or the depth of the entrenched power of his opponents.

The colonel increasingly transfers his romantic energies from nostalgia for his lost youth to the visionary imagination of a perfected Southern society in the microcosm of Clarendon. His vision of the future, like his imagination of the life of the town as "a scene from a play," too easily assumes that social facts will give way before idealistic visions that he, like the stage manager of the play, can readily impose upon them. French is not so completely immersed in his idealism that he fails to acknowledge the hard social realities beneath the idyllic appearances of Clarendon. But his temperamental predisposition to see things in ideal terms thoroughly colors his reform aspirations and strategies, calling our attention to the precarious relationship between ideals and realities, vision and practicality in the reform project itself. Even after the colonel is well embarked on peeling the rotten social onion of Clarendon, he continues to overestimate (as Chesnutt increasingly felt about his own efforts) the effect upon entrenched social attitudes and institutions that he can have by providing "some point of contact with the outer world and its more advanced thought" (90)—even though that thought *is* amply reinforced by financial muscle—and to underestimate the strength of the opposition, which is chiefly embodied in the corrupt and ubiquitous businessman, banker, and politician, Bill Fetters. French blithely assumes, for instance, that all that is needed "to rescue Clarendon from the grasp of Fetters" is a "year or two of continuous residence" that "the colonel could, if need be, spare. . . . " "The forces of enlightenment, set in motion by his aid," the colonel imagines, would naturally meet with little resistance in vanquishing "the retrograde forces represented by Fetters" (118). French's cavalier idealism is confirmed by his rising tendency to view himself in ideal terms, as a white knight appointed to deliver the village from its evil oppressor—a tendency that increases in direct proportion to the escalating formidability of the local opposition. Increasingly, French lives not in the real Clarendon but "in the Clarendon yet to be, a Clarendon rescued from Fetters, purified, rehabilitated; and no compassionate angel warned him how tenacious of life that which Fetters stood for might be" (120).

Nowhere is the depth of French's reform idealism, and its problematic relationship to historical reality, more fully exposed than in the dream from which the novel derives its title. Despite having failed that day to induce Clarendon's civic leaders to enforce the law and prosecute the members of a lynch mob, the colonel dreams that night the dream of Progressive reform:

> As the colonel slept this second time, he dreamed of a regenerated South, filled with thriving industries, and thronged with a prosperous and happy people, where every man, having enough for his needs, was willing that every other man should have the same; where law and order should prevail unquestioned, and where every man could enter, through the golden gate of hope, the field of opportunity, where lay the prizes of life, which all might have an equal chance to win or lose.
>
> For even in his dreams the colonel's sober mind did not stray beyond the bounds of reason and experience. That all men would ever be equal he did not dream; there would always be the strong and the weak, the wise and the foolish. But that each man, in his little life in this our world might be able to make the most of himself, was an ideal which even the colonel's waking hours would not have repudiated. (280–81)

The colonel envisions an agnostic City of God, an economic utopia in which every individual is guaranteed equal opportunity and equal protection under the law. His vision—as perhaps visions must be—is of the accomplished ideal of a completely reconstructed Southern society, without reference to the practical obstacles, strategies, and processes along the road to reform. The qualifications of "reason and experience" that the second paragraph places upon the utopia of the first only serve to reemphasize the degree to which French characteristically sees reform ideals not merely as guides to principled action but as fully achievable realities; in the colonel's philosophy, to expect absolute equality would be naive but to expect the establishment of completely equal access to resources and opportunities in the relatively near future appears perfectly reasonable. The colonel fully expects Clarendon, given but a little more time, to conform fully to his idealistic vision of a perfected South.

The next morning, the colonel's dream is abruptly shattered by one final encounter with the intransigent social realities with which his hubristic idealism never fully manages to come to terms. He finds on his piazza the disinterred casket of Old Peter, whom French has buried in the family plot of the segregated cemetery at his son's request and over the opposition of the citizenry. Pinned to the coffin's lid, a barely literate note instructs him to "Berry yore ole nigger somewhar else. . . . Niggers by there selves, white peepul by there selves, and them that lives in our town must bide by our rules" (281). This enactment of "the kind of depravity that knew no sense of taboo, which made war on the dead as well as the living" (Andrews 254), convinces the colonel to abandon his half-finished projects and return to the North. The colonel's dream of a color-blind and law-abiding economic utopia has collided decisively with the one cultural reality that remained most completely impervious to constructive social change, whether at the hands of a wealthy Northern industrialist or of an author of ethically purposeful fiction, in the decades surrounding the turn of the century: race. Chesnutt's close juxtaposition of the novel's fullest expression of reformist idealism with its defeat by recalcitrant social forces, reinforced (as McWilliams convincingly argues) through the rhetorical undercutting of the colonel's augustly phrased vision by the "brutal simplicity" (176) of the mob's note, underscores the terms of his critique of the reform temperament and its relationship to the reform project—including Chesnutt's own overly ambitious efforts to single-handedly reverse the relentless slide into Jim Crow by means of his fiction writing. To suggest that *The Colonel's Dream* amounts to anything less dire than a pessimistic assessment of the immediate possibilities for Progressive social change in the South would fly in the face of reason. But the novel presents the demise of the colonel's dream as a defeat of his unrealistic, overly optimistic, untempered expectations rather than of the goals of reform. Despite the "bounds of reason and experience" within which French professes to be working, his romantic absolutism is tempered neither by reason nor experience. Unable to bend before the force of what, after all, is only the last and most brutal sign of the same immovable racism that has obstructed all his efforts, the colonel's resolve breaks instead. Unwilling to compromise even provisionally with Southern actualities in his pursuit of a fully realized ideal, French's disposition cannot accept the always incomplete, unavoidably processional nature of any substantive social change. "And so *the colonel* faltered, and, having put his hand to the plow, turned back" (293, emphasis mine), Chesnutt concludes in the novel's final paragraphs. The failure of reform in *The Colonel's Dream* results neither from the necessarily idealistic vision that motivates it, nor from the reformer's tactics per se, nor even primarily from the racism of the townsfolk. Instead, failure arises from the inappropriately binary habit of mind that will not allow the dialectical negotiation between ideals and realities that fosters any successful reform.

In constructing his critique of French's reformist idealism, Chesnutt in part critiques himself. Just as French thought to transform Clarendon by the sheer force of his own will, imposing his rational vision of a transformed society upon a citizenry dazzled by its justice and wisdom, the young Chesnutt had been ambitious to write the book that would so illuminate the truth about the postwar South that it would transform Southern society as radically as had *Uncle Tom's Cabin*. In *The Colonel's Dream*, an older, disillusioned author seems to acknowledge a defeat of his literary ambitions parallel to French's:[22] as one character retrospectively assesses the colonel's efforts, "you see, suh, they were too many for you. There ain't no one man can stop them folks down there when they once get started" (292). But while the novel clearly does wish its readers to confront the full horror of darker Southern realities masked by the ubiquitous rhetoric of an emergent "New South,"[23] it also maintains a scrupulous distinction between the individual reformer and the collective project of reform, between the actuating vision of a reconstructed society and the piecemeal, fragmentary, disillusioning work of trying to enact it in the "materials" of an actual society. Chesnutt's insistence on the temperamental romanticism that both enables the colonel's dream and disables the colonel from accepting the terms under which progress toward that ideal must be purchased should be read as evidence of the novelist's acknowledgment of similar tendencies in himself and as an indication of his acceptance of a scaled-down definition of success in his social-ethical artistic endeavor. Chesnutt's novel diagnoses the failing of a certain type of reform temperament as a warning to those—himself included—who would engage in reform; it does not represent his dismissal of the larger Progressive project of which the colonel's and his own efforts constitute a part. If it is true that Chesnutt's literary career ended with the publishing failure of *The Colonel's Dream,* it is also true that he continued his reform activities after the demise of his career as a published writer of fiction, on a more diversified plan and on both the local and the national stages. As a businessman, an essayist, a correspondent, a public speaker, and even, once again, as an (unpublished) fictionist, Chesnutt continued to pursue the path of reform as the "exemplary citizen" that Howells (as Crisler, Leitz, and McElrath suggest by their choice of his phrase as the title of their collection of Chesnutt letters) had seen in Booker T. Washington but might better have recognized instead in Chesnutt.[24]

Similarly, the defeat of Colonel French does not spell in any absolute or permanent sense the defeat of his dream; the novel figures numerous small, incomplete, provisional implementations of elements of his reform vision. Employment on fair and equal terms has been given to blacks and poor whites, albeit temporarily. A succession of individuals—the black schoolteacher, Henry Taylor; the young lawyer, Caxton; and the prospective inventor, Ben Dudley; as well as Laura Treadwell and her niece Graciella among them—have been influenced if not completely won over by the ideals the colonel has attempted to enact and will continue, each in his or her own fashion, "to carry on the work which you have begun" (285), as Laura Treadwell pledges. Clarendon's citizens, from the top to the bottom of the social scale, have been forced to confront Progressive ideas about work, education, money, politics, and justice, even if the immediate results are primarily reactionary. In short, by the time the colonel's naive expectation of single-handedly bringing about the birth of a new society is shattered, Chesnutt has already shown us a dozen different ways in which that shattered ideal has begun to be enacted in genuine if limited ways. The novel's final narratorial exhortation to reform, which most critics have considered an optimistic intrusion unwarranted by the novel's events,[25] should be read in the context not only of the colonel's final defeat but of the full range of the novel's depiction of reform. Duly noting French's failure,

Chesnutt asks: "But was not his, after all, the only way? The seed which the colonel sowed seemed to fall by the wayside, it is true; but other eyes have seen with the same light, and while Fetters and his kind still dominate their section, other hands have taken up the fight which the colonel dropped" (293). The author proceeds to list a few of the signs of change in the South upon which reformers must pin their hopes: the growth of industry, government intervention in peonage, the rulings of a minority of progressive judges against "the infamy of the chain-gang and convict lease systems" (293), the beginnings of a public voice in support of education. Despite the colonel's personal abandonment of the task, the collective project of social transformation stumbles tentatively onward. "Slowly, like all great social changes, but visibly, to the eye of faith, is growing up a new body of thought, favourable to just laws and their orderly administration. In this changed attitude of mind lies the hope of the future, the hope of the Republic" (294). All success in Southern reform depends, Chesnutt concludes, upon patience with the slow pace of change and contentment with incremental steps—in short, upon a "changed attitude of mind" in reformers that would both maintain a vital faith in actuating ideals and accept their less than ideal translation into the terms of social reality. In *The Colonel's Dream*, Chesnutt confronts the paradox of reform—and the paradox of his own literary career—to which Colonel French never reconciles himself: meaningful social change depends on a motivating vision that can never be fully accomplished in reality; nevertheless, its impossibility in any absolute sense negates neither the vision nor its imperfect enactments.

Chesnutt opens his final novel with a prefatory dedication: "To the great number of those who are seeking, in whatever manner or degree, from near at hand or far away, to bring the forces of enlightenment to bear upon the vexed problems which harass the South, this volume is inscribed, with the hope that it may contribute to the same good end" (v). *The Colonel's Dream* squarely faces the cold fact that the novel's Progressive ideals are likely to collide with a wall of social resistance that seems to utterly negate its reason for being—that the worst suspicions Chesnutt entertained in *The Conjure Woman* concerning the limits of literature's mediatory capacities across cultural boundaries would be confirmed once again by the audience rejection that *The Colonel's Dream* seems almost to predict for itself. The novel nevertheless pursues its Howellsian aesthetic agenda, adding itself to the accumulation of small, tangible literary efforts to push society toward a sympathetic understanding of its Others and to act constructively upon that recognition. If *The Colonel's Dream* acknowledges in advance its own probable failure to transform Southern society, it nevertheless reaffirms Chesnutt's lifelong commitment to the reform goals that stand at the center of his Howellsian literary project.

5
Willa Cather and the Anti-Realist Uses of Social Reference

Unlike either Sarah Orne Jewett or Charles W. Chesnutt, Willa Cather forged a literary relationship to W. D. Howells that was primarily oppositional. Cather grew up and was educated in a literary world thoroughly permeated by the presence of Howells and still occupied with working out the far-reaching implications of his conception of literature's social and ethical purposes. But as she moved fitfully toward a literary career, her juvenile tastes ran to adventure-romance fiction and her later models were drawn primarily from British and European literature—not from American examples and emphatically not from works that deliberately pursued socially ameliorative goals. As far as American literature was concerned, Cather revealed her already well-entrenched Romantic and formalist aesthetic values when she wrote in 1895: "With the exception of Henry James and Hawthorne, Poe is our only master of pure prose" (*Stories* 986). As the literary young lions of the turn of the century increasingly relegated Howells to the role of cultural whipping boy (even as they extended his practice of a socially responsible literature into the more overtly political territory of the social exposé), Cather had ample precedent for dismissing the looming presence of "the Dean" as a symbol of an outmoded and irrelevant artistic dead end. By the second decade of the twentieth century, the rapidity of social and artistic change had already transformed Howells's role from that of partisan spokesperson for a radical aesthetic movement to cultural icon for a moribund literary Establishment; the explicit topicality and polemic of the newly ascendant fictive exposé exceeded the terms of Howells's prescription for a socially engaged, ethically constructive literature. Yet the new fiction derived nonetheless from a literary ethos for which Howells had been the primary advocate, and his influence, if increasingly obscured by his waxing status as cultural icon, was nonetheless unavoidable for any writer of Cather's generation. Her early fiction in particular occupies significant common ground with Howells despite her pointed rejection of the writer and his aesthetic.

In fact, Cather's fiction during the period of her transition from journalism to literature (roughly 1911 through 1913) comprises the younger author's struggle to move toward the aesthetic delineated in these later essays by freeing the social subject matter and mimetic prose style that in key respects she shared with Howells from the expectations of social-ethical purpose that Howells's earlier aesthetic had assigned to them. Close attention to three of these works in particular—the apprentice-work short story entitled "Behind the Singer Tower" (1912) and Cather's first two novels, *Alexander's Bridge* (1912) and *O Pioneers!* (1913)—reveals a deliberately chosen trajectory away from the residual elements of the Howellsian model of public social-ethical mediation through literature and toward an aesthetic that emphatically opposed Howells's conception of literary purpose even as it pursued a homologous literary representation of subject matter. In these works, Cather seeks to purge a transparent, socially referential prose of its lingering valences of Howellsian social-ethical purpose, subordinating social reference to subjective experience and heroic idealism, and Realist mimesis to mythic resonance. Cather's progress toward her unique aesthetic in these early works constitutes a struggle against the powerful model of literary enterprise that was Howells's major legacy to the writers of the early twentieth century.[1]

Cather and Howells

As one might expect given the clear generational divide between the two writers, Willa Cather's personal involvements with William Dean Howells were slight. Unlike either Charles W. Chesnutt, whose brief but intense relationship with Howells was decisive in the development of his career, or Sarah Orne Jewett, who remained the object of Howells's periodic social visits to South Berwick long after their editor-author relationship was concluded, Cather seems to have seen Howells personally only twice. She and Howells both attended Mark Twain's seventieth birthday party in 1905, and she was present also at Howells's seventy-fifth birthday party in 1912. Both events were large, widely publicized celebrations designed in some measure to exploit the celebrants' literary celebrity as a means of promoting the publishing industry. Neither occasion, therefore, would have been likely to alter Cather's sense of Howells as person or as author, and no record exists of the two writers having met. Cather's attitude toward Howells was, at best, ambivalent. As the author of a large body of undeniably important writing and as the primary cultural symbol for American literature during the years of Cather's education, Howells commanded a certain respect as a monument to recent American literary history. But Cather, as an aspiring literary journalist first in Lincoln and Pittsburgh and ultimately in New York, confronted the dean of American letters with comments ranging from the lukewarm to the openly hostile. A favorable 1896 review of James Herne's *Shore Acres,* for instance, asserts that "It comes nearer than any other play to doing for New England life on the stage what Howells has done for it in fiction" but immediately undercuts the oblique compliment by claiming that the play "remind[s] one that realism is not absolutely a synonym for evil" (qtd. in Curtin 469, 470). Elsewhere, Cather refers to Howells as "mild though undoubtedly great" (qtd. in Curtin 115), yet that same year she limits his abilities in character creation to only "very common little men in sack coats" (qtd. in Slote 407). In her 1895 review of *My Literary Passions* she seems bitterly affronted that Howells should dare to write about literary loves that she herself shared, concluding cuttingly that " 'Passions,' literary or otherwise, were never Mr. Howells' forte" (qtd. in Curtin 259). Cather biographer James Woodress attests that Cather "probably was generalizing from Howells" (128) in writing that modern authors "are not large enough; they travel in small orbits; they play on muted strings. They sing neither of the combats of Atridae nor the labors of Cadmus, but of the tea table and the Odyssey of the Rialto" (qtd. in Woodress 129).

Ironically, the domestic "tea table" trope would twice reappear in contexts that paint Howells and Cather with the same brush: first in Frank Norris's famous denunciation of Howellsian Realism as "the drama of a broken teacup" (qtd. in Cady, *Realist* 219) and later in Lionel Trilling's savaging of Cather's "mystical concern with pots and pans" ("Cather" 155). But Cather's later fictional interest in the domestic derives not from its Howellsian value as ethically useful documentation of shared social experience but from its status as a symbolic language expressive of the ideal, mythic, and essentially subjective basis of reality. And just as the two writers' literary uses of the domestic radically differed so too did their understandings of the relations between journalism and literary fiction. Like Cather, Howells usually assumed a ready distinction between journalism and literature, but where Howells's conception of literary purposes sought to move literature onto a plane of everyday social and economic experience and into a realm of ethical purposes that it shared with the documentary journalism of social exposé, Cather vehemently and repeatedly rejected any such alliance. As editor of the *Atlantic,* Howells had after all introduced to a national audience (as chapter one notes) both the new fiction of commonplace social experience and some of the pioneering examples of political exposé, including for example Henry Demarest Lloyd's unmasking of the predatory Standard Oil monopoly. For Cather, this association of Realist fiction with socially and politically activist journalism constituted a forfeiture of any claim Realists such as Howells might make to the honorific status of literature. Progressive fiction's overstepping of the polemical limits with which even Howells was comfortable confirmed Cather's suspicions of any literature that could coexist peaceably with mere journalism. Her experiences as the managing editor of *McClure's Magazine,* a journal known for its muckraking efforts at social and political reform, reconfirmed the division in her mind between a Howellsian sense of social purposes, which she regarded as the rightful province of journalism, and true literature, whose purposes (as this chapter shall demonstrate) opposed those of journalism in almost every way. But despite the consistency of Cather's stated views on these matters, the three works of her career transition dealt with in this chapter reveal a writer who nevertheless had to work to achieve in fiction the anti-journalistic, anti-Realist, and anti-Howellsian aesthetic that she envisioned from early in her career.

Social Purpose and Romantic Idealism in "Behind the Singer Tower"

Within the Cather canon, "Behind the Singer Tower" demonstrates a closer connection to a Howellsian vision of literary purpose than does any other Cather work. In its employment of current events, its concern with class and ethnicity as modes of social knowledge, and its inclusion of an unmistakable element of social protest, the story is the exception that proves the rule of Cather's emerging anti-Howellsian aesthetic. Woodress identifies the tale as "the only fictional evidence in her canon that the social policies and contents of [McClure's] had filtered into her blood" (216). Likewise, Marilyn Arnold asserts that the story reflects "a social consciousness fully compatible with the editorial spirit of McClure's" (92), and Cather herself, in a letter accompanying the story's submission to the editor of the Century, labeled her tale "yellow" (qtd. in Woodress 215). Woodress suggests that Cather's story derives from accounts of "the infamous Triangle factory fire in Manhattan in 1911," noting that the story "was written while McClure's was running a series of articles on the appalling lack of fire escapes in New York's high-rise buildings" (216).[2]

Building upon such muckraking analogues, "Behind the Singer Tower" enacts a Howellsian intervention in public discussion of contemporary social and political concerns that attempts to promote constructive social reform by encouraging readers' sympathies with the victims of the twin disasters that the story recounts. Employing a framing device that allows Cather to document the responses of a representative group of New Yorkers in the wake of the second disaster, the story tells first of the immolation of the Mont Blanc Hotel and with it the deaths of more than three hundred hotel guests. Six city professionals—including a narrator who, significantly, is himself a journalist—float in a boat in New York Harbor the evening after the fire and discuss the event and its implications. The journalist-narrator employs a dense description of social and material facts that Cather's later writing would ruthlessly prune to their most concentrated and symbolically suggestive forms but that here are presented as valuable in and of themselves. The description of the quantities of expensive "upholstery and oiled wood" that helped this "complete expression of the New York idea in architecture" (44) go up in flames, the detailed de-

piction of the progress of the fire and its material effects ("foolish fire escapes in its court melted down"), and the story's registration of the fire's
cost in human lives and of its economic and social consequences all seem
more typical of Howellsian Realism than of Cather's signature aesthetic
values. "By morning," the journalist-narrator of the frame story tells us,
"half a dozen trusts had lost their presidents, two states had lost their gov-
ernors, and one of the great European powers had lost its ambassador. So
many businesses had been disorganized that Wall Street had shut down for
the day" (44). The narrator, under the palpable influence not only of the
McClure's fire-escape articles but of exposés of contemporary labor conditions, contextualizes the event in terms of other such "fires in fireproof
buildings." These, he notes, introducing issues of class that the internal
story will address more explicitly, "had occurred only in factory lofts" and
had resulted in the deaths of immigrant workers "obscure for more reasons
than one; most of them bore names unpronounceable to the American
tongue; many of them had no kinsmen, no history, no record anywhere"
(45). The event thrusts the city's residents, represented by the newspaper-
men, engineers, lawyer, and doctor aboard the boat the next evening, into
"a kind of stupor" (43) from the depths of which they—and with them the
story itself—contemplate the public and social significances of their shared
experience of the disaster.

The narrative's close attention to contemporary networks of social,
economic, and political interrelationship, and of public ethical implications, places the tale squarely in Howellsian aesthetic territory in ways that
are confirmed by the internal story that the journalist's narration frames.
Among the six passengers in the harbor is the engineer Fred Hallet, who
amplifies the relatively muted overtones of social protest in the frame with
his recitation of an earlier disaster at the Mont Blanc, with which he was
personally involved. Hallet, who had worked on the excavations for the
Mont Blanc's foundation when the hotel was built, recounts an equipment
failure that killed a number of immigrant laborers and that could have
been prevented by the project's chief engineer, Stanley Merryweather. Hallet tells of his brief friendship with an Italian immigrant laborer named
Caesaro, who is one of those killed when the cost-conscious supervising
engineer, despite Hallet's repeated urgings, refuses to authorize the replacement of worn cables on a crane. The cable eventually snaps, dropping a

fully loaded clamshell on six workers and crushing them to death. Hallet, whose stake in Caesaro's death has become both professional and personal, angrily confronts Merryweather and eventually takes it upon himself to begin legal action on behalf of Caesaro's family, ensuring that Caesaro receives proper burial and that the family receives full monetary compensation for his death. Cather's characterization of Hallet relies heavily on descriptive markers typical of Howellsian social Realism. The journalist-narrator of the tale's frame defines Hallet as an American social "type," whose personality is formed by the convergence of his memberships in particular social, ethnic, regional, and class niches. Cather contrasts the "intelligent" (47) Hallet, an Anglo-American of old and (by implication) Protestant Bostonian stock, with the "successful" (47), and Jewish, Merryweather. While the conscientious Hallet is "a soft man for the iron age," "always tripping over the string" attached "to every big contract in New York" (50), Merryweather is "the most successful manipulator of structural steel," along with business and politics, in the city (47). In every way, Merryweather is the social foil for Hallet's representation of the New England Anglo-American Protestant gentleman. Merryweather is the symbol of the new, rising, urban-industrial United States; he is "handsome and jolly and glitteringly frank and almost insultingly cordial, . . . quick and superficial, built for high speed and a light load" (47). He is the quintessential child of the advertising age, while Hallet brings to the story the moral consciousness and earnest concern figured in much cultural iconography as belonging to a lost, antebellum social order.[3]

As a narrator, Hallet is a surprisingly Howellsian voice to have proceeded from the pen of a writer who was barely tolerant of Howells's socially conscious aesthetic. In sharp contradistinction to Merryweather's unswerving pursuit of capitalist self-interest, Hallet's concerns center upon the social and ethical meanings of the unlikely friendship between a college-educated Anglo-American and an uneducated, Catholic, southern European manual laborer. Hallet's principled and cultured extension to Caesaro of his friendship and advocacy, which provides him with material for his narratorial speculations on the moral implications of contemporary cultural change, serves to move the tale toward apparent fulfillment of a Howellsian prescription for ethically purposeful social fiction. Hallet's rather unlikely personal connection with Caesaro humanizes the immigrant, working-class Other, demonstrating for a middle-class audience resembling Hallet and his fellow passengers more than Caesaro the possibility of a sympathetic, human connection across ethnic and class boundaries. Like any number of Howells's fictive ethical conjecturers, Hallet explicitly asks his listeners and Cather's readers to imagine themselves in the places of Caesaro and his fellows, and to ponder the ethical implications for their own social and political stances:

> Suppose we went to work for some great and powerful nation in Asia that had a civilization built on sciences we knew nothing of, as ours is built on physics and chemistry and higher mathematics; and suppose we knew that to these people we were absolutely meaningless as social beings, were waste to clean their engines, as Zablowski says; that we were there to do the dangerous work . . . and that these masters of ours were as indifferent to us individually as the Carthaginians were to their mercenaries? I'll tell you we'd guard the precious little spark of life with trembling hands. (49)

The voice is reminiscent of a long train of Howellsian middle-class moral commentators (including, as we have seen, Annie Kilburn, Reverend David Sewell, Elihu Emerance, and Elmer Kelwyn) who struggle uncomfortably for a sympathetic understanding of the Others that were upsetting existing social and political arrangements in contemporary America. Hallet's voice is the voice of the Howellsian conscience, and his retrospective assessment of the first Mont Blanc disaster merges with the tale's muckraking elements to guarantee both readerly sympathy for the victim and readerly outrage against the reckless arrogance of industrialists like Merryweather.[4] The story Cather tells through Hallet, in other words, is calculated to promote sympathy for the urban immigrant Other and lead to constructive social action by the frame tale's internal audience and by the published story's readership.

Clearly social-ethical literary purposes are nowhere else in Cather's oeuvre more evident than in this story, and yet the Howellsian thrust of "Behind the Singer Tower" uneasily coexists with a second, more prototypically Catherian set of aesthetic purposes that increasingly competes for control of the tale's thematic trajectory. The story's impact as social exposé is diluted by a persistent counteraction in the direction of romantic idealism.[5] More particularly, Cather's development of both Hallet and the story's major thematic thrust betrays a bifurcation in her intentions between a Howellsian sense of social-ethical aims and a new conception of literary purpose that transforms social materials into symbolic counters on a plane of suprasocial human idealism. Although the story's frame unfolds in detail the events and social meanings of the Mont Blanc fire, Cather deploys her fictive materials in such a way that their function as mediums of mood and atmosphere for both characters and readers initially predominates over their overtly social-ethical functions. Before any details are revealed, Cather's journalist-narrator inducts readers into the emotional aura that the events of the story have already created for the story's characters. The narrator and her companions are "all tired and unstrung and heartsick," relaxing their "tense nerves" into "a kind of stupor" (43) in the cool darkness of the bay. Although "there was probably no less activity than usual" in the harbor, writes the narrator, "to us, after what we had been seeing and hearing all day long, the place seemed unnaturally quiet and the night unnaturally black" (43). Gradually, the projection of the passengers' emotions upon the physical setting is transformed rhetorically into an emotional aura inherent in the physical setting. "There was a brooding mournfulness over the harbor," the journalist continues, "as if the ghost of helplessness and terror were abroad in the darkness. One felt a solemnity in the misty spring sky where only a few stars shone, pale and far apart, and in the sighs of the heavy black water that rolled up into the light" (43). As important as the facts and social significations of the hotel fire and the excavation disaster eventually prove to be, the frame's narration initially emphasizes not the social meanings of the story's content but its evocation of the subjective qualities of the experience for those involved in it.

Cather uses this emotional scene-setting as a platform from which to launch the story's second major thematic idea, which battles with the Howellsian impulse for control of the story. The frame introduces a "question" (43) about the cost, measured in human life, of the juggernaut of urbanization, with all its attendant social upheavals. The journalist writes:

The city itself, as we looked back at it, seemed enveloped in a tragic self-consciousness. Those incredible towers of stone and steel seemed, in the mist, to be grouped confusedly together, as if they were confronting each other with a question. They looked positively lonely, like the great trees left after a forest is cut away. One might fancy that the city was protesting, was asserting its helplessness, its irresponsibility for its physical conformation, for the direction it had taken. (44)

Hallet takes up this "question" again in closing the story. It gains no further definition in the course of the tale, yet its presence is palpable. The historical fact of New York City, with its array of looming skyscrapers, symbolizes teeming masses of human life existing in radically new and confusing patterns of social interrelationship, which the content of Hallet's narration will shortly proceed to delineate via one particularized, representative incident. But while the plot and character relationships of the story attempt to develop this theme in terms of Howellsian social-ethical complicity, Cather undercuts this scheme by simultaneously trying to develop the theme in ideal terms, transferring the significance of social relationships into a realm of romantic abstraction of human character and possibility. The result is something akin to Jewett's *Deephaven:* a narrative whose dual aesthetic impulses interfere with rather than reinforce each other.

In concluding his tale of Caesaro, Hallet passes seamlessly from description of the contrasting extremes of contemporary urban society—the metaphoric "cellar" and heights of the Mont Blanc (53)—to a refiguring of his subject matter in heroic terms that bypass the particularities of history and society. He has already shown an imaginative tendency in this direction by figuring contemporary industrial labor abuses in terms of classical antiquity ("the Carthaginians . . . [and] their mercenaries") and a hypothetical orientalism ("some great and powerful nation in Asia"). Now he takes a further step toward the obliteration of historical distance and difference. Viewing the city symbolically, from a cosmic distance, as it were, Hallet reflects that "Wherever there is the greatest output of energy, wherever the blind human race is exerting itself most furiously, there's bound to be tumult and disaster" (53). Abruptly shifting back to sociohistorical grounds, he wonders aloud what attracts men like Caesaro to the tumult, danger, and disaster of a place like New York. In answer to his own question he reverts to the plane of transhistorical human destiny, eliding the more mundane economic and political motives that brought most immigrants to the United States: surely all of this confusion, destruction, and death is but the necessary birth pangs of "something wonderful coming" (53). "What it will be is a new idea of some sort. That's all that ever comes, really. That's what we are all the slaves of, though we don't know it. . . . Even Merryweather—and that's where the gods have the laugh on him— every firm he crushes to the wall, every deal he puts through, every cocktail he pours down his throat, he does it in the service of this unborn Idea" (54). Marilyn Arnold argues that this final summation from Hallet caps a successful thematic integration of a "double thrust" (96) toward social commentary and an ideal explanation for social inequity. "The dream so nobly conceived" of the idealized city "sacrifices humanity to its realization, but out of that sacrifice can arise the phoenix of its justification" (96). Taking issue with Curtis Bradford, who emphasizes the story's socially purposive elements and thus finds in it Cather's rejection of the city and its enabling prop, the machine (546–47), Arnold argues that Hallet voices "some other human need" (96) that ultimately outweighs all considerations of individual human lives and historical relationship.

While Arnold rightly acknowledges the story's suggestion of a transhistorical "other human need" that parallels the story's sociohistorical depiction of the modern city, she overstates the degree to which Cather succeeds in integrating the two contrary impulses that comprise the tale's "double thrust." The pull toward the ideal in Hallet's comments conflicts with the logic of the social exposé that has driven his story until this point. The tale goes to great lengths to establish the culpability of Merryweather and his sort in the needless deaths of Caesaro and others like him; it takes pains to establish the preindustrial Anglo-American morality of Hallet against the racially tainted, dollar-driven amorality of a madly capitalizing American society; it builds its plot and themes from the Howellsian impulse toward publicly responsible representation of a broad swath of social subgroups. The logic of the tale of Hallet, Caesaro, and Merryweather dictates that the answer to the story's central question should drive home the case for some concrete political or social reform, or at least of a moral change of heart on the part of Hallet's own auditors. Instead, Hallet's final half-page of speculation attempts to resolve all such social and ethical issues by reverting to ideal terms that sidestep the social realities the story has worked so hard to document. According to Hallet's summation, everything that happens within the sociopolitical web of everyday historical existence—contrary to the logic of social consciousness that underlies the content of the tale itself—matters only in terms of the aggregate, timeless ideal of human endeavor that it signifies. Hallet thus erases the historical reality of thousands of individual, immigrant Caesaros, burying it beneath an essentialized Idea of the City that justifies their deaths as inevitable contributions to the creation of a symbol of collective human ideals and aspirations. The story's opposing investment in social-ethical purposes evaporates in a cloud of cosmic irony. The text's persistent dodging back and forth between social-ethical and idealistic interpretations of the story Hallet tells reflects Cather's own parallel efforts to make her story's social materials express ideal meanings that render historical details inconsequential. For Cather, working in this early fiction toward an aesthetic of her own, what matters ultimately in the myriad details of social history and material existence—as she would later indicate more explicitly in such quintessential aesthetic pronouncements as "The Novel Démeublé," "Escapism," and "Light on Adobe Walls"—is their potential to suggest something eternally valid and temporally transcendent about human experience.[6] "Behind the Singer Tower" offers a unique glimpse into a young writer still in the midst of transition not only from a career in journalism to a vocation as literary artist but also away from the residual gravitational pull of an older sense of literary purposes toward a pared-down use of socially referential prose in the service of an aesthetic of mythic idealization. The transition would continue in Cather's first novel, *Alexander's Bridge*.

Social Reference and Romantic Selfhood in *Alexander's Bridge*

Published the same year as "Behind the Singer Tower," Cather's first novel takes a giant step toward subordinating Howellsian influences to a narrative mode more typical of the novelist's fully developed aesthetic. In *Alexander's Bridge*, Cather attempts to transform the social exteriorities that a Howellsian model of literary enterprise would deploy as ethically purposive instruments into symbolic material for the expression of personal, interior realities on a heroic scale. Bartley Alexander is anything but a socially representative figure of quotidian American life; he is unambiguously constructed as a romantic hero, whose downfall gains significance and emotional impact not through its meanings for the society in which it occurs nor for its use-value in the day-to-day social-ethical dilemmas of its readers but through its emotional resonances with ideals of human possibility. The novel adopts topical materials that might easily have been treated in the socially purposeful ways that their analogues had been—albeit inconsistently—in "Behind the Singer Tower" and instead suppresses their potential uses along such Howellsian lines. Yet the vestiges of that older sense of literary purpose persist in subtler ways, particularly in the book's incomplete adjustment of a socially descriptive narrative prose to its central project of heroic idealization. Where "Singer Tower," however, founders on the mutual incompatibility of the two prongs of its thematic "double thrust," *Alexander's Bridge* succeeds in establishing a clear and consistent aesthetic intention but cannot consistently harness to its service the narrative tools Cather inherited from Howellsian social Realism. The lingering pull exerted by the example of Cather's literary forebears interferes with her ability to use socially referential prose to promote the kind of readerly identification with her romantically heroic central character that the novel pursues.

From its first chapter, the novel clearly signals its intended center: the internal drama of its heroic protagonist, the bridge builder Bartley Alexander. Cather draws Alexander as an embodiment of heroic ideals rather than the product of historical processes. His very name, as David Stouck points out, "deliberately evoke(s) images of conquest on an epic scale. . . . Like the archetypal hero of epic and romance, Alexander is self-engendered and self-sustaining" (*Imagination* 9, 13). Cather presents her hero virtually without a history or a social background other than his mythic identification with "the West." In chapter one, conversation between Alexander's wife and his former professor prepares us for the arrival of a larger-than-life figure who for the moment remains offstage. They speak of Alexander as "a natural force" (286), "a powerfully equipped nature" (287), a natural enigma with "the fascination of a scientific discovery" (287). He is impervious to the efforts of others to define him, but his sheer forcefulness demands their attention, absorption, admiration. To what Cather once called his "pagan . . . crude force" (qtd. in Woodress 218), the novelist attaches a profession calculated to enhance his heroic status, appropriating the heroic mystique associated with the figure of the engineer in the turn-of-the-century American imagination to suggest ideals of power, invention, and masculine creativity.[7] This field of symbolic associations encourages readers to experience the central character more as a volatile aggregation of heroic ideals than as a concrete, flesh-and-blood person in a socially constructed world. As Cecelia Tichi has argued (73–80), Cather's deployment of Alexander's profession shows virtually no interest in the mundane elements of actual engineering practice, emphasizing instead the engineer-hero's aura of quasi-mystical power and creativity. In keeping with the novel's heroic conception of its main character, the first chapter identifies the source of the hero's downfall, toward which the entire narrative progresses, as an internal fatal flaw rather than as the result of any particular sequence of historical causes and effects. "I always used to feel," Professor Wilson informs his former pupil, "that there was a weak spot where some day strain would tell. . . . The more dazzling the front you presented, the higher your façade rose, the more I expected to see a big crack zigzagging from top to bottom . . . then a crash and clouds of dust" (284). Wilson disclaims this vision by casting it in the past tense, but his words nevertheless reinforce Alexander's monumental characterization and foreshadow his demise in almost mythic terms. Whatever subsequently develops in the story of Alexander's life will transpire as the working out of the hero's innate and unavoidable fate rather than as an individual's negotiations with history and social experience. Unlike the typical Howells character, struggling through a world defined by imperfect and imperfectly understood social interactions and moral compromises, Alexander has no ethical choice but instead is subject only to his personally allotted heroic fate.

When Alexander himself appears, the internal perspective that rapidly follows upon the first chapter's external heroization of him reinforces Cather's focus upon the interior and the ideal and away from the social and historical. What appears from the outside as a natural force is from Alexander's own perspective an ineffable but powerful sense of his own essential selfhood:

He remembered how, when he was a little boy and his father called him in the morning, he used to leap from his bed into the full consciousness of himself. That consciousness was Life itself. Whatever took its place, action, reflection, the power of concentrated thought, were only functions of a mechanism useful to society; things that could be bought in the market. There was only one thing that had an absolute value for each individual, and it was just that original impulse, that internal heat, that feeling of one's self in one's own breast. (299)

Where a Howellsian conception of literature's public purposes depended on an idea of selfhood as the product of conditioned ethical choices occurring within a field of social experience, Catherian selfhood is presented here as a Platonic given, a pre-social, subjective self-consciousness as an irreducible "original impulse." The subjective self is made visible and accessible to other subjective selves through the external circumstances of social relationship, but the self precedes and informs social experience, rather than vice versa. For Cather, just as "any art [is] but an effort to make a sheath, a mould in which to imprison for a moment the shining, elusive element which is life itself,—life hurrying away past us and running away, too strong to stop, too sweet to lose" (Song 552), the essential selfhood of any individual is made visible by the "sheath" of social relationships and material expressions that manifest it imperfectly to others. All such externalities, therefore, are at best treacherous signs of the reality of an individual's life. Professor Wilson expresses this Catherian philosophy of selfhood when he states that "however one took [Alexander], however much one admired him, one had to admit that he simply wouldn't square" (286). The mysterious and subjective force of an individual's selfhood, particularly for a great soul like Alexander, cannot be fully or accurately expressed by its temporal manifestations. Social externalities are limitedly expressive but not constituent of one's selfhood, and thus the proper focus of the novel for novelist and for readers is Bartley Alexander's subjectivity and its resonance in terms of the human ideals that subjectivities share and that make people (fitfully) aware of each other. Cather thus inverts a Howellsian conception of the relationship between exterior and interior realities, granting the essential, individual soul full precedence over every social circumstance. In Alexander's Bridge, all social reality—a primary focus and an end in itself for Howellsian fiction—becomes material for the expression of Bartley Alexander's heroic selfhood. Alexander is first a principle, and he is a socially defined individual only for purposes of that principle's manifestation to other characters and to readers.

A character-centered novel like those of Howells, *Alexander's Bridge* is built upon an alternative sense of the nature and significance of selfhood that both constitutes an opposing conception of literary purpose and calls for a correspondingly altered use of narrative mimesis to communicate characters' realities to readers. To represent the drama of Alexander's fatally divided selfhood, Cather represents three major classes of social materials: general social description; depiction of the relationships between Alexander and his wife and between Alexander and his lover; and portrayal of Alexander's participation in his profession, the primary sign of which is the half-built and fatally flawed bridge that gives the novel its title. In each case, Cather tries to harness narration of social and material realities to her central purpose of heroic idealization. But in each case, the legacy of the Howellsian sense of literary instrumentality collides with Cather's romantic idealism to produce a split focus in the novel. Having abandoned Howellsian social-ethical purposes, Cather has yet to purge her novel of those elements of social documentation which, stripped of their Howellsian valences and having no corresponding purpose in Cather's new aesthetic schema, become merely extraneous. Despite her novel's clear indications of its counter-intention to Howellsian goals, the lingering presence of those goals in shared novelistic materials alternately produces two results: it prompts social description that does not serve the ends required by the novel's heroic design, and it causes Cather, in the effort to pare her narration down to its heroically suggestive essentials, to omit externalities that might actually help readers participate in Alexander's subjective drama.

A number of lengthy passages fall in the first category, describing social situations and introducing minor characters that digress from the primary task and contribute nothing to the establishment of Alexander's selfhood. When Alexander first arrives in London, for example, the purposes so clearly signaled in the first chapter require his reintroduction to Hilda Burgoyne, Alexander's once and future lover. Paired with his marriage, the reestablishment of his relationship with Hilda constitutes a major symbol of Alexander's fatally divided selfhood. But in pursuing this limited character-development task, the narrative digresses into details of the London theater scene and genteel society, a particular play and its audience, and a number of minor characters, none of which bears any integral relationship to the exposition of Alexander's soul. Cather introduces by turns a jabbering literary dabbler named Mainhall (who suggests Alexander's visit to the theater where Hilda is presently acting), a crusty playwright called MacConnell (who also is in love with Hilda), and an obligatory sample of the English nobility (Sir Harry Towne, and Lord and Lady Westmere). None of these characters helps us see Alexander more clearly. Their ostensible function is to move the engineer toward his lover and to establish her reputation as an actress and social star. But their narration, here and in the later party scenes, outstrips these modest functions as Cather is drawn to gratuitous flights of social description for its own sake. Within the context of Cather's romantic idealist aesthetics, clearly established in this novel by the symbolic centrality of Alexander himself, these passages and others like them are intrusive. Some of them, as David Daiches notes, are "memorable" in their own terms, but they are "not . . . properly associated with the emotional situation" they are meant to reinforce; they are "workman-like pieces . . . without any organic function" (11) within Alexander's internal drama. Such passages recur throughout the London portion of the book; they are never substantial enough to form a legitimate focus of attention in and of themselves, but they are too persistent and developed to be fully subordinated to Alexander's internal, ideal drama. Alexander himself is temporarily lost in the details of the social description the narrative employs to reveal him.

Another prime example of this narrative phenomenon occurs in the fourth chapter, when Alexander visits one of Hilda's Sunday afternoon gatherings and the novel spends two lengthy paragraphs in gratuitous description of the assembled guests. A representative excerpt will serve to establish the tenor of the whole passage:

> The editor of a monthly review came with his wife, and Lady Kildare, the Irish philanthropist, brought her young nephew, Robert Owen, who had come up from Oxford, and who was visibly excited and gratified by his first introduction to Miss Burgoyne. Hilda was very nice to him, and he sat on the edge of his chair, flushed with his

conversational efforts and moving his chin about nervously over his high collar. Sarah Frost, the novelist, came with her husband, a very genial and placid old scholar who had become slightly deranged upon the subject of the fourth dimension. On other matters he was perfectly rational and he was easy and pleasing in conversation. He looked very much like Agassiz, and his wife, in her old-fashioned black silk dress, overskirted and tight-sleeved, reminded Alexander of the early pictures of Mrs. Browning. (303)

Where Howells, for instance, would deploy such characters in order to develop their potential for social representation and ethical interrelatedness, Cather divorces their socially descriptive properties from their narrative function within the novel. None of these characters bears any relation to Alexander, whose soul is the novel's thematic raison d'être; none of them reappears in the novel. Yet Cather, operating under lingering Howellsian influences, cannot resist the impulse to introduce and describe them despite the fact that doing so does not serve her own aesthetic goals. The shadow of Howellsian literary purposes, with their understanding of human reality as fundamentally a matter of social and ethical interaction, sporadically entices Cather away from her mythic-heroic design and for no reason that helps us focus more clearly on the heroic figure she has established as the novel's center. The novelist herself later condemned her practice in *Alexander's Bridge,* attributing it to the Realist-descended prevalence of novels of the "drawing-room" filled with "smart people or clever people" ("Novels" 963–64). "My first novel was very like what painters call a studio picture. It was the result of meeting some interesting people in London. Like most young writers I thought a book should be made out of 'interesting material', and at that time I found the new more exciting than the familiar" ("Novels" 963). In eventually rejecting this approach, Cather wrote in the same essay, she was following advice she received from her publisher when he rejected her third novel, *The Song of the Lark,* on grounds of its overspecification of the social: "the full-blooded method, which told everything about everybody, was not natural to me and was not the one in which I would ever take satisfaction" (965).

Another variety of this inability to match social mimesis to mythic design prevails in the delineation of Alexander's relationship with Hilda Burgoyne in the novel's central chapters. Alexander's ruminations about Hilda delineate her function in his heroic struggle well before we meet her. She represents his lost youth, his sense of his own "original impulse," now falsified by the mundane routines of middle age and social convention. She is a standing reminder of that unified selfhood that he fears he has lost forever, and his love for her is identical to his longing for the subjective spark of his vanished sense of essential identity. The middle chapters detail their relations with each other rather exhaustively, as they meet repeatedly in London and New York and as Alexander gradually realizes that his lost integrity cannot be restored by means of a love affair. But beyond her ideal significance in the drama of Alexander's soul, Hilda has little to do in the novel, and the protracted attention the narrative grants to the dynamics of their relationship again bears no integral connection to Hilda's primary function as the expression of Alexander's character. Since Alexander's divided selfhood is a matter of internal preordination rather than social relationship and ethical choice, the romance Cather manufactures between the two lovers seems superfluous on every level but the symbolic. The external focus on their relationship, which occupies significant portions of six central chapters, distracts us from the heroic intention at the core of the novel by basing itself on a competing source of characterological significance. Cather's narrator must continually remind us, as it were manually, of the relationship's symbolic meaning in the hero's ideal drama. The overspecified details of Hilda and Alexander's outings and trysts are simply unnecessary to fulfillment of Hilda's announced symbolic significance in Alexander's interior drama.

Conversely, the novel's depiction of Alexander's wife, Winifred, who forms the other symbolic pole of the hero's divided self, manifests Cather's impulse away from Howellsian Realism and toward the interior drama of heroic ideals by causing the author to underspecify rather than overspecify social externalities. Both Hilda and Winifred function not primarily as characters in their own right but as expressions of Alexander's fatally divided soul; both are signs of his preexistent, internal disharmony rather than causes of his downfall. Just as the affair with Hilda expresses Alexander's longing for his youthful sense of self, his marriage to Winifred too has primary reference to his own internal economy and exists to express the dis-ease of his soul rather than to become an independent focus of attention. But where the overspecified narration of the Alexander-Hilda relationship distracted from its primary function, the underspecification of Alexander's marriage to Winifred prevents it, too, from fulfilling its function. The reader sees very little of either Winifred or her relationship with her husband over the course of the novel, and when Winifred does appear, she is narrated in abstract terms of her significance for Alexander's heroic stature that obliterate her independent existence as an individual character. In the first chapter, for example, Cather introduces Winifred not as a flesh-and-blood woman but as an emblematic great soul, whose symbolic stature is fully commensurate with her place beside the great engineer. Her appearance expresses her strength and purity of character in only the most general terms: her eyes are "like a glimpse of fine windy sky that may bring all sorts of weather" (281), and there is "the suggestion of stormy possibilities in the proud curve of her lip and nostril" (282). She is described impressionistically through Wilson's appraising eyes as he looks for clues to the mystery of Alexander's character, and so what little we learn of Winifred reflects ultimately on Alexander more than it does upon her. Her presence heralds the appearance of the great man whom she matches in sheer greatness of soul; she is present only to help establish the terms of her husband's mythic ideality. Even her conversation, despite Wilson's stated wish of "getting to know" her (281), almost exclusively concerns Alexander. Once this introduction is past, one scarcely hears of Winifred until she arrives at the scene of her husband's collapsed bridge to claim his body in the final chapter, when once again Cather deploys her inherent greatness of soul to reflect upon Alexander's heroic stature. As Wilson notes in the epilogue, "nothing can happen to her after Bartley" (351), and so she devotes herself to the perpetual preservation of his memory. "She never lets him go," Wilson continues. "It's the most beautiful and dignified sorrow I've ever known. . . . Its very completeness is a compensation. It gives her a fixed star to steer by. She doesn't drift. We sat there evening after evening in the quiet of that magically haunted room, and watched the sunset burn on the river, and felt him" (350). Winifred exists in the novel solely as a symbolic counter for her husband's greatness. Strikingly absent from her portraiture is any narration of the mundane details of relational interchange that comprise the daily reality of marriage. When the text does occasionally give us glimpses of Alexander and Winifred's marriage—most notably in the holiday scenes that follow closely upon the initiation of his affair with Hilda—they startle with their uncharacteristic concreteness, seeming out of harmony with the abstract schema that dominates the novel's presentation of the relationship elsewhere. The author's use of Winifred to further her portrait of Alexander overcompensates for the pull toward social specification that derails her narration of the Alexander-Hilda affair, relying almost exclusively on an abstract portraiture of ideals to substitute for mimetic representation.

The almost entirely opposed strategies of narrative representation that Cather employs for Hilda and for Winifred index the author's struggle to find the appropriate narrative means to her heroic-idealist aesthetic goals in *Alexander's Bridge*. Both approaches, however, succeed in resisting Howellsian practice and intent in at least one major respect: the two women symbolize the engineer's personal struggle virtually without reference to the ethical implications of Alexander's relationships to either of them. His infidelity has no significance in the novel except as an expression of a preexistent fatal flaw *in himself*. The text gives its readers no encouragement to scorn the "other woman" nor to pity the wronged wife, much less to grapple with the intricacies of Howellsian ethical decision-making. Instead the novel focuses attention on Alexander's lonely, doomed grappling with his own duality of soul, which is emphatically not a conflict of conscience but a struggle for reintegration of his fragmented selfhood on a plane of original ideality. Alexander is not an Annie Kilburn or a David Sewell, struggling with the ethical implications of their actions for others and for the society they collectively comprise; instead, he is a tragic hero whose fate is a matter not of moral choice but of an elemental "tragic flaw," purgation of which cannot be achieved by ethical choice and conscientious action but only by his death, the collapse of the flawed structure of his selfhood that Wilson had intuited in the novel's first chapter.

The third major material expression of Alexander's heroic selfhood occurs through his professional life and its most prominent sign, the cantilevered Moorlock bridge whose ambitious span and disastrous flaw symbolize, like his relationships with Winifred and Hilda, the divided interior life of its engineer. The choice of engineering as her hero's profession enables Cather not only to tap the heroic valences of a cultural archetype but also to add to them the further mystique of artistic creation.[8] Alexander's bridge-building is a figure of creative artistry on a monumental scale that matches his outsized soul. Winifred's description of her husband's first bridge, which is a mere dress rehearsal for the Moorlock bridge whose collapse ends the novel, is calculated to surround Alexander with an aura of high-Romantic heroic sublimity: "It is over the wildest river, with mists and clouds always battling about it, and it is as delicate as a cobweb hanging in the sky," a graceful yet sturdy material representation of the "force . . . that is the thing we all live upon. . . . the thing that takes us forward" (287) and that Alexander's acquaintances sense so strongly in him. But despite the fact that the Moorlock Bridge is "a spectacular undertaking" and "the most important piece of bridge-building going on in the world" (297), for Alexander it has become "the least satisfactory thing he had ever done" (298) because, like its predecessor, it expresses the current state of his soul, mirroring the same sense of lost selfhood that is expressed in his relationships with the women in his life. The midlife transformation of boundless creative energy into the mechanical drudgery of business as usual forms a large part of Alexander's dissatisfaction with himself; instead of being the ambitious and confident creator that he was in his youth, "the man who sat in his offices in Boston was only a powerful machine" (299), a drudge "being built alive into a social structure [he did not] care a rap about" (285). Alexander's work as an engineer, like the bridge itself, exists as a projection of himself, and its decline mirrors his own internal disintegration just as the bridge's final collapse symbolizes his fatally divided self.

Cather clearly invents the bridge that gives the novel its title as a primary symbol of her hero's mythic selfhood. But its effectiveness in that capacity suffers from her reluctance or inability to exploit the full descriptive and dramatic potential of Alexander's work, in very much the same way that the underspecification of Winifred undermined her symbolic function. The ideal schema of the novel and Cather's growing awareness of social Realism's inefficacy for fulfilling that schema prevent her from sufficiently narrating the artist-engineer's involvement with his work to involve her readers emotionally in its symbolic significance. The reader never sees the creative hero expressing his soul in the materials of art, and so his artistry is never completely realized. Despite the symbolic centrality of Alexander's profession and the bridge it produces, Cather must periodically step in to remind us that Alexander does indeed actively participate in his vocation. Chapter one, for instance, announces the existence of the half-completed

Moorlock Bridge and explains Alexander's intention to attend a sketchily defined "meeting of British engineers" (283) in London because the bridge is in the British Dominion of Canada. The ensuing three London chapters are devoted to Alexander's relationship to Hilda, with no mention of either the engineers' meeting or its significance for Alexander's project. Thereafter, all mention of Alexander's professional life occurs at the peripheries of the narrative: "Alexander was very busy," the narrator informs us. "He took a desk in the office of a Scotch engineering firm on Henrietta Street, and was at work almost constantly" (296–97). Later mentions of his professional duties proceed in similarly general, flat terms: "During the fortnight that Alexander was in London he drove himself hard. He got through a great deal of personal business and saw a great many men who were doing interesting things in his own profession" (325). Alexander's mentions of the Moorlock project itself are equally nondescript. He informs Wilson, for instance, that "the Moorlock Bridge is a continual anxiety" (312), but the passage adds nothing to Alexander's meditation in chapter one on the audacity of this engineering feat and its lack of meaning for him. The symbolic program of the novel intends Alexander's engagement in the work of his profession and in the building of this particular bridge to express his tragic-heroic character. But Cather's overcompensation for the lingering counter-pull of Howellsian intentions robs her of the opportunity to harness social description to anti-Realist goals. Cather does not allow the reader—as she would, for instance, in her depictions of the opera singer Thea Kronberg in *The Song of the Lark* and the pioneer Alexandra Bergson in *O Pioneers!*—to see firsthand the social and material expressions of Alexander's selfhood, making them visible extensions of character. So eager is she to make her novel cohere on a plane of romantic idealization that she shies away from fully appropriating the realm of social and historical reality to those aesthetic purposes for fear of losing them in the tide of lingering Howellsian influence.

And yet *Alexander's Bridge,* despite its revealing failures to adjust literary representation of the social to mythic-ideal purposes, does go far toward resisting Howells's call for a public, socially responsible fiction and appropriating its materials for her alternative aesthetic. The denouement of *Alexander's Bridge* draws upon Cather's recollection of the August 1907 collapse of the Quebec Bridge across the St. Lawrence, an episode ripe for treatment as a fictive social-ethical debate or industrial exposé. The disaster, which resulted from a combination of inferior materials, irresponsible management, and sheer bad luck (as telegraph messages between the site supervisor and the designing engineer miscarried) and which took the lives of more than eighty laborers and a supervising engineer, seems tailor-made for literary treatment as a socially conscious and ethically conscientious social novel. But Cather's strategic changes to the historical record in her fictionalization of the event indicate her resistance to the Howellsian pressure toward a socially and ethically purposive fiction. First, as already noted, Cather subordinates the bridge and its collapse to their significance in terms of the heroic ideality of Alexander's internal struggle rather than of social interdependencies and their ethical implications. "This is not the story of a bridge and how it was built," Cather told the New York *Sun,* "but of a man who built bridges" (qtd. in Woodress 218), and so she relegates narration of the inevitably collective activity of bridge-building itself to a bare handful of paragraphs in the novel's final chapter. Second, Cather alters the Quebec Bridge events to suppress any lingering valences of muckraking content or Howellsian ethical intent. Where contemporary journalistic reports of the disaster and the ensuing inquiry by a Canadian Royal Commission dwelt at length on the contributing causes and ended by placing blame squarely upon Alexander's historical analogue, Cather's account downplays both the material causes of the Moorlock collapse and the readerly impulse to understand these events in terms of Alexander's moral culpability.

A number of critics have faulted the novel's use of the bridge disaster as inadequately causally connected to Alexander's conflicts and actions. David Daiches argues, for instance, that Alexander's death along with his bridge's collapse represents "no real resolution" (10) of the conflicts that they symbolize. Edward Wagenknecht concurs (developing an argument originally propounded by Raymond Thornberg), asserting that Cather's use of the Moorlock Bridge as a symbol of Alexander's "moral collapse" is "the weakest" (*Cather* 67) aspect of the novel because it inadequately establishes Alexander's professional responsibility for the bridge's collapse. Similarly, a contemporary review by H. L. Mencken, reading the novel simplistically as the story of a man "torn hopelessly between a genuine affection for his wife . . . and a wild passion for his old flame," accordingly denounces the bridge collapse as "a mere evasion of the problem" (96). Such readings respond to the residual double-focus in Cather's novel, privileging the novel's inconsistently executed social-historical representations despite cues to read the work as a drama of heroic ideals rather than as social fiction. But, as is the case in the hero's relationships to his wife and lover, the collapse of Alexander's bridge is the external representation of his fatally flawed character rather than an example of ethical failure. Cather works in her narration of the bridge disaster to move our consideration of events away from a framework emphasizing ethical decision-making and temporal consequences. Even though the bridge expresses Alexander's divided selfhood, the novel minimizes the taint of negligence that might thereby attach to Alexander's heroic soul by transferring it, in a textual transaction that occupies only a few scattered lines, to an engineering assistant who observes the signs of structural stress but neglects to halt construction promptly. The scapegoat's possible culpability and remorse are presented as wholly incidental to the real significance of the event as the climax of Alexander's tragedy. The historical material from which Cather builds her novel is closely akin to that from which she had created "Behind the Singer Tower," but in *Alexander's Bridge* she goes further toward subordinating these potentialities to her own emergent aesthetic design.[9]

Cather's first novel successfully suppresses those elements of her fictional materials that would most readily lend themselves to social-ethical treatment under a Howellsian sense of literary purpose, subordinating them to her own mythic idealization of her hero's internal struggle. The lingering influence of Howellsian Realism, however, causes her to vacillate between social over- and underspecification, giving *Alexander's Bridge* its curious double-focus. Having gone so far toward purging her fiction of overt social-ethical purpose, Cather had yet to fully implement a viable mode of harnessing the representations of social materials to altered and decidedly un-Howellsian literary purposes. While the leftover literary tools of Howellsian Realism lend themselves to a literature that promotes encounter on a social plane shared by reader, author, and characters, *Alexander's Bridge* struggles with only partial success to involve its audience in the life of its central character on the basis of an altered conception of selfhood and on an intersubjective plane of shared archetypes. Cather's second novel, *O Pioneers!*, would move decisively toward full resolution of the tension between a Howellsian sense of literary goals and an aesthetic that rejects any such idea of public purpose in favor of what Cather biographer E. K. Brown has called a "vision of essences" (258).

The Idealization of Social History in *O Pioneers!*

Jewett, Regionalism, and Cather's Aesthetics

The title of Cather's second novel, which invokes images of the late-nineteenth-century Euroamerican settlement of the American West, invites the sort of reading that for decades kept Cather pigeonholed in the literary historical category of prairie regionalist. Many of the book's early reviews settled upon its supposed portraiture of Plains life before the official closing of the frontier as the central strength and purpose of the novel. A July 1913 New York *Herald Tribune* article, for instance, praised Cather in terms reminiscent of those that Howells had used in praise of an earlier generation of regional Realists: "With a steady hand this author holds up the mirror of fiction to a people of our land little, if at all, seen therein before: the Scandinavian and Bohemian pioneers. . . . In her clear smooth glass, we see these Old World pioneers adapting themselves to new conditions, identifying themselves with the prairie soil and becoming a voice in our national life" (qtd. in Stouck, "Historical" 296). The terms of the reviewer's praise are staunchly mimetic, valuing Cather's novel primarily for the window it provides upon a hitherto unrepresented regional subculture for a curious national audience. While the article does not explicitly invoke the ethical dimension of Howells's aesthetic, it nevertheless adheres to Realist assumptions about the purpose and mode of literary representation of social-historical materials. As the Hanover, Nebraska, of *O Pioneers!* was succeeded in Cather's next novels by Moonstone, Colorado, and by Black Hawk, Frankfort, and Sweet Water, Nebraska, critics found it progressively easier to relegate Cather and her work to the ever-declining status of regionalism, ignoring the generically atypical mode of its aesthetic engagement with the social history of the Plains. As Jo Ann Middleton notes, amplifying comments by Bernice Slote and Edward Wagenknecht, "The designation of regional writer, coupled with a deceptive simplicity of style, served to relegate Cather to a relatively minor role" (20) in American literary history. Similarly, Wagenknecht writes that once "Cather had firmly placed Nebraska on the American literary map with *O Pioneers!* and *My Antonia,* it became so easy to think of her as a 'regional' writer that some readers were even disappointed in some of her later books because they did not deal with her 'own' material" (*Cather* 16). Yet, as Bernice Slote has argued, "In one sense Willa Cather was not at all a regional writer. . . . She was not interested in showing a region, in demonstrating individual differences or local color, but she used regional materials because they were her deepest emotional resources" (7) and, I will argue, because they provided her with usable material for the enactment of the mythic-idealist aesthetic toward which we have seen her working in both "Behind the Singer Tower" and *Alexander's Bridge.* Reading the first of Cather's prairie novels as the culmination of her progressive struggle against the literary inheritance of Howellsian aesthetic values uncovers the particular means she used to turn the social Realist's literary materials to decisively anti-Realist aesthetic purposes. It also reveals the sources of her novels' continued power to convince readers of their historical verisimilitude even as they pursue aesthetic goals that rank accurate social representation exceptionally low on the scale of literary value.

   O Pioneers! constitutes Cather's first fully successful embodiment of an aesthetic, many of whose key assumptions are already apparent in the transitional works previously considered, that would remain remarkably consistent in its root values over the rest of her career. A brief rehearsal of the author's later expressions of her principles of literary art in her essays on aesthetics should prove useful in understanding Cather's resolution in her second novel of inherent tensions with Howellsian aesthetics. The earliest of Cather's important aesthetic documents is the essay entitled "The Novel Démeublé," which explicitly denounces the "over-furnished" (834) nature of most modern fiction. Particularly in light of the parallel self-condemnation of her practice of "building . . . external stories" ("Preface" 941) in *Alexander's Bridge,* the literary principle of "unfurnishing" the novel expressed in "The Novel Démeublé" indicates clearly the new aesthetic approach she adopted in her next novel. Ranking the writer's powers of "observation" and "description" as "a low part of his equipment" (834), Cather argues that a truer realism consists not of the cataloguing of social and material objects and explanation of their interrelationships—not in "mere verisimilitude" (836)—but in simplification of fiction's "material in-

vestiture" (836) to the bare minimum necessary to communicate "the emotional aura of the fact or the thing or the deed" (837). Citing Balzac's
densely and voluminously descriptive prose as an example, she writes: "In
exactly so far as he succeeded in pouring out on his pages that mass of brick
and mortar and furniture and proceedings in bankruptcy, in exactly so far
he defeated his end. The things by which he still lives, the types of greed
and avarice and ambition and vanity and lost innocence of heart which he
created—are as vital today as they were then. But their material surround-
ings, upon which he expended such labour and pains . . . the eye glides
over them" (835). Novelists, unlike journalists, she continues, should not
merely document the world but should instead "interpret imaginatively the
material and social investiture of their characters; to present their scene
by suggestion rather than by enumeration" (836). Similarly, Cather had
written two years earlier in "On the Art of Fiction" that the "dazzling
journalistic successes" of the turn-of-the-century Realist novel "were really
nothing more than lively pieces of reporting" whose "sharp photographic
detail" (939) might have been momentarily gratifying but contributed
little to the true aims of art. "Art, it seems to me, should simplify. That,
indeed, is very nearly the whole of the higher artistic process" (939).
Cather's oft-repeated admonitions to simplify literary representation of social material and to maintain a strict line of demarcation between the purposes of the journalist and of the novelist were to gain an explicit denunciation of literary ethical purpose when Cather revisited the issue in 1936,
under pressure from Depression-era Left critics: "When the world is in a
bad way, we are told, it is the business of the composer and the poet to
devote himself to propaganda and fan the flames of indignation. But the
world has a habit of being in a bad way from time to time, and art has
never contributed anything to help matters" ("Escapism" 968). The novelist's proper approach to social injustice, she continues, is through provision
of deep access to individual human suffering, not through journalistic exposé or political tract. The novelist cannot be held accountable to the
ephemeral concerns of social and political ethics; instead, literary art depends on the writer's "freedom" from any and all "considerations and purposes which have nothing to do with spontaneous invention" (972). The
sources of power of literary art are ideal and emotive rather than material
and documentary: "Religion and art spring from the same root and are

close kin. Economics and art are strangers" (972), and "Industrial life has to work out its own problems" (969) without the inept aid of literature. Such pronouncements, spanning the two decades after publication of *O Pioneers!*, not only make explicit the rejection of a Howellsian social-ethical aesthetic that we have already seen displayed in Cather's transitional writing, but they also provide a useful conceptual matrix for understanding her aesthetic transformation of Realist social materials into the alternative aesthetic of her second novel.

During the years immediately preceding Cather's full-time dedication to her literary career, she received early confirmation of these anti-Howellsian aesthetic tendencies from a source that at first glance defies expectation: Sarah Orne Jewett. Jewett's friendship with and mentorship of Cather were brief but intense. The two women met in 1908 at the home of Annie Fields, Jewett's longtime friend and companion and a fixture of New England cultural life, while Cather was on long-term assignment in Boston for *McClure's*. Cather became a frequent visitor and correspondent, and Jewett became a valuable source of criticism and encouragement as the younger writer published her early short fiction and contemplated a career change. Jewett died a little more than a year after Cather met her but not before imparting to her two clusters of valuable advice. The first of these, surprisingly, counseled Cather in approved Realist fashion to write from firsthand experience of what she knew—in short, to write from the powers of observation and description that Cather would come to rate so low: "I want you to be surer of your backgrounds,—you have your Nebraska life,—a child's Virginia, and now an intimate knowledge of what we are pleased to call the 'Bohemia' of newspaper and magazine-office life. These are uncommon equipment" (*Letters* 248). The second element of Jewett's advice, however, pertained not to the fictionist's choice of literary material but to much more subjective decisions concerning the emotionally evocative qualities, for both author and audience, of the writer's treatment of her subject matter. Jewett counseled Cather to write not only from personal experience but from her own highly individual sense of emotional comfort with her creativity and a sense of spiritual connection with a transhistorically conceived audience: "You need to dream your dreams and go on to new and more shining ideals, to be aware of 'the gleam' and to follow it," finding "your own quiet centre of life" from which to write; "in short, you must write to the human heart, the great consciousness that all humanity goes to make up" (249).

It is the Swedenborgian aspect of Jewett's aesthetic, then, rather than its Howellsian social-ethical elements, to which Cather responded. She found even in Jewett's counsel to write what she knew not primarily a nudge in the direction of particular sets of social material waiting for her literary transcription but a hint that the delicate emotive evocations at which true art aimed would be best served by those essentials of Cather's personal experience in which she was most fully invested emotionally. Significantly, while Cather's next novels turned, as Jewett had counseled, to her "Nebraska life," and while her late novel, *Sapphira and the Slave Girl*, would make use of her early childhood experiences in western Virginia, Cather left her knowledge of the magazine office untapped as an artistic source, presumably because of the (for her) decidedly unartistic taint of journalism attached thereto. When Cather eventually came to write her impressions of Jewett, her fiction, and her literary advice, she identified as the essence of Jewett's achievement—and as the importance of Jewett for her own aesthetic development—only the most subjective, evocative, emotional aspects of the older writer's regionalism, pointedly ignoring its participation in a Howellsian aesthetic of cross-cultural mediation for social-ethical purposes. "The thing that teases the mind over and over for years," Cather quoted Jewett, "and at last gets itself put down rightly on paper—whether little or great, it belongs to Literature" ("Jewett" 849). Jewett's literary achievement, Cather asserts, arose from "her love of the Maine country and seacoast [which] was the supreme happiness of her life" (853). But her fiction succeeds not on the basis of accurate local documentation or social mediation; instead "Her stories were but reflections, quite incidental, of that peculiar and intensely personal pleasure" (853). To the extent that readers respond to Jewett's art, they are apprehending the author's "very personal quality of perception" (857) and emotion rather than its "material and social investiture" in the incidental details of Maine coastal life. Cather's version of Jewett subordinates all regionalist detail, and with it all lingering sense of Howellsian social purposes, to aesthetic ends that privilege the subjective, emotional evocation of a shared sense of ideality as the true basis of reality and as the proper province of literary art.[10]

Acting upon her understanding of Jewett's advice and example, in *O*

Pioneers! Cather turned simultaneously toward the subject matter provided her by a childhood and youth spent on the Divide and away from the lingering impulse to treat such social materials in accordance with a Howellsian aesthetic. She conducted her campaign on three interrelated fronts: the heroic portraiture of essential selfhood in Alexandra Bergson, the mimetic subordination of social-historical subject matter to a mythic-ideal conception of its ontological basis, and the abandonment of linear plot and narration in favor of a radically mythic-idealist narrative form.

The Material Investiture of Self and Society

As she had in her portraiture of Bartley Alexander, Cather reveals Alexandra Bergson's essential selfhood via its "material investiture" in the social, historical, and physical actualities of late-nineteenth-century life on the Great Plains. But where the earlier novel had attempted to express the greatness of Alexander's soul by inserting him as a heroic archetype into a narrative otherwise controlled by a social-Realist narrative logic, *O Pioneers!* succeeds in making its narration of Alexandra's relationships to her family, neighbors, and—above all—to the land fully serve the novel's heroic idealist purposes. Where Alexander's embodiment, through the details of his professional practice, his bridge-building, and his relationships with his wife and his lover, had been by turns under- and overspecified so that the novel's social descriptions took on a distracting life of their own, Alexandra Bergson and the instruments of her material investiture are mutually commensurate and seamlessly fused to one another.

This fusion is particularly evident in the novel's construction of Alexandra's relationship with the land. She alone among the book's major characters has the inherent capacity to fully divine the "enigma" (148) of the wild prairie that none of the settlers has yet learned to farm successfully. "It was like a horse that no one knows how to break to harness, that runs wild and kicks things to pieces" (148). Her unique vision of the land respects its essential power and mystery while envisioning its potential for productive human cultivation in harmony with, rather than in opposition to, its inherent qualities. In fact, this essential matching of her nature with that of the land enables both of them, as it were, to give themselves to each other. As Alexandra recommits herself to the family farm after having briefly considered selling out because of an ongoing drought, the novel portrays the event in terms of this mythic union of woman with land: "For the first time, perhaps, since that land emerged from the waters of geologic ages, a human face was set toward it with love and yearning. It seemed beautiful to her, rich and strong and glorious. Her eyes drank in the breadth of it, until her tears blinded her. Then the Genius of the Divide, the great, free spirit which breathes across it, must have bent lower than it ever bent to a human will before. The history of every country begins in the heart of a man or a woman" (170). The history to which the passage refers is the incidental expression of this ideal melding of nature with human will rather than the product of social and political events. Alexandra transforms "The Wild Land" of the novel's first section to the "Neighboring Fields" of section two as an expression of her "faith" (170) in the land rather than a pursuit of material gain. While she does indeed have a secure grasp of the economics of farming—she, rather than her brothers, has the intelligence to "tell about what it had cost to fatten each steer, and . . . guess the weight of a hog before it went on the scales" (149)—her real investment in the land is an imaginative involvement of herself with the ideal of cultivation rather than a pursuit of monetary or social success.[11] She is gifted with the imagination of Cather's archetypal pioneer, which confers the capacity "to enjoy the idea of things more than the things themselves" (161)—an imaginative capacity that echoes Cather's aesthetic values. Her mind is "slow, truthful, steadfast" (168) like the land itself, with no trace of the mere "cleverness" (168)—a consistently derogatory term in Cather's critical writing—that sees in the land only an opportunity for financial speculation. "It was because she had so much personality to put into her enterprises," the narrator tells us, "and succeeded in putting it into them so completely, that her affairs prospered better than those of her neighbors" (237). Where Bartley Alexander's character had sought expression in things smaller than himself, Alexandra's heroic ideality and the mythic essence of the land are mutually expressive; when Alexandra is most herself, the boundary between her identity and the spirit of the earth virtually disappears so that the land and its closest human associate share a single identity. In the wake of the epiphany that closes the book's first section, she "felt as if her heart were hiding down there, somewhere, with the quail and the plover and all the little wild things that crooned or buzzed in the sun. Un-

der the long shaggy ridges, she felt the future stirring" (173). Cather constructs Alexandra's selfhood via its material investiture not in the physical
landscape but in the already humanly idealized conception of the land; her
selfhood is built on mythic foundations.

Lesser souls, too, are understood in *O Pioneers!* as essential selves rather
than as the products of historical circumstance, and they, too, are made
manifest through, rather than constituted by, social and material appearances. But where Alexandra's great soul required expression by nothing less
immense than the life force of the earth, the selves of smaller persons like
her brothers are expressed in the ephemeralities of passing social relationships, economic exchanges, and politics; their expressibility in such paltry
materials is a primary index of their inherent smallness. Cather describes
the brothers' essential characteristics early in the novel, and the changes
they undergo as they age are mere variations on the limited set of innate
themes of personality with which they were born. While Alexandra's heroic
selfhood compels her to merge with the prairie in a mythic expression of
the idea of culture, Lou and Oscar remain constitutionally unable to participate in their sister's prophetic vision. When in time of drought she proposes bucking conventional wisdom and buying more land instead of selling out, they resist on grounds that have as much to do with fear of their
neighbors' opinions as they do with economic analysis. In fact, whenever
Alexandra innovates in pursuit of her vision—proposing to build a silo
instead of a conventional barn, to replace the pigsty with a field and a
shelter, to plant wheat instead of the usual corn—Lou and Oscar blindly
resist for fear of being seen as fools. As a young man, Oscar is "as indolent
of mind as he was unsparing of his body," hardworking but subject to a
"love of routine [that] amounted to a vice" and to a stolid persistence in
"always doing the same thing over in the same way, regardless of whether
it was best or no" (165). His prosperity in later life changes him not one
jot: he remains radically suspicious of change and devoted to conformity,
and he has grown wealthy through sheer physical determination, on the
coattails of his sister's vision. Similarly, Lou begins life "fussy and flighty"
(165), frenetically active but unfocused in his actions, flitting from one
uncompleted farm task to another with no clear sense of priority. In midlife these native traits find their "natural field" in politics, and Lou accordingly "neglects his farm to attend conventions and to run for county

offices" and gains a neighborhood reputation for being "tricky" (185). Neither brother is a mere allegorical representation of the human character traits they bear; both are individualized, realized characters. But their individuated characteristics are nonetheless subordinate to the innate qualities that make them who they are and that are unchangeable by external forces of social and historical change or ethical choice. They do not change or develop; by midlife "they have simply, as Alexandra said of them long ago, grown to be more and more like themselves" (185). To read them aright, one must read through temporal appearances to the essential qualities of selfhood that they convey. If Cather's representation of their selfhood tends toward expression through its material investiture in mundane social and economic transactions, it does so only because Lou and Oscar's souls, in stark contrast to Alexandra's, are petty enough to be so expressed.

Similar principles govern the novel's representations of regional history and society. Cather strategically elides, for instance, all narration of the decades of hard work—the physical labor, the deeds and mortgages, the materials and invoices and daily decisions—that bring Alexandra's vision in "The Wild Land" into fruition as the accomplished fact of "Neighboring Fields." If one reads the novel, as many readers have, as social history, this narrative elision appears to be a serious artistic failing. A contemporary review by Frederick Taber Cooper, for instance, reads *O Pioneers!* as a "history of the conquest of prairie land" (112) and accordingly faults Cather's omission. "Now, the story of how Alexandra fought her battle and won it," Cooper writes, "might have been well worth the telling; but this is precisely the part of her history which Miss Cather has neglected to chronicle. Instead, she has passed over it in leaps and bounds, and when we once more meet Alexandra, it is in the midst of prosperity, with all her brothers save the youngest happily married, her land increased by hundreds of acres, all yielding fabulous harvests, and Alexandra herself on the threshold of her fortieth year" (112). The slightly derisive tone of Cooper's description of the miraculous changes that have been wrought on the Bergson farm during the decades between the novel's first two sections has its roots in readerly expectations that derive from Realist purposes and conventions: Cooper, along with numbers of critics and readers following him, expects linear narration and dense description of the actual mechanisms by which first-generation settlers turned prairies into farm fields—literary representation via what Cather called the "full-blooded method, which told everything about everybody" ("Novels" 965). But Cather's mythic history of Alexandra Bergson and the prairie has very little to do with the socio-historical processes by which Alexandra's vision has come to material expression, except as they reveal her soul in communion with the humanized ideal of the land. The narrative movement directly from visionary ideal to accomplished reality demonstrates Cather's paring away of all matters of historical process and progress as mere excrescences of the mythic reality of her chosen subject matter, ephemeral manifestations of the ideal that Alexandra and the land together symbolize. When the narrative turns in the early chapters of "Neighboring Fields" to description of the accomplished artifact of Alexandra's vision in the Bergson farmstead, it does so sparingly, deploying selected instances of material and social reality as signs of transhistorical reality rooted in the ideal. Unimportant in and of themselves, the particulars of the farm gain significance only because in them "*you feel* again the order and fine arrangement" that they materially express; "*You feel* that, properly, Alexandra's house is the big out-of-doors, and that it is in the soil that she expresses herself best" (178, emphasis mine). The meaning of temporal events and objects, in other words, resides in the reader's emotional apprehension of their mythic connectivity with the heroic properties of Alexandra's soul, not in their status as historic actualities.[12]

In her narration of Plains farm and village society, too, Cather employs the objects of social representation that constituted the core of Howellsian literary content and purpose to strikingly contrary ends, as temporal symbols of transhistorical realities rather than as primary loci of meaning in and of themselves. These aesthetic purposes, despite the vivid impressions of regional reality to which they lead, have virtually nothing to do with making Nebraska farm culture known to outside readers via Howellsian social mediation, nor with chronicling the history of pioneer settlement of the western frontier, nor do they call for an explicitly ethical response from readers. Instead, Cather's novel makes regional history serve literary purposes that proceed from an alternative vision of the relation of selfhood to society and history and that call for a concomitant shift in readers' involvement with literary representation. To the extent that local society constitutes a center of attention for the novel at all, it does so in emblematic rather than historical terms. The novel depicts individuals and their actions as signs of the essential qualities of the life of the people as a group, as David Stouck notes, directing our attention "in the epic manner" by "continual reference to people in the background" toward "the activities of a whole people" (*Imagination* 25). Local society is thus presented as a collective entity defined by the aggregate expression of the group's innate and informing qualities, just as individuals manifest their essential selfhood in social and material terms. Chapter one, for example, describes a gathering of farmers and their wives in the Hanover general store in terms that studiously avoid the individuated descriptions that had derailed the intended function of Cather's London scenes in *Alexander's Bridge*. Here, Cather makes her readers view the details of village life from the middle distance, emphasizing the "groupness" of the farmers' actions as momentary revelations of the informing spirit of the *volk* rather than as examples of a subcultural Other that are sociologically interesting in their own right. The novel creates our impression of the farm people gathered in the store by revealing glimpses of disarticulated light, motion, and speech rather than by constructing a more inclusive and linear descriptive architecture more typical of Realism. References to "rough-looking countrymen in coarse overcoats, with their long caps pulled down to their noses" (139), to "a red or a plaid shawl flash[ing] out of one store into the shelter of another" (139), to "farm people . . . checking over their groceries and pinning their big red shawls about their heads" (144), to "three big Bohemians . . . drinking raw alcohol, tinctured with oil of cinnamon" (144) occur in widely dispersed, almost random patterns. The shoppers are revealed neither as individuals nor as representatives of the various social categories to which they belong but instead are referenced momentarily by gender, nationality, occupation, activity, or appearance to suggest the aggregate qualities of the group rather than to delineate its constituent parts.

A similar representational strategy prevails in the often discussed vignette of the French horsemen in "The White Mulberry Tree" section of the novel. The passage narrates a procession of young men from the settlement called Sainte-Agnes as they ride to meet the bishop, who is traveling from Hanover to conduct a service of confirmation in the French Catholic church, which is scheduled to occur as the villagers simultaneously mourn the death of one of their fellows. Unlike the description of the Hanover farmers, this passage is presented as a set piece:

> When the word was given to mount, the young men rode at a walk out of the village; but once out among the wheatfields in the morning sun, their horses and their own youth got the better of them. A wave of zeal and fiery enthusiasm swept over them. They longed for a Jerusalem to deliver. The thud of their galloping hoofs interrupted many a country breakfast and brought many a woman and child to the door of the farmhouses as they passed. Five miles east of Sainte-Agnes they met the bishop in his open carriage, attended by two priests. Like one man the boys swung off their hats in a broad salute, and bowed their heads as the handsome old man lifted his two fingers in the Episcopal blessing. The horsemen closed about the carriage like a guard, and whenever a restless horse broke from control and shot down the road ahead of the body, the bishop laughed and rubbed his plump hands together. "What fine boys!" he said to his priests. "The Church still has her cavalry."
>
> As the troop swept past the graveyard half a mile east of the town,—the first frame church of the parish had stood there,—old Pierre Séguin was already out with his pick and spade, digging Amédée's grave. He knelt and uncovered as the bishop passed. The boys with one accord looked away from old Pierre to the red church on the hill, with the gold cross flaming on its steeple. (262–63)

At first glance, the passage appears to be a socially representative description of local cultural practice. But closer attention to the descriptive technique reveals a contrary set of aesthetic purposes. The passage emphasizes the group rather than its constitutive individuals, describing the movement of the troop of horsemen across the plain as symbolic spectacle. Visual and temporal details are subordinated to their collective emotional effects on the scene's witnesses; the reactions of the farm women and children and of the bishop himself to the passing procession serve as guides to readers' emotive responses, and the insertion of the solitary figure of the grave digger points to the symbolic significance of the pageant in terms of the eternal interrelation of life with death. The passage subordinates regional and historical specificity—its status as description of a turn-of-the-century temporal reality that is Nebraskan, French, and Catholic—to its evocation of a feeling of participation in a sort of group soul. The life of the group evoked by description of these particular moments in time in turn evokes a transhistorical reality that transcends even the boundaries of the particular culture. Just as the individual artifacts and activities of a culture comprise the material investiture of the collective soul of its people, the culture as a whole is but the temporal expression of an eternal and universal human reality. To read Cather's literary representation of social and historical realities as they want to be read is to enter into a shared feeling, an intersubjective apprehension of an order of reality that ontologically precedes any particular material expression of itself.

The formal innovation of *O Pioneers!* also occurs on this plane of shared emotional participation in mythic ideals, so clearly indebted to the example of Jewett. The cumulative absences of any unifying plotline or consistently linear narration or a program of social mediation in the novel have led critics from the first to question its formal and conceptual unity. Cather's friend Elizabeth Sergeant, for example, the novel's first, prepublication reader, noted its lack of a "sharp skeleton" (97), an observation with which Cather partly seems to have agreed. More recently, Phyllis Rose writes: "If you approach *O Pioneers!* as a naturalistic account of the conquest of new land, four-fifths of the book is anticlimactic, even irrelevant, and you must wonder why the story of the adulterous love of Emil Bergson and Marie Shabata and their murder by her jealous husband is taking up so much space in a book about pioneers" (126). As Rose's comment suggests, the perception of disunity stems both from the earlier noted narrative elision of the process by which Alexandra settles the prairie and from the presence of two major subplots that bear no obvious relationship to each other, at least in terms of story per se. The latter disharmony arises in part from the book's genesis as two independent texts: one entitled "Alexandra" and concerned primarily with its eponymous heroine, and the other entitled "The White Mulberry Tree" and recounting Emil and Marie's ill-fated love. On both counts, the novel's perceived disunity derives in large measure from the familiar readerly disposition to misunderstand Cather's literary use of prairie social materials as consonant with that of Howellsian Realism. But

Cather's intentions, as have already been established, are anything but "naturalistic," and the elusive unity of the book's two halves occurs on the same basis of material investiture of essential selfhood that we have seen at work in Cather's characterization of Alexandra and her brothers and in her use of social description.

Rose is on the right track when she posits the shared basis of both stories in their appeal to "the largest, strongest, most elemental emotions" (126). Yet Cather herself defended her book's relative formlessness not in terms of the representation of emotions per se but as an attribute of the shape and feel of the book's "hero" (Sergeant 92), which she identified as the land whose "soft, light, fluent, black" character "influences the mind and memory of the author and so the composition of the story" (Sergeant 97). In Cather's cosmology, the land signifies (as we have seen) not merely a material fact but a mythologized vision of human investment in nature, an ideal of culture. Alexandra symbolizes that ideal so that she and the land itself are mutually expressive of each other. The essential selfhood of Emil and Marie are likewise commensurate with key aspects of a mythologized conception of the land, and their expression of transcultural, transhistorical human ideals—like that of the French horsemen vignette—makes them of a single piece with the Alexandra sections of the novel.

Marie Shabata's inherent vitality and sexualized generosity mark her from the first as a soul whose genius matches that of the Divide. The text repeatedly associates her with the restless energy of prairie fauna, describing her as a wild "creature" (205), "a little brown rabbit" (203) springing up from the grass, "a white night-moth out of the fields" (260) fluttering in the moonlight. Her nature expresses itself physically in quick movements and lithe physical appearance and socially in impetuous speech, irrepressible cheerfulness, and impulsive generosity. When Alexandra's friend Carl Linstrum observes the two women together, the scene comprises a symbolic portrait of two contrasting faces of nature:

> They made a pretty picture in the strong sunlight, the leafy pattern surrounding them like a net; the Swedish woman so white and gold, kindly and amused, but armored in calm, and the alert brown one, her full lips parted, points of yellow light dancing in her eyes as she laughed and chattered. . . . The brown iris, he found, was curiously

slashed with yellow, the color of sunflower honey, or of old amber. In each eye one of these streaks must have been larger than the others, for the effect was that of two dancing points of light, two little yellow bubbles, such as rise in a glass of champagne. Sometimes they seemed like the sparks from a forge. She seemed so easily excited, to kindle with a fierce little flame if one but breathed upon her. (204–05)

The narrative vocabulary of this portraiture is vividly impressionistic, employing Marie's physical appearance and mannerisms, like Alexandra's, as signs of her spiritual correspondence with the land. Sitting beneath the white mulberry tree where she and Emil will eventually be hunted and shot like wild animals by Marie's jealous husband, she says: "I feel as if this tree knows everything I ever think of when I sit here. When I come back to it, I never have to remind it of anything; I begin just where I left off. . . . I'm a good Catholic, but I think I could get along with caring for trees, if I hadn't anything else" (212). Again like Alexandra, but in a slightly different register, Marie's selfhood is part and parcel of her relationship with nature; she exists in communion with the natural elements of which her own nature is but the human extension. In like fashion, Emil's essential selfhood expresses itself in the social realm first via his boyhood faith in Alexandra's vision of the land and later through his irrepressible passion for Marie. Seeing the two young people together, Carl sees not two individuals but "two young things abroad in the pasture in the early morning" (201). When Alexandra later laments Emil's death, asking herself, "Why did it have to be my boy?" (288), Carl responds to her query: "Because he was the best there was, I suppose. They were both the best you had here" (288). Second only to Alexandra herself in Cather's scale of human ideality, Emil and Marie require material investiture on a scale commensurate with the greatness of their innate qualities.

Like the expressions of themselves in the sheaths of their physical and social existence, their love for each other too gains novelistic expression in terms that defy a Howellsian conception and literary construction of social reality. Cather treats both Marie's marriage to Frank Shabata and her adulterous relationship with Emil not according to a social and ethical understanding but as the inevitable expressions of essential selves in their intersubjective aspect. The novel emphasizes the "waste" (205) of Marie's unhappy marriage to the surly, jealous, and self-absorbed Frank Shabata, contrasting the natural fitness of the young lovers for each other with the fundamental mismatch between Frank and his wife. While Marie's soul lives in close correspondence to the spirit of the prairie, Frank is inclined toward city life and hates nearly everything about the farm. "Frank would be all right in the right place," observes Marie. "He ought to have a different kind of wife, for one thing" (233). The novel presents marriage not as a social institution, a site for communicative negotiation between individuals who shape and are shaped by their interactions with each other, but as the social expression of the sum of its constituents' separate beings. A good marriage, like the union projected at the end of the novel between Alexandra and Carl Linstrum, consists of the matching of souls whose essential qualities are complementary but whose union does not diminish their individuality. A bad marriage, like Marie and Frank's, fails because it expresses the essential disparity between the individual souls of its participants. In either case, the marriage itself exists, again, merely as the social investiture of a mythic and subjective reality that is pre-social in origin. After Emil's and Marie's deaths, Alexandra does indeed voice a mild, conventional condemnation of their adultery, but the emotional momentum of the novel's narration of the lovers' relations with each other and with Frank Shabata runs overwhelmingly in the opposite direction. Frank and Marie's selves oppose each other almost absolutely, while Marie and Emil's love is the elemental attraction between like natures. It is impervious to any exertion of individual ethical or social or religious sanction; neither Emil's attempts to put Marie out of his mind by traveling to Mexico nor Marie's struggles to remain faithful to her husband by focusing on the dictates of her church can ultimately withstand the force of natural affinity that pulls them together. Nor does the text (Alexandra's uncharacteristic moral nostrums notwithstanding) encourage us to condemn the fact. Within the mythic calculus of this novel, the social sanctions in favor of Marie's continued marriage weigh little against the essential attraction of like natures. Carl counters Alexandra's petty moralizing with an account of the affair that puts it back into the mythic context in which the novel has developed it. Marie, he asserts, was one of those "women who spread ruin around them through no fault of theirs, just by being too beautiful, too full of life and love. They can't help it. People come to them as people go to a warm fire in winter" (288). In response to Alexandra's query about why he had not warned her of the developing affair, Carl asserts that Marie and Emil's love was inevitable, "was something one felt in the air, as you feel the spring coming, or a storm in summer. I didn't *see* anything. Simply, when I was with those two young things, I felt my blood go quicker, I felt—how shall I say it?—an acceleration of life" (288). Socially and ethically defined concepts like marriage and adultery, Carl implies, are simply the wrong categories of analysis for understanding the convergence of Emil and Marie's natures and their collision with Frank's opposing selfhood.[13]

Earlier, noting her essential incompatibility with her husband, Marie had lamented the apparent fact that "you almost have to marry a man before you can find out the sort of wife he needs; and usually it's exactly the sort you are not. Then what are you going to do about it?" (234). In "The Bohemian Girl," another important story dating from this period of her career, Cather answered that question by allowing the spirited woman smothering in a lifeless marriage simply to escape with the lover more suited to her soul. *O Pioneers!* so strongly establishes the natural fitness of Emil and Marie for each other that the whole weight of their mythic characterization points to a like solution for them. But Cather's choice of a tragic rather than a comedic ending for the Emil-Marie subplot, founded as it is upon the narrative logic of essential selfhood that informs the novel's characterization of Alexandra as well, gives their story a further mythic resonance that reinforces its symbolic consonance with Alexandra's story.

By ending "The White Mulberry Tree" in death rather than elopement, Cather not only maintains the idealist logic that informs the novel's representation of all temporal events and social relationships but also fuses Emil and Marie's story definitively with that of the land itself, the novel's main character and the ground of being that the young lovers share with Alexandra. The final chapter of the section begins with a lengthy account of the material aftermath of Frank's jealous rage: detailed, almost naturalistic descriptions of Emil's and Marie's damaged bodies lying in the blood-stained, flattened grass beneath the mulberry tree. From this physical evidence the living quickly piece together the chain of recent events. "But the stained, slippery grass, the darkened mulberries," the narrative continues, "told only half the story. Above Marie and Emil, two white butterflies from

Frank's alfalfa-field were fluttering in and out among the interlacing shadows; diving and soaring, now close together, now far apart; and in the long grass by the fence the last wild roses of the year opened their pink hearts to die" (272). This impressionistic tableau tells no story at all in any conventional narrative sense. Instead, the scene evokes the other "half" of the story via a natural symbolism of the paradoxical unions of individuality with procreation, of life with mortality, moving the novel's representation of reality once again off the plain of Realist social specification and into the realm of the ideal. The murder is not the stuff of individual will, ethical choice, and temporal cause-and-effect but is the collision of eternal ideals whose presence precedes and informs all mere personal or social existence in Cather's fictive world. The material fact of Emil's and Marie's deaths becomes a mythic apotheosis of their souls in spiritual union with the land—precisely like the death that the novel, hard on the heels of its announcement of her coming marriage, foresees for Alexandra: "Fortunate country, that is one day to receive hearts like Alexandra's into its bosom, to give them out again in the yellow wheat, in the rustling corn, in the shining eyes of youth!" (290).

In *O Pioneers!* Willa Cather entered her mature aesthetic mode, finding the means to free herself from the residual gravitational pull of a Howellsian sense of literary purpose and to put into literary practice the romantic "vision of essences" that would guide the rest of her career. As a professional journalist and editor, she had been immersed in a literary world still reacting to the strong model of public artistic enterprise promulgated by Howells. In the crucial works of her transition from journalism to fiction, we see her struggling to wrest the materials of social and historical externality away from their permeation with Howellsian assumptions and harness them instead to an aesthetic vision of mythic ideality. If Cather's literary-historical relationship to Howells is more tenuous than either Jewett's or Chesnutt's, the literary-cultural influence of the Howellsian ideal on her work is no less palpable for consisting on her part primarily in a process of deliberate rejection. Cather's productions in the years 1911 through 1913 chart a trajectory away from the overt social-ethical purposes she only partially subverts in the muckraking story "Behind the Singer Tower," through the partially successful appropriation of social reference to heroic portraiture in *Alexander's Bridge,* to the mythic evocation of human ideality via mimetic prose in *O Pioneers!* These works reveal the complexity of Cather's relationship to Howells as well as prefigure her resistance to periodically resurgent calls for an ethically activist social fiction later in the century. Reading these works through the lens of the Howellsian aesthetic against which Cather struggled reveals how her works, which reject the ethically invested goals of cross-cultural communication of local social realities endorsed by Howells, nevertheless sustain a popular conception of Cather as a Great Plains regional Realist. Such a reading also replaces the popularly prevailing perception of Cather as self-created romantic original with a considerably more complex portrait of an artist unevenly constructing a new aesthetic from the materials and influences left her by a previous literary generation.

6
Implications

〜

An earlier version of this book concluded abruptly at the end of the chapter on Cather, a fact that one reader rather generously interpreted as an intentional indication of the open-endedness of the book's project. It was not that—at least not intentionally; yet the inquiry pursued here is in fact fundamentally open-ended. Arguments about one of the larger contexts for this book, the moral effects of novels and novel reading, are as old as the novel form itself, and this debate has been so ubiquitous as to become an almost continuously present informing influence in the novel whether or not individual novels address it explicitly. The idea of literature as an art form that carries with it the strong presumption of serving moral teaching purposes for its readers, and whose ethical impacts, too, extend far beyond the personal moralities of individual readers, has been a continuous influence on novels and novelists throughout the form's history. This book has picked up and followed one specific strand of that idea: the particularly powerful and, for a time, influential conception of an aesthetic consciously built upon principles of social, rather than merely personal, ethics. The implications of that social-ethical aesthetic lead in many different directions over several decades of American literary and cultural history. The depth and longevity of Howells's influences (despite their rapidly shifting valences in American culture over the years) guaranteed a long life for his aesthetic, and its essentially pragmatic—and Pragmatist—conception of

literature's ethical use-value for its readers and their society easily accom-
modated the exigencies of new social and artistic circumstances and visions
as other writers encountered its influences. Other candidates for inclusion
in this study included at one time or another, for instance, Hamlin Garland, who championed Howellsian ideas while pushing them in his fiction
(*Main-Travelled Roads*) toward a robust literary populism and in his critical theory (*Crumbling Idols*) toward recognition of the author-centered
subjectivism of any literary representation of reality; Henry James, who in
The Bostonians and *The Princess Cassamassima* began novels that aimed in
a Howellsian mode straight at the heart of contemporary social and political issues only to end them as individual dramas of emotional suffering and
redemptive renunciation; and John Dos Passos, whose revolutionary narrative techniques in the *U.S.A.* trilogy welded high-Modernist aesthetics to
the call for political action and radical social change. The American novel
in the later twentieth century has found other ways than Howells's to
address—or to evade—its responsibilities for engaging readers ethically in
contemporary social realities, and the question therefore is open regarding
how far the inquiry begun in this book might be continued toward the
present. One hope for this book is that it might encourage reexamination
of other texts and authors in and beyond the late nineteenth century for
the shaping influences of the debate about literature's modes of intervention in public discussion of contemporary social and ethical issues.

This book began as an inquiry into the tension in the fictions of Howells
and other turn-of-the-century American writers between the demands of
aesthetics per se and of verisimilitude in the representation of a putatively
objective reality—what chapter one discussed under borrowed terms as the
idiogenicity and allogenicity of the literary text. When a writer sets out to
construct a truthfully mimetic representation of an "objective" material
and social world, and when s/he does so employing the tools, techniques,
and inherited forms of literary art, with their inherent insistence on ac-
countability not only to external realities but also to internally generated
economies, how does the writer negotiate these competing demands? Is the
novel thus produced an inevitable botch, a fatal compromise between in-
compatible ends? Is there some available accommodation that allows both
truth-to-life and art qua art to occur harmoniously? Is the dichotomy itself
a false distinction, a product of our later critical and philosophical assump-

tions rather than a problem of which turn-of-the-century writers were conscious? Such questions remain eminently worth answering, both as theoretical and as textual-critical issues, and this book aims to shed some light in that direction even though its controlling terms have shifted significantly since the book's inception. When I began to sift Howells's critical writing for traces of this tension between aesthetics and mimetic representation, I discovered that Howells himself had already confronted a major phase of the question as he worked toward his formulation of Realist aesthetics. For Howells, questions of representation were experienced first not as abstract issues of ontology, epistemology, or hermeneutics but as matters of vital ethical concern: literature's representation of contemporary social actualities had real consequences for readers, individually and in their collective identity as the social and political body of the American democracy. I found the sense of social and ethical urgency in Howells, built on the assumptions that fiction really mattered and was consequential in more substantial and wide-ranging ways than as mere personal entertainment or as a profitable publishing enterprise, uniquely compelling in a time when our culture and, I would argue, a large sector of the academic critical establishment has essentially written off fiction as a serious and constructive intervention in contemporary life.

Any conception of the literary enterprise that posits the writing of fiction as Howells did, as in part an act of conscious authorial entrance into a public conversation, necessarily focuses upon authorial intention as an important dimension of literary writing. This book thus seeks to take seriously a literary fact that many critics over the past few decades have considered a critical taboo. Since the common denominator in the book's five widely different chapters is the response to a conscious and conscientious understanding of literature's ethical purposes in and for American society, my treatment of texts by each of the authors included herein tends to privilege the more or less conscious purposes they held for their works, rather than the works' expressions of either their authors' personal psychologies or the more invisible assumptions and ideologies of the culture at large. And since all five chapters are concerned in one way or another with individual authors' variations on a particular, if loosely constructed, conception of aesthetic values, the book emphasizes, too, each fiction's embodiment of more or less consciously held aesthetic intentions. Despite the death of the author, anyone who has written or known someone who has knows that writers do write, at least in part, to communicate their intentions. And readers accordingly continue to be guided as a matter of course by the pragmatic assumption that part of the reading process involves interpreting authors' intended meanings. This is not to say that the range of a text's meanings is contained or exhausted either by the author's conscious intentions or by the reader's knowledge of them; rather, the literary text proceeds from a complex calculus of conscious and unconscious, individual and cultural, intellectual and emotional imperatives. But if authorial intention never constitutes the sum total of literary creativity it does nevertheless constitute its initial and in some sense controlling impulse. In our increasingly abstract critical approaches to the interactions of the literary artifact with the cultural networks of value and meaning in which it unconsciously participates, we have unwisely neglected intentionality as a decisive element in the literary creative act and as a legitimate avenue of critical approach to the literary text. It is a necessary one for a study rooted in a Howellsian aesthetic of social and ethical purpose.

The trend of much of the recent scholarship in Realism and Naturalism has been toward the critical mining of literary texts for evidence of their authors' largely unconscious participations in cultural, historical, economic, and social patterns only dimly understood, if at all, by the participants themselves. This work has been crucial in revitalizing the study of turn-of-the-century authors and texts. But much of it, too, seems counterproductively invested in a post-Foucauldian sense of ethical defeat, permeated with the sense of literary authors' inescapable complicity in structures of social and political power that have always already co-opted the texts that seek to resist them. The critical overvaluation of these invariably conservative complicities reduces the ethical intentions that power so much nineteenth- and early-twentieth-century writing to just so much obtuseness or hypocrisy on the part of its authors. Such stances implicitly claim for the critic an intellectual and moral perspicuity that the benighted subjects of his or her study could never achieve for themselves; these stances assume—and perhaps the assumption itself is an occupational hazard—that the critic knows the true implications of the author's novel so much better than the author does as to constitute a de facto assertion that critics have in fact freed themselves of the culturally induced myopias that mar the works we study, that our authoritative assertions are somehow exempt from the moral compromises and contradictions that express themselves in Realist writing and undermine their ostensible purposes from within. But perhaps most troubling of all, such criticism often comes close to an implied denial of literature's capacity to play any constructive role whatsoever in shaping the ethical and political commitments of its readers and the society they comprise, figuring the literary text and author instead as mere instruments and registers of extraneous sources of power. By so doing, they not only misrepresent the works and authors they treat but, more importantly, they shrink the ethical ground upon which nonacademic audiences share the possibility of a socially useful engagement with literary texts. I hope that this book will play some small part in reopening for critics, teachers, and readers a range of possibilities for reading literature as a meaningful and conscious intervention in vital contemporary public conversations—not, as the content of the preceding chapters should make clear, as a means of suppressing the problematic nature of that intervention but as a way of recognizing in it a live possibility for literary writing then and now.

Fundamentally, then, this book attempts to find a way—without bypassing the insights afforded by an ever more theoretically sophisticated set of critical approaches to turn-of-the-century American literature—to write a kind of criticism that is more sympathetic to the Howellsian principle of literary practice that constitutes its subject than most recent scholarship has been. I have sought, therefore, to interpret these four authors' works from within their own theoretical perspectives as far as possible, without sacrificing a genuinely critical stance and while recognizing the ultimate impossibility of that ambition in any final sense. The danger inherent in such an approach is that, by sharing too many of the principles and assumptions of the subject authors of the study, the critic may lose the intellectual distance necessary to form a genuinely critical opinion. I have undertaken this study, however, on the hypothesis that the antithetical danger is a more real and present one: that a critic who is too unsympathetic to the fundamental values of the subjects of his study is thereby too detached from them to have any real hope of understanding them.

Notes

Chapter 1

1. The preface to *Literature and Life,* from which Howells's comment is excerpted,
   dates from a decade later than the *Editor's Study* columns that form the subject
   of this chapter, and so I have relegated to this note Howells's elaboration of the
   idea: "I have never been able to see much difference between what seemed to
   me Literature and what seemed to me Life. If I did not find life in what pro-
   fessed to be literature, I disabled its profession, and possibly from this habit,
   now inveterate with me, I am never quite sure of life unless I find literature in
   it" (iii). Despite the time lag, Howells's critical thinking after the *Editor's Study*
   remained remarkably consistent, and its expressions here and elsewhere (most
   notably in the 1899 lecture entitled "Novel-Writing and Novel-Reading")
   usually correspond neatly with the earlier work.

2. The list of scholars devoting significant critical attention to Howells's shifting
   social and political ideas during this period would include Edwin Cady, Robert
   Hough, Louis Budd, Everett Carter, and Clara and Rudolf Kirk, among others.
   This list does not include all the scholars who have acknowledged the impact
   of Howells's social-ethical commitments on his work (Amy Kaplan comes immediately to mind), but it constitutes the core of those who concern themselves
   directly with the development of Howells's social and ethical thinking in his
   work as critic, editor, and essayist, rather than as novelist—the focus of this
   chapter. See especially: the first chapter ("Christian Socialism") of Clara M.
   Kirk's *W. D. Howells, Traveler from Altruria;* Clara and Rudolf Kirk's coauthored
   William Dean Howells, which includes specific discussion of the *Editor's Study*
   (117–26); Robert Hough's *The Quiet Rebel: William Dean Howells as Social*

Commentator, which includes chapters on Howells's tenure, during the matura-
tion of his social-ethical commitments, at the *Atlantic* and *Harper's;* Everett
Carter's discussion of the progress of Howells's social and critical thinking in
Howells and the Age of Realism (88–102, 170–98); Louis J. Budd's exploration
of Howells's Republican social beliefs as expressed in his work at the *Atlantic;*
and Edwin Cady's impassioned assertion, in *Young Howells and John Brown,* of
the ongoing influence of Howells's youthful experience of social and political
radicalism in Ohio's abolitionist Western Reserve (85–104). Finally, so many
sections of Cady's two-volume Howells biography, which remains the standard,
are indispensable to this discussion that I will make no attempt to specify them
further.

3. Edward Wagenknecht's further note on Howells's agnosticism correctly insists
   that while the term "agnostic" may be denotatively correct, it is misleading in
   its implication of active religious disbelief (244). Howells's agnosticism was
   that of an empiricist skeptic who yet recognizes that science has no basis for
   authority to pronounce on realities that, should they exist at all, exist beyond
   the realm of direct empirical experience (245–46). Thus Howells's agnosticism
   is a circumstantially limited will to believe or, as Howells himself wrote, "a perpetual toleration of mystery as thinkable" (qtd. in Wagenknecht 244). (On
   Howells's agnosticism, see also Wagenknecht 235–48 and Hough 30, footnote)
   Concerning the ethical dimensions of Swedenborgianism, see Rodney D.
   Olsen's discussion of William Cooper Howells's Swedenborgian equation of
   goodness with other-centered, communally useful service (16–19).
4. See especially the Ohio chapters of Lynn's and Cady's biographies, as well as
   Cady, *Brown* 7–18, 47–62, and more recently, Olsen 95–98, 101–04, 173–76.
   For primary documents from Howells's Ohio years, see Thomas Wortham.
5. See also Hough 20–29, Budd 41–58, Bassett 15–29.
6. See Hough 29–39, Kirk and Kirk 108–14, Wagenknecht 263–77, Carter 176–
   85, Alexander 67–69, 71–81, 83–98, Kirk, *Traveler from Altruria* 15–33, Garlin 97–163, Cady, *Realist* 64–81, 147–63, Lynn 282–96, Eble 97–101, 114–22.
7. Similarly, John Bassett asserts of Howells and Samuel Clemens that "They were
   perhaps more conscious of their writing as communication than as art, both
   being trained as journalists with one eye always on their audience" (8). Bassett
   attributes to this journalism-born "sensitivity to audience" (8) both authors'
   commercial success, an insight worked out at greater length in Daniel Borus's
   Writing Realism, which traces "the realist writing process" to "the consolidation
   of the literary marketplace as the locus of literary production, exchange, and
   circulation" (24). In order to avoid the marketplace's equation of literary value
   with popularity, according to Borus, Howells sought a compromise with marketplace valuation, locating the value of literature simultaneously in the economically "privileged condition of its producer" (63) and in "the sum of [the] individual tastes" (64) of its readership. The novel, therefore, "had to establish itself

as authentic and unmediated communication" (61) in order to claim for itself status as a serious and democratic enterprise operating independently of the vagaries of consumers' desires.

8. The challenge posed to Howells's naive conception of literary mimeticism by the advent of deconstruction and other manifestations of poststructuralist interpretive theory needs little rehearsal here. The net effect of these developments has been to emphasize the self-referential nature of language, unmooring words from their referents, making of language a primarily self-referential closed system of infinitely deferred meaning and thus digging an insuperable gulf between human subjectivity and extralinguistic reality. The implications of these ideas for scholarly thinking about Realism have been neatly summarized by Amy Kaplan: "From an objective reflection of contemporary social life, realism has become a fictional conceit, or deceit, packaging and naturalizing an official version of the ordinary. From a style valued for its plain-speaking vernacular, realism has adopted a rhetorical sophistication that now subverts its own claims to referentiality. From a progressive force exposing the conditions of industrial society, realism has turned into a conservative force whose very act of exposure reveals its complicity with structures of power." (*Social* 1) Kaplan's study attempts to negotiate the spaces between these dichotomous conceptions of realism. My study (as the introduction and the remainder of this chapter should help to clarify) accepts—as a matter of pragmatic (and Pragmatist) convenience though not as hermeneutic certainty—a number of assumptions about the referentiality of language and about its potential to effect social change that much contemporary theory regards as fatally unsophisticated but which nevertheless underwrote Howells's conception of literature's social-ethical purposes and was shared in large measure by the other authors referenced in this book as well.

9. Several recent critics have addressed questions related to late-century transformations in the authorial sense of literary vocation. Daniel Borus, for example, who traces Howells's conception of the literary occupation to the development of a market economy, will receive extended discussion later. (See especially 57–64, "Literary Value and the Postbellum Market.") Additionally, Michael D. Bell, Alfred Habegger, and Rodney D. Olsen all devote attention to the consequences for Howells of nineteenth-century definitions of the gendered spheres of occupation. Bell's reading of the *Editor's Study* concludes that Howells "was torn between the sin of art and the socially sanctioned imperatives of worldly, 'masculine' success," at a time when "'authorship,' in a social sense, [was] a kind of 'sin,' an abandonment of responsibility and 'manhood'" (25). Habegger, interpreting Howells's youth and early career in the context of feminine domination of the midcentury literary market, traces the antisentimentalist strain of Howells's novels to his culturally generated anxieties about being regarded as a "sissy" because of his literary pursuits. Olsen devotes an important chapter, entitled "Woman's Sphere" (137–63), to the psychological efforts

required by young Howells, still in Ohio, to reconcile the conflicting claims of cultural orthodoxy regarding gendered spheres of occupation and his own persistent literary ambitions. (On realism and gender, see also Borus 110–14.) None of these accounts coincides precisely with my point here, but Olsen's insight into the early importance of Swedenborgian teaching to Howells's sense of vocation prefigures his mature conception in the *Editor's Study;* Swedenborgianism's understanding of "moral purpose as social utility" (19) through selfless devotion to others, Olsen observes, "required a moral, communal context for the literary vocation" (89).

10. On contemporary assumptions about the nature and use of language, see also Elsa Nettels (21–23).

11. Howells's choice of a nonfiction work as one of his first exemplars in the *Editor's Study* of a literary style commendable under the new aesthetic simultaneously suggests the closeness literature ought to bear to "real life" and (as Howells does throughout the *Study*) borrows for Realism the public—and masculine— respectability more readily accorded to nonfiction, by treating both fiction and nonfiction alike with the same seriousness and according to the same aesthetic yardstick. His praise of Grant seeks to accrue to the new aesthetic some of the public approbation granted the practical-minded, results-driven, and undeniably successful military man. Grant's writing, Howells implies, is part and parcel of his practical, public achievements just as Realist fiction must participate fully and effectively in the public issues and events of its own day. Howells thus draws freely upon the public and patriotic respectability afforded the manly business of war to stake a claim for the vocational power and importance of the literary profession.

12. I borrow the term "idiogenetic" from Lee Baxandall and Stefan Morawski, who use it (as I do) to distinguish between the literary text's internally reflexive aspects and its "allogenetic" engagements with "non-aesthetic givens" outside the text itself (1, 9).

13. Borus borrows the term from Raymond Williams, defining it as the "complex of relationships" formed by authors "with their material, their audience, and the society as a whole" as they engage "in the process of producing a text" (8).

14. Reasoning similar to Borus's undermines Amy Kaplan's argument about Howells's "mass-mediated realism" (*Social* 15–43), which I have not treated at length primarily because she concentrates not on Howells's critical writing but on *A Modern Instance.* According to Kaplan, the rise of mass-market journalism "can be seen as a direct threat to Howells' conception of realism, threatening by virtue of its very similarity to that realism" (*Social* 30). Realism and journalism, Kaplan maintains, both attempt to appeal to a socially stratified audience by "uniting them through the medium of the market rather than through mutual recognition of a community" (*Social* 30). Kaplan's argument, in my opinion, relies too much on interpretation of a single novel to demonstrate Howells's

putative anxiety over the threat posed by journalism. She cites little of Howells's critical writing and even less biographical information in support of her central point and thus suppresses (as does Borus) the more apparent roots of Howells's model of literary enterprise in his social-ethical commitments.

15. Michael Bell makes a similar point with direct reference to Howells's critical writing: "*Criticism and Fiction* apparently mattered far less to its author as an aesthetic manifesto than as an attempt to work out his own status as a writer, to reconcile the culturally divergent identities of 'artist' and 'man' by presenting authorship as one of what Jefferson called the 'real businesses of life'" (35). Bell's analysis of this phenomenon is considerably less nuanced than either Olsen's or Habegger's, giving his formulation of Howells's struggles to reconcile gender ideology with vocation the flavor of a reductio ad absurdum. His concern to establish the romantic figure of the alienated artist as the model for all worthy literary endeavor forces him to reduce Howells's efforts to unite art with everyday life to a merely personal, unconscious psychological wrangle rather than a conscious, aesthetic decision.

16. Borus, too, notes a related tendency "in the book world . . . to use 'literary' as a derogatory adjective": "[P]ublishers and the new business men and women of the pen used the expression to signify threats to democratic equality . . . [and] to connote an excessive concern with niceties of expression, pathetic insistence on outmoded formalities of composition, and dry, lifeless subject matter" (45). With the possible exception of the last, such connotations closely match Howells's denigration of the terms of art. However, Borus's attribution of the derogation of the literary to the newly entrepreneurial nature of the literary marketplace, in keeping with his thesis, seems to overlook important distinctions between the motives of publishers and those of an author like Howells, who employed this critical strategy as much in the service of social-ethical ends as in the furtherance of market goals.

17. The primary arguments for using the *Editor's Study* instead of *Criticism and Fiction* may be found in Cady's edited collection, *W. D. Howells as Critic* (74–76), in Pizer (xviii–xix), and most extensively in Carter (185–90). For the idea of Howells as "culture critic," see Cady, *Critic* (2).

18. Any statement of these ideas as a binary opposition risks recapitulating the mistake that derails Bell's reading of *Criticism and Fiction*. Nevertheless, for the sake of clarity of argument I let the preceding sentences stand, with the following disclaimers and qualifications: Any given literary work, regardless of its relative level of formal conventionality or experimentation, necessarily participates simultaneously both in a network of exterior reference to the world of nature and society (allogenicity) and in one of aesthetic autonomy and self-referentiality (idiogenicity). To restate what may perhaps be obvious: the meanings of a literary work arise both from its adoption and variation of aesthetic conventions of genre, form, style, and so on, and from its reference to the world

external to art. In fact, aesthetic conventions themselves can make sense only within the larger frames of social reference within which they must exist. While it may be useful as a theoretical convenience to conceive of literary allogenicity and idiogenicity separately, to do so is not to imply that they can occur separately; allo- and idiogenicity are two aspects of a single phenomenon rather than separate and distinct ontological qualities. The differences between literary and critical practices that privilege the idiogenetic and those that favor the allogenetic are always differences of tendency and degree rather than unconditional opposition.

Chapter 2

1. The query from which Tolstoy derived the title of his book *What Is to Be Done?* (1886) belonged originally to the crowds surrounding Jesus, as recorded in the third chapter of the New Testament book of Luke, who wanted to know what actions to take in response to his prophecy of impending divine retribution for their society's general wickedness. Jesus's responses demanded the people's active commitment to social justice toward the poor, providing Tolstoy, whose example and ideas were increasingly important to Howells during the 1880s and '90s, with the starting point for his theologically based social criticism.

2. Stowe poses, and then proceeds to answer, her own rhetorical question: "But, what can any individual do? Of that, every individual can judge. There is one thing that every individual can do,—they can see to it that *they feel right*. An atmosphere of sympathetic influence encircles every human being; and the man or woman who *feels* strongly, healthily and justly, on the great interests of humanity, is a constant benefactor to the human race. See, then, to your sympathies in this matter! Are they in harmony with the sympathies of Christ? or are they swayed and perverted by the sophistries of worldly policy?" (624) Succeeding paragraphs counsel her Christian readers to follow up their right sympathies with prayer and concrete social action, primarily defined in terms of refugee resettlement and education. In Stowe's theology, right feeling presupposes righteous action—the former is unavailable except through performance of the latter.

3. Gary Scharnhorst reviews the evidence for Howells's probable personal acquaintance with Horatio Alger and for his conscious satirical rewriting of the "Alger country-boy myth" (16) in *The Minister's Charge,* particularly as embodied in Alger's two-part narrative, *The Young Outlaw* and *Sam's Chance.* Edwin Cady notes that "the hero's story is as close to Horatio Alger as Howells ever came" but that the resemblance is "on the surface" only (*Realist* 4); Howells's purposes in the novel go well beyond rote rehearsal of the American success myth, particularly insofar as Sewell rather than Barker is the focus of the novel's attention.

4. Wai Chee Dimock provocatively interprets Sewell's championing of the utili-

tarian moral principle he calls (in *The Rise of Silas Lapham*) the "economy of pain" as a countermanding principle to the doctrine of complicity: "On the one hand, there is a movement toward expanded connectedness, which implicates everyone and makes everyone responsible for everyone else. Complementing it, however, is a movement in the opposite direction, a movement that restores limits, that tries to minimize not only suffering but also the obligations that suffering entails" (103). I am arguing, on the contrary, that Sewell's and the latter novel's difficulty is not how to evade or limit the moral responsibilities entailed by the recognition of complicity but how to act constructively upon those responsibilities within a divided and alienated society.

5. Daugherty's essay is perceptive in a number of ways that intersect with my argument's assertions of the essentially skeptical and anxious mode of Howells's engagement with Tolstoy's question. Of particular interest is her discussion of Howells's evolving relationship with Tolstoy's work and philosophy before, during, and after the writing and publication of *Annie Kilburn*. Daugherty argues that *Annie Kilburn* "begins as a defense of the Russian author [but] undermines not only Tolstoy's social ideas but the theory of realism that Howells himself was expounding in his 'Editor's Study' columns" (22). While Daugherty's understanding of the substance of Howells's theory—"that individuals can achieve a common vision and sense of purpose and that there is a divine truth revealed by the light of common day" (25)—is different from mine (as detailed in the previous chapter), I agree wholeheartedly with her that *Annie Kilburn's* significance results in large measure from its revealing extension and complication of the aesthetic ideas Howells developed in the *Editor's Study*, partly under the influence of Tolstoy.

   Also useful is Daugherty's summary of the relatively small portion of previously published commentary on the novel, none of which postdates 1973 ("Limits" 40, n. 33). The most substantial treatment of the novel and its genesis is Edwin Cady's in *The Realist at War* (64–67, 82–91), followed in shorter form by Kenneth Lynn's (289–96). Both biographers (more recently joined in yet briefer form by John Crowley in *The Dean of American Letters,* 9–10) understand the novel in the context of Howells's discovery of Tolstoy, his research into labor conditions in the mills at Lowell, his unsuccessful defense of the Haymarket anarchists, and the worsening health of his daughter, Winifred. Cady, however, finds in the novel "a magnificent power to command the reader's imagination to see, hear, and reflect" on "the puzzle of how to make the American Dream real in modern times" (83), while Lynn sees the "enormous defeatism of the novel" (294) as a mark of Howells's failure to make the novel "an instrument for widening the bounds of sympathy between social classes in a strife-torn decade" (296).

6. Chase's landmark study, for its part, seems to value *The Vacation of the Kelwyns* primarily because it can be made to fit his thesis that romance is the defining

characteristic of the best of American literature. Chase finds Howells in general lazy, prudish, and lacking in imagination, and declares offhandedly that he was "always making great refusals" because "he never tried hard enough" (177). Nevertheless, Chase pronounces *The Kelwyns* "quite possibly his best" (177) novel because it embodies for him something "akin to romance as we find it in Shakespeare's late plays" (183).

7. I am relying here on John Crowley's dating of Howells's renewed efforts to complete *The Children of the Summer* rather than Cady's and Lynn's 1910 dating; Crowley's is the most complete (though brief) published summary of the process. See *The Dean of American Letters,* 84. Cady and Lynn may have been misled by the 1911 flurry of Howells's correspondence with his publisher concerning last-minute changes to page proofs of the novel, which was actually advertised prematurely in Britain in 1911 before Howells had made the final decision to withdraw it. See Donald R. Smith's unpublished annotated edition of the novel, i and ii. See also Smith's account of Howells's vacation experiences in Shirley, Massachusetts, during the summers of 1875 and 1876, which provided much of the raw material for the novel and for Howells's 1876 *Atlantic* article about his experience with the Shakers at Shirley.

8. In *The Dean of American Letters,* John Crowley gives a comprehensive account of the destruction of Howells's literary reputation during the early twentieth century and its lasting detrimental effects.

Chapter 3

1. Karen Kilcup and Thomas Edwards provide an excellent, detailed analysis of the history of Jewett criticism in the introductory essay to their edited volume, *Jewett and Her Contemporaries.* See "Confronting Time and Change: Jewett, Her Contemporaries, and Her Critics," 1–27.

2. See especially 119–26 on the parallel social uses of regionalism and the vacation for the rising leisure class, and 145–54, in which Brodhead applies these insights more specifically to Jewett's career, concentrating primarily on *The Country of the Pointed Firs.*

3. Technically, Helen Denis is the sole narrator of *Deephaven,* but in fact she comprises with Kate Lancaster a sort of hybrid narrator. The two women experience everything in the book together, and although Helen alone writes about their experiences, she relies heavily on the more voluble Kate for the content of her narration. Here and throughout, therefore, I refer to Kate and Helen collectively as "the narrators."

4. For further information on Jewett's summer visits to the coast and her use of them in *Deephaven,* see especially Blanchard (85).

5. Jewett notes her adoption of the sketch form in an oft-quoted 1873 letter to Horace Scudder, in which she confesses a lack of "dramatic talent" and ability

for plot construction. "It seems to me I can furnish the theatre, and show you the actors, and the scenery, and the audience, but there never is any play! I could write you entertaining letters perhaps, from some desirable house where I was in most charming company, but I couldn't make a story about it." She therefore finds the sketch more conducive to her strengths in description and characterization: "I am certain I could not write one of the usual magazine stories. If the editors will take the sketchy kind and people like to read them, is not it as well to do that and do it successfully . . . ?" This early and decisive artistic choice arose in part, as Paula Blanchard notes, from Jewett's correspondence with Howells concerning the early *Deephaven* sketches, published in the *Atlantic* between 1873 and 1876. See Cary, *Letters* 29, and Blanchard 61–62.

6. The latter quotation is from a letter of May 22, 1893, to Frederick M. Hopkins that seems to have served as a prototype for the 1894 *Deephaven* preface. See Cary, *Letters* 83–85 and n. 6. The maxim from Plato may be found in this letter also, as well as in letters to Samuel Thurber (Cary, *Letters* 164) and Elizabeth McCracken (Jewett, *Letters* 228).

7. Donovan appends the following sentences as further evidence of Jewett's "sense of writerly purpose": "When I was, perhaps fifteen, the first city boarders began to make their appearance near Berwick; and they so misunderstood the country people, and made such game of their peculiarities, that I was fired with indignation. I determined to teach the world that country people were not the awkward, ignorant set that those persons seemed to think" (405).

8. Howells's 1877 *Atlantic* review of *Deephaven,* too, confirms the essential congruity of social and aesthetic purposes between author and editor: "No doubt some particular sea-port sat for Deephaven, but the picture is true to a whole class of old shore towns, in any one of which you might confidently look to find the Deephaven types." The narrators' "sojourn is only used as a background on which to paint the local life" and the narration itself records "the very tint and form of reality" informed by a "conscientious fidelity" which produces "a sympathy as tender as it is intelligent" (25).

9. Jewett pinned a parallel piece of advice, from Gustave Flaubert, above her writing desk: "Écrire la vie ordinaire comme on écrit l'histoire" ("Write about daily life as you would write history") (qtd. in Blanchard 84). While this quotation from the French Realist raises too many issues about differences between Howellsian and other varieties of Realism to be unambiguously useful here, Jewett seems to have understood by it a second piece of counsel toward referential documentation of commonplace realities in literature. See Blanchard's discussion.

10. From this fact, more than any other, derives the long-running arguments over possible distinctions between "local color" and "regionalism," and over regionalism's and/or local color's fraught relationships to the two or more distinct cultures to which they inevitably belong. The discussion usually reverts to some

version of the local color versus regionalism distinction found, for instance, in Donald Dike (although Dike eschews the term "regionalism" altogether): local color writers "were related to local material in two dissimilar ways," Dike writes. The first sort write as "tourists," exploiting "the eccentric and pictur- esque" aspects of "a local community, struck by its singularity, its differences from the norm of their own social group," which includes their audience. The second sort (regionalists) "identified themselves with the community which was their subject matter" and sympathetically rendered local difference as "cultural relativists," granting local culture a validity equal to that of the metropolis (82).

More recently, Judith Fetterley and Marjorie Pryse, redefining regionalism as a women's literary tradition distinct from traditional conceptions of both "local color" and "regional realism" (xi), nevertheless adopt the older distinction be- tween the empathetic, insider regionalist narrator and the exploitive, outsider local color narrator (xvii–xviii). See also Richard Brodhead's extended discus- sion of nineteenth-century American regionalism generally (107–41) and more particularly of Jewett as regionalist (142–76). Brodhead grants brief attention to the social leveling effect of the fact that the primary prerequisite for regional- ist authorship was mere familiarity with an obscure or semiobscure subculture, but most of his argument is weighted toward regionalism as an upper-class, culturally appropriative act.

The regionalist debate significantly predates these modern authorities. As Ann Douglas Wood points out, Howells used local color women writers as exemplars of the new Realism in the very first of his *Editor's Study* columns for *Harper's Monthly;* "In sum, the best of the women Local Colorists . . . were in the literary vanguard of their day as Howells understood it" (4), she concludes. For Howells, as numerous *Editor's Study* columns avowed, the value of such writing was closely tied to the fact that it was produced by insiders writing from local points of view, guaranteeing not only the mimetic accuracy of individual works but the presence of literary reports from numerous different regions and subcultures of the nation, thus maximizing the writing's social-ethical use-value in two distinct ways. Further, to cite just one more historical example, Howells's disciple Hamlin Garland, in pushing Howellsian ideas of local literary perspec- tive to more subjectivist extremes, calls the literature of the insider "local color," not regionalism. (See *Crumbling Idols,* especially essays five and six, entitled "Local Color in Art" and "The Local Novel," respectively.) For fuller discussion of these issues, see also: Bowron 273–75; Pryse, "Reading"; Pryse, "Distilling"; Fetterley, "Not in the Least."

11. Significant strands of argument in both Brodhead and Michael D. Bell (175– 204) depend upon this assertion that Jewett belonged to a "high-art" tradition embodied most significantly by Henry James. Both critics likewise depend on serious misreadings of W. D. Howells's relation to this tradition: Brodhead by uncritically assuming Howells's full alliance with James as a symbol and propo-

nent of a putative high culture, and Bell, conversely, by declaring Howells's supposed opposition to "art" and especially to women's art. That both readings can emerge from a single writer's work testifies to the powerful sway that Howells's status as cultural icon ("the Dean of American Letters") continues to exert over scholars' often decontextualized readings of a narrow selection of his texts. Both Brodhead and Bell establish their dubious readings of the meaning of Jewett's career and writing in part upon suspect readings of Howells that are, in turn, founded more certainly upon the received cultural valences of "the Dean" than upon contextualized understanding of his writing. The effects of the literary character assassination inflicted upon Howells in the early decades of the twentieth century and ably investigated by John Crowley in *The Dean of American Letters* (see especially chapter five) thus continue to hamper the critical enterprise.

12. Significantly, Howells shared Jewett's awareness of contemporary Swedenborgianism but could not grant it his full belief as she did. As Donovan points out, Theophilus Parsons "became a neighbor of William Dean Howells (on Concord Avenue in Cambridge) in July 1873" ("Swedenborg" 732). Another Boston acquaintance, Henry James Sr., was a Swedenborgian as well, as was Howells's own father. The son shared his father's interest in Swedenborgian ideas throughout the latter's lifetime, corresponding periodically about the philosophy and about the junior Howells's inability to place his faith in it. Howells's rationalist skepticism rendered him permanently doubtful about the mystical aspects of Swedenborgianism, but its ethical aspects played an important role in the formation of his aesthetic. In effect, Howells became, in the phrase of his biographer Edwin H. Cady, an "ethical Swedenborgian." See Cady, *The Road to Realism,* especially 145–51.

13. Julia Bader makes this comment about the writing of Jewett and her contemporaries generally, asserting that their fictions often include such "scenes of dissolving vision" (198).

14. Sarah Way Sherman treats Jewett's literary and biographical involvements with the myth of Demeter and Persephone at length. Here, though, I am primarily interested in the immediate use of the myth by Kate and Helen as a mediatory narrative tool.

15. Judith Bryant Wittenberg foregrounds Jewett's narratorial choices in *Deephaven,* suggesting that the book is "Jewett's exploratory metafiction" in which the "author overtly considers various aspects of her narrative craft, exploring such basic artistic issues as the posture of the writer *vis-a-vis* her material" (153). While the scope and conclusions of Wittenberg's study differ from mine, her insight into *Deephaven's* experimentation with narratorial configuration supports my argument. Most recent critics of *Deephaven* take for granted its narrative limitations and turn their attention to Helen and Kate as characters within the tale Helen tells. See, for example, Ann Romines and especially Judith Fetter-

ley (in "Reading *Deephaven* as a Lesbian Text"), who reads the book as the suppressed record of Helen's lesbian attachment to Kate. My reading, on the other hand, focuses more centrally on Kate and Helen as narrators rather than characters, although the success of their narration depends in part on their filling both roles simultaneously.

16. Zagarell makes a related point in her investigation of what she calls "the cosmopolitanism of regionalism's representation of rural life" ("Troubling" 645): Zagarell reads the lighthouse episode as evidence of *Deephaven's* "fantasized erasure of postbellum class tension and of working-class presence in upper-class domains" (646). Her reading points once again to the problematic status of the regionalist narrator but, to my mind, overemphasizes the text's complicity in a regionalist project of cultural imperialism while suppressing the genre's capacity as a vehicle for the communication of genuine cross-class understanding.

17. Romines makes a similar point about the quality of Kate and Helen's interaction with the rituals that she sees as the central constituents of Deephaven's collective life. Try as they might to enter the local life unreservedly, Romines asserts, "the two young protagonists quietly crash into a transparent, unbreakable partition" (205), erected by themselves, which reduces their attempts at full participation to "ritual as spectator sport; ritual as a kind of sympathetic voyeurism" (209).

18. Bill Brown devotes significant attention to this aspect of regionalism, contextualizing Jewett's practice of the genre in terms of contemporary developments in history and, especially, anthropology.

19. See Donovan, *Jewett* 134, and Cary, *Letters* 91.

20. An implied but not usually explicit crux of much of the criticism of *The Country of the Pointed Firs* is the relative emphasis placed upon the narrator's dual statuses as character and narrator. While an earlier round of feminist criticism (for example, Ammons, *Conflicting;* Fetterley and Pryse; Zagarell, "Narrative") tended to emphasize the former in order to recover the book's celebration of communities of women, recent work in the wake of Richard Brodhead (for example Ammons, "Material" and Zagarell, "Difference") tends in the opposite direction in order to emphasize the cultural appropriation and colonization enacted by Jewett's regionalism. Other criticisms that make the narratorial insider/outsider status an explicit focus of attention include: Allison T. Hild, who explores the problematic dualism of the narrator's orientation to the two subcultures in which she claims membership; Josephine Donovan, who maintains that despite the narrator's "strong desire" to become "an active participant" in the local life, "she is fundamentally cut off from this world, and must return in the end to her urban, modern world" ("Theory" 221); Ann Douglas Wood, who contends that "the narrator . . . is very clearly an author in search of material" (29); and Sarah Way Sherman, who writes that the narrator's "adoption in this little world" of Dunnet Landing may by the end of the book have made

her "a foreigner in both worlds, loyal to each but unable to accept the limitations of either" (256). A major reason for the aesthetic success of Jewett's book, I am arguing, is precisely that Jewett manages to fuse the roles of participant-character and observer-narrator so unobtrusively.

21. The narrative shape to which I am here referring as spherical is not unlike the "vortical, centric, weblike" (46) form that Elizabeth Ammons discusses in *Conflicting Stories*. But Ammons keys her discussion to Jewett's feminist resolution "of the conflict she felt between . . . allegiance to the world of mother and entrance into the world of men" (45) rather than to an aesthetic allied to Howellsian literary social-ethics and addressed to the obstacles posed to that aesthetic by the problems inherent in regionalist narration. The choice of the sphere as a figure for *Country*'s functional narrative form—a figure for which I continue to search for a more apt replacement—is my attempt to suggest that the fundamental nonlinearity of the narrative yet continues to serve social and ethical purposes outside the text in the world of socially situated readers, where the narrative's communication of alien local realities to real readers will serve culturally mediatory ends. In other words, the figure of the sphere is intended to convey both the text's internally constitutive formal networks and its relatedness to external networks of literary communication.

22. Ammons employs this insight within an essentialized feminism that her more recent work on Jewett has sought to modify. In her earlier account of Jewett's book, Ammons writes that Littlepage's tale "symbolizes the narrative structures men inherit from each other" (49), which are "self-indulgent, learned, male-focused, aggression-based" (48). Ammons's interpretation of Littlepage as a negative, patriarchal, anticommunal figure (48–50) seems to have become the orthodox explication among many feminist scholars, but she herself complicates this reading in her more recent essay on material culture and imperialism (see "Material" 106–08).

Chapter 4

1. For discussion of Chesnutt's relationship to progressivism and to the Progressive movement, see William L. Andrews (*Literary Career*), Helen M. Chesnutt, J. Noel Heermance, Frances Keller, and Ernestine Pickens.

2. As should be clear from the preceding discussion, Richard H. Brodhead makes a false distinction when he asserts: "Chesnutt conceives of writing as a largely autonomous zone of verbal creation. . . . The most powerful writers among Chesnutt's black contemporaries—Booker T. Washington and Frances Harper come to mind—think of writing as ancillary to a primary work of public speaking and they mentally subordinate such speech to larger goals of moral and social betterment. But Chesnutt, like his high-cultural white contemporaries, dissociates literary art from such transliterary aims and makes it more of an

end" (*Cultures* 178). Brodhead's misstatement arises from the particular purposes of his argument, which places Chesnutt's career in the contexts of a "high-
cultural" literary writing catering to the new American leisure class and of contemporary debate between Washingtonian proponents of practical industrial
education for African Americans and champions (including Chesnutt) of
"classical" education on the Northern model. Brodhead explicates Chesnutt's
adoption of a literary career as evidence of his acculturation in the particular
"culture of letters" that enabled the rise of a self-interested, self-improving black
professional class. In order to do so, however, he downplays until later in his
essay the importance of the pervasive sense of literary purpose that forms an
important part of the "high" culture of letters within which Chesnutt wrote.
Eventually, Brodhead returns to the Chesnutt journal passage I have quoted
above, deploying it as a corrective to his earlier reading of Chesnutt's literary
self-conception, as well as to Washington's critique of classical education for
blacks: "Washington was wrong to think that liberally educated black professionals were self-interested only. The incipient black professional class of this
time differed from its white social cognate in its inevitable heavy consciousness of its race's social plight and in its linking of individual achievement
with duty toward its race" (*Cultures* 195). From this sense of duty, Brodhead
argues, arises Chesnutt's particular sense of his own literary vocation. To this
argument I would add only that Chesnutt's feeling of literary duty and his
"practice-governing idea of what writing *is* and *does*" (*Cultures* 195) arise not
only from the culture of the classically educated black professional class but also
from the inevitable negotiation with Howellsian literary culture's ideal of literature as a tool for social-ethical change.

3. As Brodhead has noted, *Uncle Tom's Cabin* was "for Chesnutt and his contemporaries the inevitable image of the novel as agent of social change" (qtd. in Chesnutt, *Journals* 50). Tourgée's radically pro-Reconstruction *A Fool's Errand* would
not result in the same groundswell of popular and political support for reform
that Stowe's book had, but its phenomenal popular and critical success in the
early 1880s seemed to Chesnutt to promise just such a decisive social impact
for that novel, as well. See Matthew Wilson for fuller critical discussion of these
two important influences and their meanings for Chesnutt's literary career and
professional self-conception.

4. See Howells, "Mr. Charles W. Chesnutt's Stories."

5. See Howells, "A Psychological Counter-Current in Recent Fiction."

6. Favorable mention of Howells's novel appears in the manuscript versions of
Chesnutt's speeches entitled "The Ideal Nurse" (373) and "The Negro in
Books" (433, 436), both of which are reprinted in Chesnutt's *Essays and
Speeches*. Joseph McElrath notes that *An Imperative Duty* is "the only novel
by Howells that one finds in the remains of Chesnutt's personal library" (246).

7. My brief account of the Howells-Chesnutt relationship is deeply indebted to

William L. Andrews's efficient summarization of its main outlines in "William Dean Howells and Charles W. Chesnutt." Andrews—problematically—attributes Howells's discontent with Chesnutt's later writing to his "neglect" of "his task as literary critic," who should properly be concerned with "the *novel* as literature" rather than with "the *novelist's* temperament and perspective" (339). This judgment relies on an overly simplistic segregation of politics from aesthetics that Howells's thinking explicitly rejects and that is probably the product of the particular critical moment (1976) of Andrews's essay. For a more recent, wider-ranging, and more fully contextualized consideration of the Howells-Chesnutt relationship, see Joseph R. McElrath. Also useful, particularly in reconstructing the finer details of the history of Howells and Chesnutt's contacts in person and in correspondence, are the footnotes to Chesnutt's half of the surviving letters between the two men in *"To Be an Author."*

8. Chesnutt's intricate relationship to Southern regionalism and to plantation-dialect fiction specifically has been a perennial hot topic for some time now. In addition to Andrews's *The Literary Career of Charles W. Chesnutt* (see especially 10–12 and 40–50), see: Eric Sundquist, who explores the signifying relationship between Joel Chandler Harris's Uncle Remus books and Chesnutt's conjure tales (323–59), focusing on Chesnutt's use of dialect as "a kind of crossroads of cultural languages" (308) that enables the "astute expression and theoretical analysis of African American vernacular and its accompanying folk beliefs during the ascendancy of segregation" (309); Robert C. Nowatzki, who offers a brief and useful contextualization of Chesnutt in terms of Page and Harris, and whose attention to the tales' framing in some ways anticipates mine; and Richard H. Brodhead, whose introduction to his edition of the conjure tales sketches the literary traditions in which Chesnutt's tales participate (2–6), a project put to more pointed critical uses in his Chesnutt chapter in *Cultures of Letters* (177–210). See also Lucinda H. Mackethan's useful overview of "Plantation Fiction, 1865–1900" in *The History of Southern Literature* (209–18), Craig Werner, Kenneth M. Price, Dean McWilliams, and Henry B. Wonham ("Curious"). Wonham provocatively questions the tendency among critics to read Chesnutt's writing in this genre exclusively as either "an expression of politically contemptible acquiescence, or of creative subversion" (56): "Is it necessary . . . as a condition of Chesnutt's quite recent ascent from obscurity to canonical status, that we forgive—and in forgiving fix—the unstable political commitments that generate so much of the power and irony of the conjure tales? And, to pursue the same question in another direction, must we demonize the arbiters of late nineteenth century critical taste—Howells, Page, Gilder, and others—who presumably stifled his trajectory toward a less ambivalent, more politically decisive form of protest fiction? Perhaps in making this critical move, we are simply voicing our impatience with the structural asymmetries of the local-color tale as a form, one that frustrated Chesnutt for many of the same rea-

sons, but that clearly suited his ambivalent racial allegiances and set in motion some of his most compelling ironies." (64) My argument concerning Chesnutt's ambivalent but pointed internal questioning of the capacities and limitations of his audience in the conjure tales contributes, I hope, to the project to which Wonham's question points.

9. The relationship of Joel Chandler Harris's work to reactionary Reconstruction politics is much more complex than is the relatively straightforward racism of Page and his ilk, as Eric Sundquist exhaustively demonstrates. Nevertheless, while Harris's texts may indeed, as Sundquist argues, authorize critical exploration of Harris's psychological investments of himself in his literary representations of black folk culture, Chesnutt employs the same literary conventions for ends that are much more overtly purposeful, socially and ethically.

10. Robert Bone observes that "the function of the outside plot is to provide a clue to the meaning of the metamorphosis, and thereby to control our reading of the fable" (81–82). More to my point, Hedin argues that *The Conjure Woman* is one of a number of nineteenth-century black texts that use frame narratives to "present within themselves, in the form of white listeners/observers, a sensitive register" (182) of the murky relationship between African-American writing and "mainstream (white) American culture" (182).

11. Brodhead argues that "No effort is made to individualize John or Uncle Julius or to naturalize the relation between them. Stock characters, they are given to us virtually *as* stock characters, as standard-issue figures of the local color form" ("Introduction" 6). Further, Brodhead writes elsewhere, "Chesnutt stays so close to generic conventions that they inevitably become revealed, though without comment or overt parody, as conventions" (*Cultures* 196). While I would not maintain that John, Annie, and Julius approach the status of fully rounded characters, the attention paid in a significant number of the tales to their individuating character traits and temperaments and to their idiosyncratic responses to frame situations contrasts markedly with the tales' generic analogues. These characters are individuated not only according to race but also by their individual relations to local and national culture and history, their distinctly specified disagreements concerning values and worldviews, their genders, and their unique economic and political assumptions. Brodhead concedes that they are "unusually rich in social markers" (*Cultures* 197); it is this social specificity that enables productive reading of John and Annie as figures of audience.

12. For an alternative account of the narratorial relationship between John and Julius, see Dean McWilliams, who finds in John and Annie's response to Julius's tales evidence of a "regular progress of the Northerners' education" (86) in matters "moral and social" and "epistemological and aesthetic" (87). McWilliams, I think, suppresses the significant differences between John's and Annie's responses, and thus overestimates the degree to which they are in fact successfully "educated" by Julius's tales.

13. Brodhead makes a similar point when he suggests that Chesnutt progressively discovered that adoption of white generic conventions in the conjure tales in some ways "constrained his work to serve the imaginative agenda of that culture, the agenda not of dismantling prejudice but of feeding an appetite for consumable otherness" (*Cultures* 206).

14. Earlier critics have noted in other ways the premium Chesnutt places upon the role of readers in the success of his project. Brodhead, for example, notes in his discussion of the tales' deliberate conventionality that "as usual this message is left completely implicit, available to those who have ears to hear it" ("Introduction" 6). Similarly, David D. Britt, in an article tellingly subtitled "What You See Is What You Get," argues that "*The Conjure Woman* is primarily a study in duplicity that masks or reveals its meaning according to the predisposition of the reader" (271).

15. Hedin asserts that the tales "are experiments in finding or creating a readership whose existence [Chesnutt] had no reason to suppose" (196). He argues that John represents Chesnutt's intended, white, male audience (205, footnote), which Chesnutt gradually decided was incapable of understanding his intentions (193–95), but he nevertheless sees John as pointing to the possible future existence of an as yet imaginary, ideal audience that Chesnutt's tales attempt to call into existence. While John certainly figures a portion of Chesnutt's actual audience, it seems likely, given the nature of late-nineteenth-century literary culture and Chesnutt's knowledge of the literary marketplace, that he wrote with a majority audience of middle-class women rather than men in view—a supposition reinforced by the internal figuration of just such an audience in the person of Annie.

16. Julius's capitulation to white generic norms in his storytelling in this tale parallels his capitulation to a generically prescribed role for himself in the tale's frame. In Henry Wonham's words, "As the loyal black retainer who facilitates a symbolic reconciliation between North and South, Julius assumes a highly conventional role in this tale, a role designed apparently to reassure Chesnutt's readers that for all the ex-slave's maneuvering for control within the contested postwar Southern domain, the conjure stories are finally contained within the ideological imperatives of the plantation tradition" (*Study* 40).

17. Scharnhorst notes that the novel "went into only two printings, indicating that no more than a few thousand copies were sold" ("Growth" 272).

18. Andrews notes that "*The Colonel's Dream* has always been the least popular and least discussed of Chesnutt's novels, partly because of its unrepresentativeness" (presumably in comparison to Chesnutt's other works) "and partly because of its more glaring aesthetic deficiencies" (*Literary Career* 257). Likewise, Dean McWilliams notes the "critical consensus" that the novel is "the least successful of the long fictions published during [Chesnutt's] lifetime" (166). J. Noel Heermance, conversely, pronounces the novel "the most impressive embodi-

ment of Chesnutt's technical artistry" (184), and Scharnhorst finds in it "a pastiche of 'parodic-travestying forms'" amounting to "a remarkably modern, multi-layered experiment" ("Growth" 271) designed to disrupt and debunk prevailing literary formulas and their accompanying cultural mythologies. Such a wide variety of aesthetic judgments on a single text indicates, at the least, that this novel needs further critical elucidation.

19. Ernestine Pickens, for example, writes that "French's failure in *The Colonel's Dream* is symbolic of Chesnutt's failure to influence public opinion in favor of blacks" (119). Similarly, Andrews asserts that Colonel French's eventual retreat from the South at the end of the novel "not only document[s] southern migrations of the time but prefigur[es] their creator's own leave-taking of the vexed contemporary southern problem in fiction" (*Literary Career* 256).

20. Predictably, Chesnutt's move toward polemic made Howells distinctly uncomfortable, as his review of *The Marrow of Tradition* and his failure to notice *The Colonel's Dream* both suggest. In the *Editor's Study,* Howells repeatedly rejected polemic as a literary mode unlikely to achieve the sort of social-ethical amelioration at which he, with Chesnutt, believed literature should aim. (The *Editor's Study* discussion of James's *The Princess Cassamassima* (77) stands as just one example of Howells's rejection of literary polemicism.) What McElrath has written about Howells's and Chesnutt's comparative literary approaches to the topic of miscegenation might reasonably be made to stand for Howells's continued expectation of Chesnutt: "what they obviously did have in common . . . was the hope that by the act of writing about [the 'Negro Problem'], and by humanizing what was for the predominantly white readership a problem in the abstract, a positive contribution might be made to narrowing the social gap between blacks and whites" 247). Accordingly, Howells's review of *Marrow* expresses his discomfort with Chesnutt's apparent abandonment of this strategy, faulting the book for its "bitter" quality, which "has more justice than mercy in it" (882) and is therefore unlikely, in Howells's judgment, to win white readers to a sympathetic understanding of its black characters. In a letter to his publishers dated December 28, 1901, Chesnutt responded: "My friend, Mr. Howells, who has said many nice things about my writings—although his review of *The Marrow of Tradition* in the *North American Review* for December was not a favorable one as I look at it—has remarked several times that there is no color line in literature. On that point I take issue with him. I am pretty fairly convinced that the color line runs everywhere so far as the United States is concerned" (qtd. in Helen M. Chesnutt 178). For further insight into Howells's discomfort with Chesnutt's later literary mode, see Howells's conflicted letter to Henry Blake Fuller regarding *The Marrow of Tradition* (*Letters* 2: 149). See Andrews ("Howells") and McElrath for fuller discussion of the Howells-Chesnutt relationship.

21. Andrews maintains that the novel "cuts two ways" (*Literary Career* 253), criticizing both the sociopathic tendencies of Southern society and the defects of north-

ern reformers' tactics. Similarly, Pickens elaborates on the novel's analysis of the failure of Progressivism to create a New South in the image of the North (89–121). Blake, more specifically, reads Chesnutt's book as a response to and partial refutation of Booker T. Washington's strategies for improving black fortunes through technical education, manual labor, and infusions of white capital.

22. Responding to the poor sales of *The Marrow of Tradition,* Chesnutt wrote to his publisher that "I am beginning to suspect that the public as a rule does not care for books in which the principal characters are colored people, or written with a striking sympathy with that race as contrasted with the white race" (qtd. in Helen Chesnutt 178). *The Colonel's Dream* abandons the former but not the latter narrative strategy.

23. Andrews (*Literary Career* 225–33) offers an overview of the origins and progress of New South rhetoric and mythmaking.

24. "Had [Howells] lived past 1920, and had he come to know Chesnutt better," the editors of *An Exemplary Citizen* write, "it is likely that he would have deemed Chesnutt the more significant figure" and acknowledged that "he more credibly modeled the attainable ideal that Howells envisioned for African Americans in a truly egalitarian society of the future" (xxxiv).

25. McWilliams, for instance, contends that "the narrator's comments at the end of *The Colonel's Dream* are unconvincing," an expression of "strained optimism" that "achieves an effect opposite to the one intended," announcing "by their inappropriateness to the narrative they conclude, the real bleakness of the moral landscape that has been portrayed" (180).

Chapter 5

1. An analogous bifurcation in the history of Cather's reception confirms the aesthetic difficulty she faced in her early fiction: on the one hand, Cather's popular readership, bolstered by the longstanding dominance in Cather studies of the "Nebraska group" of critics (informally aligned with the tellingly named Willa Cather Pioneer Memorial in Red Cloud) tends to read Cather as the quintessential fictive historian of Euroamerican settlement of the Great Plains. These readers made Cather's pioneer books, especially *O Pioneers!* and *My Antonia,* perennial bestsellers even during the decades before Cather won her current centrality to the American literary canon. An increasingly far-flung host of academic readers, however, has discovered a number of alternative Cathers whose interest in prairie subject matter is thoroughly ancillary to other imperatives, from Modernist aesthetics to British Romanticism to lesbian gender politics. These newer approaches have little in common with each other aside from their marked difference from popular and traditional understandings of Cather's work. But that difference itself points to the tension inherent in the Cather canon between social materials deriving from a nineteenth-century Real-

ist tradition and saturated with concomitant readerly expectations, and aesthetic ends that exceed and/or run counter to those expectations.

2. Joan Wylie Hall, in an essay focusing on the Conradian dimension of Cather's story, provides a summary of the spate of articles in *McClure's* in 1911 exposing urban fire hazards in New York City. See 82.

3. Among other methods, Cather uses anti-Semitic stereotyping to characterize Stanley Merryweather as the representative of the aggressive, acquisitive, new American businessman and to contrast him to Hallet as a socially representative "type." Merryweather is the son of "a professor who knew too much about some Oriental tongues I needn't name to be altogether safe" (47), and he marries "a burgeoning Jewish beauty" (48) in order to further his career. His craven and opportunistic character traits are clearly defined by Hallet as "racial characteristics" (44) rather than personal ones, and Cather draws the other Jewish character in the story—Zablowski, "a young Jewish doctor from the Rockefeller Institute" (44)—as an involuntary sympathizer with Merryweather's temperament, making him the butt of Hallet's gibes. The final sentences of the story make it clear that Zablowski stands along with Merryweather—at least for the white, Anglo-Saxon, Protestant narrator—for the class of materialist connivers who will inherit the new American capitalist society that Hallet sketches in alternative, idealistic terms. Hallet's anti-Semitism goes a long way toward counteracting for a contemporary audience the effect of his generous if condescending relationship with that other, more socially acceptable "other," Caesaro, and makes it more difficult to sympathize with Hallet—as the story clearly means us to—in his social-ethical predicament. Regrettably, this unintended effect likely would have been an issue for far fewer of Cather's contemporaries than it is for us. I must nevertheless take issue with James Woodress's assertion that the inclusion elsewhere in Cather's fiction of non-Jewish villains and "good Jews" along with her "unflattering Jewish figures" absolves her of anti-Semitism. Woodress acknowledges that Cather had "what one might call a typical Midwestern bias against Jews in the aggregate," but he concludes that "to call her anti-Semitic is to exaggerate considerably." (See 283–84 and note.) By contrast, Loretta Wasserman offers a nuanced reading of Cather's treatment of Jews in "Behind the Singer Tower," suggesting that the author deploys Zablowski as a vehicle for the ironization of Hallet's inability to extend his principled sense of justice to a Jew (7–8). While I am not fully convinced by Wasserman's argument, her interpretation does indicate in yet another way the degree to which Cather's story is atypically invested in issues of intercultural relationship and social justice.

4. The resemblance is not absolute; Cather deprives Hallet of the ironic self-criticism that Howells nearly always employs to deepen and complicate the characterization of his ethical spokespersons.

5. I frequently recur in this chapter to the term "idealism" as a label for Cather's

aesthetic principles. The word is inadequate as a descriptor of a complex aesthetic, but I mean it to stand as shorthand for Cather's consistent assertion that the core of both human and literary experience lies outside and beyond the network of linguistically specifiable social and material realities. This central idea constitutes a fundamental assumption of almost all Cather scholarship, even when that scholarship objects to scholars' too uncritical acceptance of Cather's intentional statements. Major Cather critics, however, trace differently the lines of historical descent and literary influence that lead to Cather's aesthetic idealism. Susan Rosowski, for instance, finds its primary roots in the British Romantics; Bernice Slote, in "First Principles: The Kingdom of Art," expands this assertion to include French and other Continental romanticists; Jo Ann Middleton traces Cather's idealism to a "modernist" interest in drawing readers into a co-creative experience that resides in the "vacuoles" or gaps in literary representation; Woodress suggests some possible American sources, from Emersonian idealism to turn-of-the-century swashbuckling romances.

6. These later aesthetic pronouncements respond more directly to the demands of Depression-era Leftist critics for an overtly political and activist fiction than they do to Howells directly. But the line of descent from Howellsian Realism through Progressivist social exposé to Marxist-influenced 1930s literary radicalism is clear, and "Behind the Singer Tower" prefigures Cather's later responses to the literary Left. For fuller discussion of Cather's later resistance to such ideas and of her articulations of literary aesthetics, see my essay on the late novel, *Sapphira and the Slave Girl,* especially 27–31.

7. See Elizabeth Ammons's "The Engineer as Cultural Hero and Willa Cather's First Novel, *Alexander's Bridge.*"

8. For discussion of Alexander as an artist figure, see Sharon O'Brien and Cecelia Tichi.

9. Accounts of the Quebec Bridge collapse and Cather's strategic revisions of its details may be found in Woodress, E. K. Brown, and most extensively in John P. Hinz. The episode occurred during Cather's tenure at *McClure's* and made headlines in all the New York papers. Journalistic coverage of the disaster assigned no immediate blame, dwelling instead upon the irony of the misdelivered telegram that arrived just hours short of preventing loss of life. Later reports, in the wake of a Canadian Royal Commission inquiry, refocused attention on the search for causes and the placement of responsibility on the principal engineer, Theodore Cooper.

10. A sample of more extensive scholarly treatments of the Cather-Jewett relationship would include those of Eleanor Smith, Sharon O'Brien (334–52), and Paula Blanchard (355–61). Jewett's extant letters to Cather may be found in Annie Fields's edition of Jewett's letters (234–35, 245–50). Cather's primary statement on Jewett is the revised and expanded version of her 1925 preface to *The Best Short Stories of Sarah Orne Jewett,* which Cather included in her essay

collection *Not Under Forty* (1936) under the title "Miss Jewett." Her account of meeting Jewett opens "148 Charles Street," which precedes "Miss Jewett" in the collection.

11. Mary Paniccia Carden makes a similar point, contextualized in terms of the novel's "negotiation with traditional gender-role expectations and male-dominant narratives of [American] history" (295), when she writes of this passage: "Here the narrator defines the vision that positions Alexandra as a hero of the earth: she understands the prairie as a growing and vital entity unto itself and honors what it is naturally inclined to grow rather than forcing incongruent production on it. She has 'faith' in the prairie, and it is this faith, this relation with the already valued earth, rather than the authority of ownership vested in the name of the father, that Cather identifies as the founding moment of American history. Alexandra's will and the spirit of the Divide are not opposed, but cooperative forces; her success is accomplished not by the violent penetration and conquest glorified in the dominant narrative of national origins but by mutual and conjoined desire" (282).

    The passage also registers one of the notable consequences (although not directly relevant to my argument) of Cather's mythic imagination of Nebraska history in *O Pioneers!*: the erasure of Native American culture. Janis P. Stout notes the "shockingly imperialistic misrepresentation" (109) constituted by this oft-quoted, thematically central passage's suppression of the recent presence of the Sioux on Alexandra's plains—a suppression that Melissa Ryan explores more fully in an essay considering the novel's repeated episodes of "confinement as a manifestation of Cather's latent ambivalence toward the pioneering enterprise" (286).

12. Hermione Lee acknowledges Cather's ability to "make us feel Alexandra as a life-force as much as an individual" (109) but suggests that the "interchange between the historical and the legendary" in Alexandra's characterization "creates difficulties for Cather" when the novel moves her "out of her pastoral context" (116). When Alexandra travels to Lincoln and the State Penitentiary where Frank Shabata serves his sentence, the movement "has an extraordinary effect, as though she has been put into another kind of novel" (117). Transplanted into the gritty world of literary Naturalism, the mythic heroine "loses all her magic powers—she can do nothing for Shabata" (117). Lee's argument points to an exception that proves the rule of Cather's usual mode of mythic characterization in *O Pioneers!*

13. For a strikingly different assessment of the novel's moral import, see James Seaton, who acknowledges the novel's avoidance of "easy moralizing" (201) but nevertheless finds in the Emil-Marie-Frank story a condemnation of a "delusive romanticism" that "leads all three to believe that they are superior people, different from their neighbors in some fundamental way" (198). Seaton attempts, unsuccessfully I think, to link this moral to the novel's demonstration "that life on

a Nebraska farm in a middle-class community can possess depth and significance" (201) and thus to root it in the novel's supposed affirmation of "bourgeois morality" (193). But the mythic logic of *O Pioneers!,* I have been arguing, values prairie society on quite other grounds than "bourgeois values" (193), which are embodied most clearly in Lou and Oscar and with which the novel has little patience. The novel's ethos, on the contrary, endorses rather than condemns a scheme of human valuation that distinguishes clearly between superior and inferior individuals, while also maintaining the respect due to whatever is most individual in each person.

Works Cited

Alexander, William. *William Dean Howells: The Realist as Humanist.* New York: Franklin, 1981.

Ammons, Elizabeth. *Conflicting Stories: American Women Writers at the Turn into the Twentieth Century.* New York: Oxford UP, 1991.

———. "The Engineer as Cultural Hero and Willa Cather's First Novel, *Alexander's Bridge.*" *American Quarterly* 38 (1986): 746–60.

———. "Material Culture, Empire, and Jewett's *Country of the Pointed Firs.*" *New Essays on The Country of the Pointed Firs.* Ed. June Howard. New York: Cambridge UP, 1994, 81–100.

Andrews, William L. *The Literary Career of Charles W. Chesnutt.* Baton Rouge: Louisiana State UP, 1980.

———. "William Dean Howells and Charles W. Chesnutt: Criticism and Race Fiction in the Age of Booker T. Washington." *American Literature* 48 (1976): 327–39.

Arnold, Marilyn. *Willa Cather's Short Fiction.* Athens, OH: Ohio UP, 1984.

Auerbach, Erich. *Mimesis: The Representation of Reality in Western Literature.* 1946. Trans. Willard Trask. Garden City, NY: Doubleday, 1957.

Bader, Julia. "The Dissolving Vision: Realism in Jewett, Freeman, and Gilman." *American Realism: New Essays.* Ed. Eric J. Sundquist. Baltimore: Johns Hopkins UP, 1982. 176–198.

Bassett, John E. *"A Heart of Ideality in My Realism" and Other Essays on Howells and Twain.* West Cornwall, CT: Locust Hill, 1991.

Baxandall, Lee, and Stefan Morawski. Editor's Preface. *On Literature and Art.* By Karl Marx and Frederick Engels. Ed. Lee Baxandall and Stefan Morawski. Documents on Marxist Aesthetics 1. New York: International General, 1974. 1–2.

Bell, Michael D. *The Problem of American Realism: Studies in the Cultural History of a Literary Idea.* Chicago: U of Chicago P, 1993.

Blake, Susan. "A Better Mousetrap: Washington's Program and *The Colonel's Dream.*" *CLA Journal* 23 (1979): 49–59.

Blanchard, Paula. *Sarah Orne Jewett: Her World and Her Work.* Radcliffe Biography Ser. New York: Addison-Wesley, 1994.

Bone, Robert. *Down Home: A History of Afro-American Short Fiction from Its Beginnings to the End of the Harlem Renaissance.* New York: Putnam's, 1975.

Borus, Daniel H. *Writing Realism: Howells, James, and Norris in the Mass Market.* Chapel Hill: U of North Carolina P, 1989.

Bowron, Bernard A., Jr. "Realism in America." *Comparative Literature* 3 (1951): 268–85.

Bradford, Curtis. "Willa Cather's Uncollected Short Stories." *American Literature* 26 (1955): 537–51.

Britt, David D. "Chesnutt's Conjure Tales: What You See Is What You Get." *CLA Journal* 15 (1972): 269–83.

Brodhead, Richard H. *Cultures of Letters: Scenes of Reading and Writing in Nineteenth-Century America.* Chicago: U of Chicago P, 1993.

———. Introduction. *The Conjure Woman and Other Conjure Tales.* By Charles W. Chesnutt. Ed. Richard H. Brodhead. Durham, NC: Duke UP, 1993. 1–21.

Brown, Bill. "Regional Artifacts (The Life of Things in the Work of Sarah Orne Jewett)." *American Literary History* 14 (2002): 195–226.

Brown, E. K. *Willa Cather: A Critical Biography.* 1953. Completed by Leon Edel. New York: Avon, 1980.

Budd, Louis J. "Howells, the *Atlantic Monthly,* and Republicanism." 1952. *On Howells: The Best from American Literature.* Ed. Edwin H. Cady and Louis J. Budd. Durham, NC: Duke UP, 1993. 41–58.

Cady, Edwin H. Headnote. *W. D. Howells as Critic.* By William Dean Howells. Ed. Edwin H. Cady. Routledge Critics Ser. Boston: Routledge & Kegan Paul, 1973.

———. *The Light of Common Day: Realism in American Fiction.* Bloomington: Indiana UP, 1971.

———. *The Realist at War: The Mature Years 1885–1920 of William Dean Howells.* Syracuse, NY: Syracuse UP, 1958.

———. *The Road to Realism: The Early Years 1837–1885 of William Dean Howells.* Syracuse, NY: Syracuse UP, 1956.

———. *Young Howells and John Brown: Episodes in a Radical Education.* Columbus: Ohio State UP, 1985.

Carden, Mary Paniccia. "Creative Fertility and the National Romance in Willa Cather's *O Pioneers!* and *My Antonia.*" *Modern Fiction Studies* 45 (1999): 275–302.

Carter, Everett. *Howells and the Age of Realism.* 1954. Hamden, CT: Archon, 1966.

Cary, Richard. *Sarah Orne Jewett.* U.S. Authors Ser. 19. New York: Twayne, 1962.

———, ed. *Appreciation of Sarah Orne Jewett.* Waterville, ME: Colby Coll. P, 1973.

——, ed. *Sarah Orne Jewett Letters*. Waterville, ME: Colby Coll. P, 1967.

Cather, Willa. *Alexander's Bridge*. 1912. *Stories, Poems, and Other Writings*. New York: Library of America, 1992.

——. "Behind the Singer Tower." 1912. *Collected Short Fiction, 1892–1912*. Ed. Mildred R. Bennett. Lincoln: U of Nebraska P, 1965.

——. "Escapism." *Commonweal* 17 April 1936. Rpt. in *Stories, Poems, and Other Writings*. New York: Library of America, 1992. 968–73.

——. "Miss Jewett." 1925. Rev. 1936. *Not Under Forty*. *Stories, Poems, and Other Writings*. New York: Library of America, 1992. 849–58.

——. "My First Novels (There Were Two)." 1931. *Stories, Poems, and Other Writings*. New York: Library of America, 1992. 963–65.

——. *Not Under Forty*. 1936. *Stories, Poems, and Other Writings*. New York: Library of America, 1992.

——. "The Novel Démeublé." 1922. *Not Under Forty*. 1936. *Stories, Poems, and Other Writings*. New York: Library of America, 1992. 834–37.

——. "On the Art of Fiction." 1920. *Not Under Forty*. 1936. *Stories, Poems, and Other Writings*. New York: Library of America, 1992. 939–40.

——. *O Pioneers!* 1913. *Novels and Stories 1905–1918*. New York: Library of America, 1999. 133–290.

——. "Preface to *Alexander's Bridge*." 1922. *Stories, Poems, and Other Writings*. New York: Library of America, 1992. 941–43.

——. *The Song of the Lark*. 1915. *Novels and Stories 1905–1918*. New York: Library of America, 1999. 291–706.

——. *Stories, Poems, and Other Writings*. New York: Library of America, 1992.

Chase, Richard. *The American Novel and Its Tradition*. Garden City, NY: Doubleday, 1957.

Chesnutt, Charles W. *The Colonel's Dream*. New York: Doubleday and Page, 1905.

——. *The Conjure Woman and Other Conjure Tales*. Ed. Richard H. Brodhead. Durham, NC: Duke UP, 1993.

——. *Essays and Speeches*. Ed. Joseph R. McElrath Jr., Robert C. Leitz III, and Jesse S. Crisler. Stanford, CA: Stanford UP, 1999.

——. *An Exemplary Citizen: Letters of Charles W. Chesnutt 1906–1932*. Ed. Jesse S. Crisler, Robert C. Leitz III, and Joseph R. McElrath Jr. Stanford, CA: Stanford UP, 2002.

——. *The Journals of Charles W. Chesnutt*. Ed. Richard H. Brodhead. Durham, NC: Duke UP, 1993.

——. *"To Be an Author": Letters of Charles W. Chesnutt 1889–1905*. Ed. Joseph R. McElrath Jr. and Robert C. Leitz III. Princeton, NJ: Princeton UP, 1997.

——. "The Writing of a Novel." *Essays and Speeches*. Ed. Joseph R. McElrath Jr., Robert C. Leitz III, and Jesse S. Crisler. Stanford, CA: Stanford UP, 1999. 549–53.

Chesnutt, Helen M. *Charles Waddell Chesnutt: Pioneer of the Color Line*. Chapel Hill: U of North Carolina P, 1952.

Cooper, Frederick Taber. Rev. of *O Pioneers!*, by Willa Cather. *Bookman* 37 (Aug. 1913): 666–67. *Critical Essays on Willa Cather.* Ed. John J. Murphy. Boston: Hall, 1984. 112–13.

Crowley, John W. *The Dean of American Letters: The Late Career of William Dean Howells.* Amherst: U of Massachusetts P, 1999.

Curtin, William M., ed. *The World and the Parish: Willa Cather's Articles and Reviews, 1893–1902.* 2 vols. Lincoln: U of Nebraska P, 1970.

Daiches, David. *Willa Cather: A Critical Introduction.* Orig. pub. Ithaca, NY: Cornell UP, 1951. Rpt. Westport, CT: Greenwood, 1971.

Daugherty, Sarah B. "Howells, Tolstoy, and the Limits of Realism: The Case of *Annie Kilburn.*" *American Literary Realism* 19.1 (1986): 21–41.

Dike, Donald A. "Notes on Local Color and Its Relation to Realism." *College English* 14 (1952): 81–88.

Dimock, Wai Chee. "The Economy of Pain: The Case of Howells." *Raritan* 9 (1990): 99–119.

Donovan, Josephine. "Jewett and Swedenborg." *American Literature* 65 (1993): 731–50.

———. "Jewett on Race, Class, Ethnicity, and Imperialism: A Reply to Her Critics." *Colby Quarterly* 38 (2002): 403–16.

———. *New England Local Color Literature: A Women's Tradition.* New York: Ungar, 1983.

———. *Sarah Orne Jewett.* New York: Ungar, 1980.

———. "Sarah Orne Jewett's Critical Theory: Notes toward a Feminine Literary Mode." *Critical Essays on Sarah Orne Jewett.* Ed. Gwen L. Nagel. Boston: G. K. Hall, 1984. 212–25.

Douglas, Ann. *The Feminization of American Culture.* New York: Knopf, 1977.

Doyle, James. "Annie Howells and *The Vacation of the Kelwyns.*" *Canadian Review of American Studies* 10 (1979): 125–35.

Eble, Kenneth E. *William Dean Howells.* 2nd ed. U.S. Authors Ser. 16. Boston: Twayne, 1982.

Fetterley, Judith. "'Not in the Least American': Nineteenth-Century Literary Regionalism." *College English* 56 (1994): 877–95.

———. "Reading *Deephaven* as a Lesbian Text." *Sexual Practice/Textual Theory: Lesbian Cultural Criticism.* Ed. Susan J. Wolfe and Julia Penelope. Cambridge, MA: Blackwell, 1993. 164–83.

Fetterley, Judith, and Marjorie Pryse. Introduction. *American Women Regionalists 1850–1910.* New York: Norton, 1992. xi–xx.

Folsom, Marcia McClintock. "'Tact Is a Kind of Mind-Reading': Empathic Style in Sarah Orne Jewett's *The Country of the Pointed Firs.*" *Critical Essays on Sarah Orne Jewett.* Ed. Gwen L. Nagel. Boston: G. K. Hall, 1984. 76–89.

Fuller, Henry Blake. "Howells or James?" 1885. Ed. Darrel Abel. *Modern Fiction Studies* 3 (1957): 159–64.

Garland, Hamlin. *Crumbling Idols: Twelve Essays on Art and Literature.* 1894. Gainesville, FL: Scholars' Facsimiles, 1952.

Garlin, Sender. "William Dean Howells and the Haymarket Era." *Three American Radicals.* San Francisco: Westview P, 1991. 97–163.

Habegger, Alfred. *Gender, Fantasy, and Realism in American Literature.* New York: Columbia UP, 1982.

Hall, Joan Wylie. "Cather's 'Deep Foundation Work': Reconstructing 'Behind the Singer Tower.'" *Studies in Short Fiction* 26 (1989): 81–85.

Hedin, Raymond. "Probable Readers, Possible Stories: The Limits of Nineteenth-Century Black Narrative." *Readers in History: Nineteenth-Century American Literature and the Contexts of Response.* Ed. James L. Machor. Baltimore: Johns Hopkins UP, 1993. 180–205.

Heermance, J. Noel. *Charles W. Chesnutt: America's First Great Black Novelist.* Hamden, CT: Archon, 1974.

Hild, Allison T. "Narrative Mediation in Sarah Orne Jewett's *The Country of the Pointed Firs.*" *Colby Quarterly* (1995): 114–22.

Hinz, John P. "The Real Alexander's Bridge." *American Literature* 22 (1950): 473–76.

Homestead, Melissa. "'Links of Similitude': The Narrator of *The Country of the Pointed Firs* and Author-Reader Relations at the End of the Nineteenth Century." *Jewett and Her Contemporaries: Reshaping the Canon.* Ed. Karen L. Kilcup and Thomas S. Edwards. Gainesville: UP of Florida, 1999. 76–98.

Hough, Robert L. *The Quiet Rebel: William Dean Howells as Social Commentator.* Lincoln: U of Nebraska P, 1959.

Howard, June. "Unraveling Regions, Unsettling Periods: Sarah Orne Jewett and American Literary History." *American Literature* 68 (1996): 365–84.

———, ed. *New Essays on The Country of the Pointed Firs.* New York: Cambridge UP, 1994.

Howells, William Dean. *Annie Kilburn.* 1888. *Novels 1886–1888.* New York: Library of America, 1889.

———. *Editor's Study.* 1886–1892. Ed. James W. Simpson. Troy, NY: Whitston, 1983.

———. *A Hazard of New Fortunes.* 1890. New York: Penguin, 2001.

———. *Life in Letters of William Dean Howells.* Ed. Mildred Howells. 2 vols. Garden City, NY: Doubleday, Doran, 1928.

———. *Literature and Life.* New York: Harper, 1902.

———. *The Minister's Charge.* 1886. *Novels 1886–1888.* New York: Library of America, 1989.

———. "Mr. Charles W. Chesnutt's Stories." Rev. of *The Conjure Woman* and *The Wife of His Youth,* by Charles W. Chesnutt. *Atlantic Monthly* 85 (1900): 699–701.

———. "Novel-Writing and Novel-Reading: An Impersonal Explanation." 1899. *Howells and James: A Double Billing.* Ed. William M. Gibson. New York: NY Public Library, 1958.

———. "A Psychological Counter-Current in Recent Fiction." Rev. of *The Marrow of Tradition,* by Charles W. Chesnutt. *North American Review* 173 (1901): 872–88.

———. Rev. of *Deephaven,* by Sarah Orne Jewett. 1877. *Critical Essays on Sarah Orne Jewett.* Ed. Gwen L. Nagel. Boston: Hall, 1984. 25–26.

———. "A Shaker Village." *Atlantic Monthly* 37 (1876): 699–710.

———. *The Vacation of the Kelwyns.* New York: Harper, 1920.

Jewett, Sarah Orne. *The Country of the Pointed Firs.* 1896. *Novels and Stories.* New York: Library of America, 1994.

———. *Deephaven.* 1877. *Novels and Stories.* New York: Library of America, 1994.

———. *Letters of Sarah Orne Jewett.* Ed. Annie Fields. Boston: Houghton Mifflin, 1911.

———. Preface. *Deephaven.* Boston: Houghton Mifflin, 1894. 1–8.

Kaplan, Amy. "Nation, Region, Empire." *The Columbia History of the American Novel.* Ed. Emory Elliott. New York: Columbia UP, 1991. 240–66.

———. *The Social Construction of American Realism.* Chicago: U of Chicago P, 1988.

Keller, Frances Richardson. *An American Crusade: The Life of Charles Waddell Chesnutt.* Provo, UT: Brigham Young UP, 1978.

Kilcup, Karen L., and Thomas S. Edwards. "Confronting Time and Change: Jewett, Her Contemporaries, and Her Critics." *Jewett and Her Contemporaries: Reshaping the Canon.* Ed. Karen L. Kilcup and Thomas S. Edwards. Gainesville: UP of Florida, 1999. 1–27.

———, eds. *Jewett and Her Contemporaries: Reshaping the Canon.* Gainesville: UP of Florida, 1999.

Kirk, Clara M. *W. D. Howells and Art in His Time.* New Brunswick, NJ: Rutgers UP, 1965.

———. *W. D. Howells, Traveler from Altruria.* New Brunswick, NJ: Rutgers UP, 1962.

Kirk, Clara, and Rudolf Kirk. *William Dean Howells.* U.S. Authors Ser. 16. New York: Twayne, 1962.

Klinkowitz, Jerome. "Ethic and Aesthetic: The Basil and Isabel March Stories of William Dean Howells." *Modern Fiction Studies* 16 (1970): 303–22.

Lauter, Paul. *Canons and Contexts.* New York: Oxford UP, 1991.

Lee, Hermione. *Willa Cather: Double Lives.* New York: Pantheon, 1989.

Loriggio, Francesco. "Regionalism and Theory." *Regionalism Reconsidered.* Ed. David Jordan. Wellesley Studies in Critical Theory, Literary History, and Culture 5. New York: Garland, 1994. 3–27.

Lynn, Kenneth S. *William Dean Howells: An American Life.* New York: Harcourt Brace Jovanovich, 1971.

Mackethan, Lucinda H. "Plantation Fiction, 1865–1900." *The History of Southern Literature.* Ed. Louis D. Rubin Jr. Baton Rouge: Louisiana State UP, 1985. 209–18.

McElrath Jr., Joseph R. "W. D. Howells and Race: Charles W. Chesnutt's Disappointment of the Dean." *Critical Essays on Charles W. Chesnutt.* Ed. Joseph R. McElrath Jr. New York: Hall, 1999. 242–60.

McWilliams, Dean. *Charles W. Chesnutt and the Fictions of Race.* Athens, GA: U of Georgia P, 2002.

Mencken, H. L. Rev. of *Alexander's Bridge,* by Willa Cather *Smart Set* 38 (Dec. 1912): 156–57. *Critical Essays on Willa Cather.* Ed. John J. Murphy. Boston: Hall, 1984. 96–97.

Middleton, Jo Ann. *Willa Cather's Modernism: A Study of Style and Technique.* Rutherford, NJ: Fairleigh Dickinson UP, 1990.

Mobley, Marilyn Sanders. *Folk Roots and Mythic Wings in Sarah Orne Jewett and Toni Morrison: The Cultural Function of Narrative.* Baton Rouge: Louisiana State UP, 1991.

Morawski, Stefan. Introduction. *On Literature and Art.* By Karl Marx and Frederick Engels. Ed. Lee Baxandall and Stefan Morawski. Documents on Marxist Aesthetics 1. New York: International General, 1974. 3–47.

Nettels, Elsa. *Language, Race, and Social Class in Howells's America.* Lexington: UP of Kentucky, 1988.

Nowatzki, Robert C. " 'Passing' in a White Genre: Charles W. Chesnutt's Negotiations of the Plantation Tradition in *The Conjure Woman*." *American Literary Realism* 27 (1995): 20–36.

O'Brien, Sharon. *Willa Cather: The Emerging Voice.* New York: Oxford UP, 1987.

Olsen, Rodney D. *Dancing in Chains: The Youth of William Dean Howells.* New York: New York UP, 1991.

Page, Thomas Nelson. *In Ole Virginia, or Marse Chan and Other Stories.* 1887. Chapel Hill: U of North Carolina P, 1969.

Petrie, Paul R. " 'Skulking Escapist' Versus 'Radical Editor': Willa Cather, the Left Critics, and *Sapphira and the Slave Girl*." *Southern Quarterly* 34.2 (1996): 27–37.

Pickens, Ernestine Williams. *Charles W. Chesnutt and the Progressive Movement.* New York: Pace UP, 1994.

Pizer, Donald. Introduction. *Selected Literary Criticism, Volume II: 1886–1897.* By W. D. Howells. Bloomington: Indiana UP, 1993. xiii–xxi.

Price, Kenneth M. "Charles Chesnutt, the *Atlantic Monthly,* and the Intersection of African-American Fiction and Elite Culture." *Periodical Literature in Nineteenth-Century America.* Ed. Kenneth M. Price and Susan Belasco Smith. Charlottesville: UP of Virginia, 1995. 257–74.

Pryse, Marjorie. " 'Distilling Essences': Regionalism and 'Women's Culture.' " *American Literary Realism* 25.2 (1993): 1–15.

———. "Reading Regionalism: The 'Difference' It Makes." *Regionalism Reconsidered.* Ed. David Jordan. Wellesley Studies in Critical Theory, Literary History, and Culture 5. New York: Garland, 1994. 47–63.

———. "Sex, Class, and 'Category Crisis': Reading Jewett's Transitivity." *Jewett and Her Contemporaries: Reshaping the Canon.* Ed. Karen L. Kilcup and Thomas S. Edwards. Gainesville: UP of Florida, 1999. 31–62.

Romines, Ann. "In *Deephaven:* Skirmishes Near the Swamp." *Colby Library Quarterly* 16 (1980): 205–19.

Rose, Phyllis. "Modernism: The Case of Willa Cather." *Modernism Reconsidered.* Ed. Robert Keily and John Hildebidle. Cambridge: Harvard UP, 1983. 123–45.

Rosowski, Susan. *The Voyage Perilous: Willa Cather's Romanticism.* Lincoln: U of Nebraska P, 1986.

Ryan, Melissa. "The Enclosure of America: Civilization and Confinement in Willa Cather's *O Pioneers!*" *American Literature* 75 (2003): 275–303.

Scharnhorst, Gary. "'The Growth of a Dozen Tendrils': The Polyglot Satire of Chesnutt's *The Colonel's Dream.*" *Critical Essays on Charles W. Chesnutt.* Ed. Joseph R. McElrath Jr. New York: Hall, 1999.

———. "Howells's *The Minister's Charge:* A Satire of Alger's Country-Boy Myth." *Mark Twain Journal* 20.3 (1980–1981): 16–17.

Seaton, James. "The Beauty of Middle-Class Virtue: Willa Cather's *O Pioneers!*" *The Moral of the Story: Literature and Public Ethics.* Ed. Henry T. Edmondson III. New York: Lexington, 2000. 193–202.

Sergeant, Elizabeth Shepley. *Willa Cather: A Memoir.* New York: Lippincott, 1953.

Sherman, Sarah Way. *Sarah Orne Jewett, an American Persephone.* Hanover, NH: UP of New England, 1989.

Slote, Bernice. "First Principles: The Kingdom of Art." *The Kingdom of Art: Willa Cather's First Principles and Critical Statements 1893–1896.* Lincoln: U of Nebraska P, 1966. 31–112.

———. "Willa Cather as a Regional Writer." *Kansas Quarterly* 2.2 (1970): 7–16.

Slote, Bernice, ed. *The Kingdom of Art: Willa Cather's First Principles and Critical Statements 1893–1896.* Lincoln: U of Nebraska P, 1966.

Smith, Donald R. "A Critical Edition of W. D. Howells' *The Vacation of the Kelwyns.*" Diss. Indiana U, 1979.

Smith, Eleanor M. "Sarah Orne Jewett and Willa Cather." 1956. *Appreciation of Sarah Orne Jewett.* Ed. Richard Cary. Waterville, ME: Colby Coll. P, 1973. 112–27.

Stouck, David. Historical Essay. *O Pioneers!* By Willa Cather. Scholarly ed. Ed. Susan J. Rosowski and Charles W. Mignon, with Kathleen Danker. Lincoln: U of Nebraska P, 1992. 283–303.

———. *Willa Cather's Imagination.* Lincoln: U of Nebraska P, 1975.

Stout, Janis P. *Willa Cather: The Writer and Her World.* Charlottesville: UP of Virginia, 2000.

Stowe, Harriet Beecher. *Uncle Tom's Cabin.* 1852. New York: Penguin, 1981.

Sundquist, Eric J. *To Wake the Nations: Race in the Making of American Literature.* Cambridge, MA: Harvard UP, 1993.

Thornberg, Raymond. "Willa Cather: From *Alexander's Bridge* to *My Antonia.*" *Twentieth Century Literature* 7 (1962): 147–58.

Tichi, Cecelia. *Shifting Gears: Technology, Literature, Culture in Modernist America.* Chapel Hill: U of North Carolina P, 1987.

Tourgée, Albion W. *A Fool's Errand, by One of the Fools.* 1879. Ed. John Hope Franklin. Cambridge, MA: Harvard UP, 1961.

Trilling, Lionel. "Willa Cather." 1937. *Willa Cather and Her Critics.* Ed. James Schroeter. Ithaca, NY: Cornell UP, 1967. 148–55.

———. "William Dean Howells and the Roots of Modern Taste." 1951. *The Moral Obligation to be Intelligent: Selected Essays.* Ed. Leon Wieseltier. New York: Farrar, Straus, and Giroux, 2000. 203–23.

United States. National Endowment for the Arts. *Reading at Risk: A Survey of Literary Reading in America.* Research Division Report no. 46. June 2004. Washington: GPO, 2004.

Updike, John. "Howells as Anti-Novelist." 1987. *Odd Jobs: Essays and Criticism.* New York: Knopf, 1991. 168–89.

Wagenknecht, Edward. *Willa Cather.* Literature and Life: American Writers Ser. New York: Continuum, 1994.

———. *William Dean Howells: The Friendly Eye.* New York: Oxford UP, 1969.

Wasserman, Loretta. "Cather's Semitism." *Cather Studies* 2 (1993): 1–22.

Werner, Craig. "The Framing of Charles W. Chesnutt: Practical Deconstruction in the Afro-American Tradition." *Southern Literature and Literary Theory.* Ed. Jefferson Humphries. Athens, GA: U of Georgia P, 1990. 339–65.

Wilson, Matthew. "Who Has the Right to Say? Charles W. Chesnutt, Whiteness, and the Public Sphere." *College Literature* 26 (1999): 18–35.

Wittenberg, Judith Bryant. "*Deephaven:* Sarah Orne Jewett's Exploratory Metafiction." *Studies in American Fiction* 19 (1991): 153–63.

Wonham, Henry B. *Charles W. Chesnutt: A Study of the Short Fiction.* New York: Twayne, 1998.

———. "'The Curious Psychological Spectacle of a Mind Enslaved': Charles W. Chesnutt and Dialect Fiction." *Mississippi Quarterly* 51 (1997–98): 55–70.

———. "Writing Realism, Policing Consciousness: Howells and the Black Body." *American Literature* 67 (1995): 701–24.

Wood, Ann Douglas. "The Literature of Impoverishment: The Women Local Colorists in America 1865–1914." *Women's Studies* 1 (1972): 3–45.

Woodress, James. *Willa Cather: A Literary Life.* Lincoln: U of Nebraska P, 1987.

Wortham, Thomas, ed. *The Early Prose Writings of William Dean Howells 1853–1861.* Athens, OH: Ohio UP, 1990.

Zagarell, Sandra. "*Country*'s Portrayal of Community and the Exclusion of Difference." *New Essays on The Country of the Pointed Firs.* Ed. June Howard. New York: Cambridge UP, 1994. 39–60.

———. "Narrative of Community: The Identification of a Genre." *Signs* 13 (1988): 498–527.

———. "Troubling Regionalism: Rural Life and the Cosmopolitan Eye in Jewett's *Deephaven.*" *American Literary History* 10 (1998): 639–63.

Index